The Lord as Guru

THE LORD AS GURU

Hindi *Sants* in North Indian Tradition

DANIEL GOLD

New York Oxford
OXFORD UNIVERSITY PRESS
1987

Oxford University Press
Oxford New York Toronto
Delhi Bombay Calcutta Madras Karachi
Petaling Jaya Singapore Hong Kong Tokyo
Nairobi Dar es Salaam Cape Town
Melbourne Auckland

and associated companies in
Beirut Berlin Ibadan Nicosia

Published by Oxford University Press, Inc.,
200 Madison Avenue, New York, New York 10016

Library of Congress Cataloging-in-Publication Data
Gold, Daniel.
The lord as guru.
Bibliography: p. Includes index.
1. Saints—India—Cultus. 2. Gurus—India. I. Title.
BL2015.S3G64 1987 294.5′61 86-23496
ISBN 0-19-504339-1

Printing (last digit): 9 8 7 6 5 4 3 2 1

Printed in the United States of America on acid-free paper

Contents

A Note on Transliteration

My aim has been to represent the North Indian pronunciation to the interested nonspecialist—sacrificing, when necessary, precision to readability. Thus, I have not added diacritics to Indic terms frequently used in English, generally known scriptures, and proper names, and when I do give exact transliterations I have opted for the less technical of conflicting scholarly conventions: *ch* and *chh* instead of *c* and *ch; sh* and *ṣ* instead of *ś* and *ṣ*. Sanskritists, moreover, will have to get used to the Hindiwallah's ways: short *a*'s at the end of syllables have normally been dropped when they are not sounded in Hindi; *ṛ* stands for the Hindi retroflex flap—when the Sanskrit vocalic *r* occurs it is represented as *ṛi*.

Acknowledgments

Not only through researching this book did I learn about the different kinds of help Indian and Western gurus can give, but also through the expanded process of putting it together.

In Chicago, Frank Reynolds listened to me and helped me formulate my ideas. Most important, he did not discourage me from attempting the grand comparative endeavor I felt called upon to undertake. Wendy O'Flaherty gave sound advice as to what needed to be clarified in the text, emphasized, or deleted. I thank her for her good stylistic judgement; her energy and enthusiasm are legendary. It is less easy to acknowledge one's wife as guru, let alone one's mother-in-law. But Ann Grodzins Gold is an anthropologist whose ethnological ear would not put up with religio-historical reverie, and Ruth Grodzins is a professional editor who went over the entire text, giving suggestions I often very irrationally ignored.

Kali Bahl took the time to go over most of my translations with me, catching several minor errors and solving two major puzzles. Norman Zide first introduced me to the academic study of Hindi religious verse and asked some interesting questions about new work on modern Hindi religious versifiers. Praise from Mircea Eliade provided encouragement.

In Banaras, Nagendranath Upadhyaya eased my way into the University bureaucracy and presented the extensive Indian scholarship on the *sant*s. His comments on the work I showed him reflected both native cultural sensibilities and detached erudition. Shyam Sundar Shukla generously shared the fruits of his academic labors on the tradition he has known since childhood. Shukdeo Singh introduced me to his wide circle of acquaintances among *sant panthī sādhū*s. Of these, Satnam Das of Kanwar has offered help that has been both academically and spiritually instructive.

Help of another order entirely has long been offered by Malik Sahib of Gwalior. *Jai Guru Dev!*

Ithaca, N.Y. D.G.
November 1986

The Lord as Guru

Introduction: *Sants*, Holy Men, and Indian Religion

The worship of a living person as a manifestation of the divine is not a phenomenon unique to India, but it has certainly thrived there. Dressed in ornate robes and offered rich foods, the Indian guru may be seen by disciples in the image of a deity, an object of intense devotion; or, rough and eccentric, he may impart yogic secrets through his gifted insight and spiritual power. The guru charms his disciples and berates them, helps them in matters human and divine, and teaches through trial and obstruction. To the disciple, the guru's actions present lessons to be cherished, and daily life around the guru is imbued with magic and mystery.

Devotion to the holy man has found some of its clearest expression anywhere among the *sant*s of North India, Hindi poet-singers remembered from the fifteenth century and still visible today. Remarkable in the history of Indian religions, *sant* tradition in some of its variants exalts the guru at the expense of ritual and gods. As the sole available source of spiritual power and object of personal devotion, the guru becomes the seat of great religious mystery. Sometimes he appears as a being within, or the supreme transcendent Lord; at other times he is described in very human terms, as if he could only be a living master. Very baldly and directly, then, the *sant*s reveal the implications of guru devotion for both personal piety and the dynamics of tradition.

Long before the first Hindi *sant*s, the mystery of the guru was crucial for many Indian devotees, but it gained added significance during the epoch in which *sant* tradition took shape. The collapse of classical empire in the middle of the first millennium of the common era had already seen the emergence of iconoclastic holy men within Hinduism and Buddhism. Just as political power was now vested in individual princes with limited domains, so spiritual power became commonly vested in individual holy men, at hand and accessible to disciples. But the emergence of the Hindi *sant*s was accompanied by a crucial new cultural and political factor: the coming of Islam. Muslim princes now ruled through much of North India, displacing their Hindu counterparts. Two centuries later the patronage of Mughal emperors would lead to a flowering of Indo-Muslim culture, but at the time of the early *sant*s both Hindus and Muslims in India were experiencing the effects of hundreds of years of political instability and religiocultural confusion. In the midst of this period of unsettledness and cultural doubt, the *sant*s arose from common, unlettered classes to transcend orthodox doctrines. To those who recognized the received traditions of neither Hinduism nor Islam as unquestionably true, the *sant*s could present the mystery of the guru as an alternative basis of faith.

Thus, while *sant* tradition has native Indian roots, those roots do not derive from Brahmanic orthodoxy. Kabir, the first and best known of the Hindi *sant*s, was a weaver, from among the most despised of Indian classes. And, like some other early *sant*s—a few of whom had even meaner origins—Kabir was nominally Muslim. Nevertheless, despite the low ritual status of the early *sant*s, the widespread popularity of their verses eventually gave the tradition a modicum of respectability. By the eighteenth century most *sant*s would come from middle Hindu castes—often from trading communities. In the nineteenth century the line of Radhasoami gurus emerged among reputable clerks and merchants to present a particular esoteric version of *sant* tradition among large numbers of devotees throughout India and beyond.

Arising from figures remembered as Muslims, but eventually spreading among ordinary Hindus, *sant* tradition has consistently eluded definitive characterization. Just where do the *sant*s stand within the diverse Indian religious landscape? Indian scholars have often emphasized the affinity of the *sant*s with one or another familiar religious tradition. Some stress the similarity of the *sant*s' songs with those of free-spirited yogis found among Buddhists as well as Hindus. Others point to elements in *sant* experience comparable to orthodox Hindu tantra or the devotion espoused in Narada's classical sutras of devotion. At the same time, few deny the multiple sources for the piety of the *sant*s, who are frequently seen as the synthesizers of Indic traditions par excellence. The Islamic elements in the *sant* synthesis have sometimes been stressed by Indian Muslims, a number of whom have long counted Kabir as at least marginally one of their own. The early *sant*s, we have been told, brought together popular Hindu and Sufi religious currents—sometimes in a highly revolutionary way. This image of the *sants*, moreover, was the first to be presented to the West.[1]

Recent Western scholars attracted to the *sants* have usually been engaged with specific problems, thus tending to avoid general interpretations. Drawn by the devotional force of the *sants'* songs, students of Hindi literature have produced careful textual studies and vivid translations. Social scientists interested in the plight of marginal groups have discovered contemporary, unorthodox religious movements invoking *sants* of the past. Absorbed in the particulars of their studies, many of these scholars have often ignored the *sants* as a tradition.[2]

Western scholars who have paid attention to the larger field of *sants*, moreover, sometimes question the very existence of a *sant* tradition at all, for the piety found in the modern groups seems to vary greatly from that suggested by the medieval poetry, and the gaps between the *sants* and the movements that invoke them often seem greater than their continuities. At the same time, poets devoted to one or another of the hallowed Hindu deities have been known to take up characteristic themes of the *sants*, a few of whom have themselves been tolerant of—if not enthusiastic about—the worship of the Hindu gods. With no set boundaries or fixed institutions, and with great diversity among individual gurus, the *sants* do not readily present themselves to outsiders as a coherent religious tradition.[3]

Nevertheless, if we examine the *sants* in the centuries between the earliest poets and the latest movements, we find that many notable gurus discovered a tradition of sorts themselves. If the boundaries of this larger *sant* tradition are diffuse and variable, the boundary markers remain consistent: the names and verses of greater and lesser *sants*. Later *sants* cite earlier ones, and large and important sectarian compilations include verse attributed to figures from beyond the immediate lineage of the *sant* to whom the sect traces its origins.[4] By the end of the eighteenth century, Tulsi Sahib, a precursor to the Radhasoamis, gave the tradition more explicit theological expression through his exposition of *sant mat,* "the teachings of the *sants*."

The relationships recognized by the *sants* among themselves present some intriguing problems of holy men and tradition, which can be missed in analytic work oriented exclusively toward early poets or modern movements. To penetrate these problems we must study materials that form a bridge between the legendary pioneers of *sant* tradition and its visible contemporary developments. Though *sants* from the seventeenth and eighteenth centuries are not always remembered as creative poets, they often managed to deal creatively with their religiohistorical situations. Tracing long lineages of gurus and disciples, they demonstrate the ways in which bonds of coherence exist among idiosyncratic holy men. Proud to inherit the legacy of low-caste spiritual forbears, they nevertheless had to reinterpret this legacy for a more Hinduized milieu. The forms of piety that thus emerged show us the immediate origins of today's *sant* movements, before their adaptation to contemporary Indian society and Western culture. Lore on eighteenth-century lineages, a fresh contribution of this book to the Western-language materials on *sant*s, will thus help us understand the images of later premodern figures in their own eyes as well as those of their contemporaries.

Studying the *sant*s as a tradition leads to questions that draw us in opposite directions. Moving outward, we will look at the *sant*s in the history of Indian religion, examining their origins, style of piety, and continuing socioreligious place. Moving inward to the dynamics of the tradition itself, we will ask questions about the structure of *sant* lineages and the ways in which individuals and small groups present themselves as part of larger collectivities. Yet, as we observe the ways in which *sant* tradition adapts common Indian religious forms and how larger socioreligious roles derive from its internal structures, we will find that our inward and outward lines of questioning are not really opposite but interdependent. Central to both, moreover, is the figure of the guru: assimilating factors from outside as he presents the *sant*s to the world, he is at once the focal point of change in tradition and the only visible object of devotion that it offers.

To present the *sant*s in their North Indian environment, I will use a set of analytic terms that highlight the distinctive characteristics of the holy man as a type of object of faith. How does the sanctity of the living guru stand out against the disincarnate divinities invoked in many premodern cultures and the ancient knowledge that informs traditional lifeways? The structural relationships among holy men and other crucial objects of worship have been presented in a separate study, where they suggest some broad religiohistorical implications of the idea of tradition among *sant*s.[5] Here the same terms will be used to describe *sant* tradition in India: the elements from its environment that it adapted, the characteristic problems of internal coherence that it faced, and its particular place in the history of Indian religion.

As a basis of faith, the *sant* stands in contrast to two other sources of salvation commonly known to Hindus. On the one hand, he differs from the great gods of Hindu mythic lore—Krishna, say, or Shiva. On the other hand, he differs from the cumulative ritual heritage understood to derive from the Vedas, which informs Hindu society. Krishna and Shiva present themselves through story, image, and drama; the Vedic heritage is understood through the practice of everyday life; the guru's grace is accessible through immediate personal contact and lasting channels established at initiation. Yet though these sources present different dynamics, all are understood as vital conduits though which the divine reveals itself to men. We thus call them immanent foci of the divine.

The *sant,* the Hindu deity, and the Vedic heritage, moreover, each represent a distinct *type* of immanent focus. The *sant,* along with other living masters, practicing saints, and worshiped gurus, we call a holy man: a man because he is alive in a body; holy because he is looked to for salvation. A holy man, moreover, always exists among other holy persons; he is a member of a class of people—both male and female—especially qualified to mediate the divine. A god like Krishna or Shiva we call a singular personality: a personality because he is a person without a definite form, a being who can be conceived in many images and adored intimately as a deity; singular because the devotee worships him as an entity uniquely divine, one without equal. The category of singular personality may then extend beyond mythic deities to include revered individuals of the past—especially figures known as founders of traditions, such as Buddha or Jesus; the personality's uniqueness may also dignify select sectarian leaders in the present. No longer holy men like others, these leaders appear as special personages whose links to a singular personality give them a supreme status among living beings. Presenting an object of faith that differs from those offered by both gurus and gods is the idea of tradition itself, as seen in the Hinduism that invokes the Vedas. As an object of faith, a cumulative tradition can be called an eternal heritage: a heritage because it is the legacy of the fathers, the ways of the venerable past; eternal because the past ways are the original ways—perfect, true, and needing no change.

As bases of both personal salvation and communal solidarity, these three immanent foci demonstrate revealed aspects—visible to all—and hidden ones, which only the wise can see. The holy man is revealed visibly in his discourses and commands, the singular personality in a scripture and a church, and the eternal heritage through the mythic and legal tradition of a venerable culture. The other, more esoteric qualities of the foci are made known only to those fit to understand: the holy man offers hidden help for his disciples and a particular cosmic mission for the universe; the singular personality presents hidden saving grace to the true church of the elect; and the complex lore of the eternal heritage holds deep meanings and teaches hidden precepts.

Presenting characteristic contrasts, the immanent foci, though emerging from Hindu phenomena, are proposed as general religiohistorical categories and will eventually be used to discuss phenomena outside the Hindu world. And as the immanent foci are identified throughout the world religions, they acquire a new comparative dimension, for they are, in fact, usually perceived in combination, thus letting us distinguish structural similarities among specific traditions.

In addition to the foci provided by the major religions as great contexts of meaning, specific traditions offer foci of their own. Thus, in religions founded by great personalities—Christianity, say, or Buddhism—we find "catholic" developments that take the cumulative ritual and textual heritage itself as mediating the divine. In the Hindu (but not the Judaic) heritage we find devotional developments focused on a singular personality like Krishna, as well as on tantric lineages of holy men. A tradition such as Shaivite tantra presents a configuration in which all three major foci are important: a living guru, embodying the personality of Shiva, is embedded in a greater Hindu heritage.

Yet even in combination the immanent foci do not exhaust all possibilities for human faith. For individuals can be found within most civilizations whose faith transcends any one configuration of foci; they see a unifying truth behind all the religious traditions of which they are aware. The divine has been revealed in all scriptures and liturgies, they say, and is realized by those who can penetrate the secret meanings of ritual, myth, and history. As a basis for even a highly syncretic tradition, of course, the totality of the world's scriptures and sacraments is highly unmanageable. So a belief in a unifying truth will be seen largely as an individual attitude or one embedded in the informing religious context of a liberal tradition still grounded in foci of its own.

Indeed, as general categories of religious perception, the foci are given specific meanings by many different types of contexts, not just those provided by identifiable religious traditions. Religiocultural contexts, continuous over time and space, reveal common idioms among variants of world religions existing in the same cultural areas—such as the North Indian variants of Hinduism, Buddhism, and Islam. Sociohistorical contexts—situations, say, of syncretism, feudalism, or collapse of empire—present grounds for comparison over disparate cultural realms.

Looking at religious traditions as configurations of foci in contexts enables us at once to identify crucial aspects of a given tradition and to compare traditions within cultural universes and among them. Viewing the *sants* in this way, then, can give us complementary perspectives on the internal dynamics of lineages and the place of the *sants* in Indian religion. Using the immanent foci as pivots, we will move from the contexts of *sant* tradition to its structure and back again, letting questions that emerge from one direction of inquiry lead us to another. We will begin with the enduring elements of North Indian religion still visible today (part I), see how they come together in the continuing *sant* tradition (part II), and by the end of the study will be able to make some conjectures about the place of the *sants* in the development of Indian religion (part III).

Part I presents the *sants* in the North Indian devotional environment in which they still stand. The continuities in religiocultural idiom that the *sants* share with the traditions around them are described in the first chapter. The second then contrasts the *sant* as holy man with the personality of Krishna and the heritage of the Vedas.

Part II explores the dynamic of holy men and cumulative tradition among the *sants*, examining some ways in which that tradition itself gives rise to distinctive singular personalities and the idea of a heritage of *sants*. The *sants* as a tradition of holy men are introduced in the third chapter, which compares two figures formative to the tradition with two from the eighteenth century: What continuities exist among *sants* as individuals who must deal in their own ways with the different religious situations that confront them? The fourth chapter examines the institutional forms of *sant* lineages. As the spiritual legacy of a *sant* of the past increasingly overshadows the immediate presence of a living guru, what do lineages in fact offer the individual and the community? From problems of socioreligious routinization we move, in the fifth chapter, to the routinized codification of inner vision. What can continuities in technical language among successive gurus tell us about the continuity of esoteric experience in *sant* lineages? The sixth chapter examines the idea of the guru in theological speculation, asking questions about the relation of doctrine to socioreligious reality in different Radhasoami groups.

Part III takes some results of this analysis of tradition among *sants* to contiguous Indian contexts in order to identify the distinctive characteristics of *sants* as Indian holy men. The institutions of guru and lineage examined among *sants* are compared in the seventh chapter to those found in other Indian traditions oriented toward the holy man: Buddhist, Hindu, and Islamic. In the eighth chapter the results of these comparisons—together with a review of the sociohistorical contexts of the early *sants*—will finally suggest a solution to the perplexing problem of *sant* origins.

I

THE CHANNELS OF GRACE AND POWER IN NORTH INDIAN RELIGION

1

The Contexts of *Sant* Tradition

The rich development of religious practice in North India can appear overwhelming not only through the variety of its forms but also through their distribution. Gods are worshiped alongside gurus; death rites are administered just down the shore from the place where pilgrims take their ritual baths. Yet almost as overwhelming as apparently dissimilar phenomena in the same place are similar phenomena in similar contexts over highly diverse regions. The diffusion of the Hindi *sant*s throughout North India demonstrates that the religious soil of its varied terrains does contain common elements; to understand the place of the *sant*s within the larger North Indian religious landscape we will need to discover what some of these common elements are. But first we must get some idea of the geographic range of our exploration.

Differences among the various regions of North India are frequently discussed both by the people who live there and by the people who study them. Natives are often quick to point out cultural styles, not only of dress and food, but also of temperament. Regional stereotypes, both kind and unkind, abound: "Punjabis are industrious (and aggressive)"; "Gujaratis have good business sense (perhaps a little too good)." The factors taken by scholars as the indices of regional differentiation are usually considerably more sophisticated than those of the natives, but frequently lead to similarly debatable, imprecise results. Alternative bases have been proposed for the general regional differentiation of Indian culture, and the various historical, anthropological, and linguistic concerns of different scholars justifiably lead them to slice up the subcontinent in different ways.[1] In practice, then, most scholarly mapping of Indian regional diversity is oriented to specific academic problems.

Our practice will be no different, and the North Indian area to be mapped out here will emerge from problems of understanding the nature of the *sant* tradition. Holy men identifying themselves with a common tradition including Kabir, Dadu, and locally formidable *sant*s spread from Bihar in the east to Rajasthan in the west, encompassing just about all of the central northern regions sometimes referred to collectively as Hindustan. By the eighteenth century, both Bihar and the Rajasthani region of Marwar gave rise to *sant*s with the same name: the two have to be distinguished in tradition as Dariya Biharwale and Dariya Marwarwale. The northern and southern boundaries of a continuous *sant* tradition, however, are less neatly marked. To the north, in the Punjab, *sant* tradition developed through Guru Nanak and his successors into the religion of the Sikhs, and gurus from Punjabi Sikh families have been very important in the Radhasoami revival of *sant* tradition today. Not only do modern Radhasoamis revere the first five Sikh gurus as *sant*s and cherish their songs, but the Sikh scriptures have a place for some early devotional poets from Guru Nanak's time and before, including, among others, Kabir, Raidas, and Namdev. Namdev himself was from Maharashtra, beyond the southern border of Hindustan, but is said to have traveled in the northern regions and to have left verses in Hindi. Mention of Namdev is found even in conservative versions of the Kabirian corpus,[2] and he and other *sant*s of Maharashtra were known to many in the Hindi *sant* tradition.

The geographical continuity of Hindi *sant* tradition, then, extends throughout the Hindustani plains into the bordering regions of Punjab and Maharashtra, regions traditionally in cultural interaction with the central areas. But in the regions at the extremes of continental India—Kashmir, Bengal, and Gujarat—we find important popular singers who spoke at times of a formless Lord but who identified little with the tradition of Namdev and Kabir.[3] The Hindi *sant*s, in their turn, generally remained silent about these figures, though most had probably heard something about the forms of piety for which their native regions were famous. For the specialized traditions of tantra in Bengal and Kashmir and of Krishna devotion in Gujarat had impact throughout the north, and will thus at times occupy us in this study. Indeed, perhaps the fabled excesses of tantric practice (and the more luxuriant ones of Vaishnava ritual) were a factor in the Hindi *sant*s' lack of solidarity with the singers of the regions where these traditions flourished.[4]

Yet the excesses of Vaishnava ritual and tantric practice derive from the same Indian religious soil that gave rise to the piety of the *sant*s, and an understanding of the diversely fertile potencies of this soil may be gained in part from a consideration of the excesses it nurtured. In this study, then, we will have occasion to discuss Vaishnava and tantric traditions as elements of the Hindu religious landscape in which the *sant*s flourished. Much of what we will say about the cultural and historical contexts of *sant* tradition, moreover, applies to religious developments throughout the northern regions, indeed, throughout the subcontinent. But while we will be looking at the *sant*s within broad Indian contexts, the *sant*s and their disciples were in fact contained within a single continuous Indian area, one that seems to have taken shape largely along linguistic lines.

Constituting the most central basis for unity within the diffuse *sant* tradition are the *sayings* of the *sant*s, the *sant bānī*—a common stock of vernacular verses by *sant*s, which have been used in the tradition as scripture. Thus, at the core of the region of study defined by *sant* tradition are areas where people speak the various languages lumped together as "Hindi"—diverse but related, and with effort usually mutually intelligible. Within this area and somewhat beyond, the common lingua franca is the dialect of Delhi, known as *khāṛī bolī* Hindi, or Hindustani. For the most part, the spread of Hindi *sant* tradition corresponds to the areas where *khāṛī bolī* is understood by large portions of the population: Hindustan itself, and parts of the bordering areas of Punjab and Maharashtra. The spread diminishes in areas where pride in regional languages is strong—most noticeably Bengal, and also Gujarat and Kashmir.

Certainly, few *sant* texts show consistent *khāṛī bolī* forms, though many do seem to show a *sant*'s own language oriented toward the widely understood *khāṛī bolī* norms. This make-do idiom does not usually provide the scholar addicted to grammatical rules with easy reading, but it does indicate something about the *sant*s' purpose for composition. More erudite poets in Vraj, Awadh, Marwar, and other places were developing local dialects into elegant literary media that would provide standard languages over sizable cultural regions. The orientation of the language of many *sant*s toward an even more widely comprehensible though workaday and commercially vulgar idiom reflects not only their own disregard for literary polish but also their desire to reach a popular audience as wide as possible.

The extant verses of the Hindi *sant*s do not date much earlier than the middle of the fifteenth century. The tradition itself, however, had certainly begun to take shape before then. The earliest important work in the Marathi *sant* tradition, its immediate predecessor, dates from the end of the thirteenth century.[5] Both Hindi and Marathi *sants*, moreover, drew directly on traditions of tantric yoga and ecstatic devotion that developed characteristic forms centuries earlier.

The patterns of socioreligious organization in all these traditions reflected pervasive secular forms of the postclassical age. Fresh foreign onslaughts and the collapse of such empire as there was introduced the new phase of Indian cultural history, which was signaled by the death of Harsha in A.D. 647. The political arena proliferated with rival units; lack of centralized communication increased regional consciousness. But just as there are important religious continuities across the geographical regions of North India, so there have been some important historical continuities within Indian society from the end of Hindu empire up to the present. Indeed, as Romila Thapar observes,

> The period from the eighth to the thirteenth centuries . . . is a formative period . . . since many institutions of present-day India began to take enduring shape during this period. Feudalism as the basis of the politico-economic structure survived in a broad sense until recent times and influenced the development of society accordingly.[6]

Thus, as the spatial parameters of our study find a focus in the Hindustani plain but move into the extremities of North India and beyond, so the temporal period focuses on the efflorescence of the Hindi *sants* from the fifteenth to the eighteenth centuries, but includes traditions emerging with the start of the postclassical age and continuing till the present day.

The Socioreligious Context: Kinship and Contract in Politics and Religion

Thapar's characterization of the politicoeconomic structure of postclassical India as "feudal" needs some clarification. Certainly there were significant differences between the postclassical Indian patterns and the medieval European polity from which the notion of feudalism is derived.[7] The manorial system and large-scale farming that existed in Europe were unknown in India. Nor did Hindus have nearly as much use for political alliance based solely on contract as they did for those based on bonds of kinship, distant as well as close. But Europeans too paid attention to kinship relations in politics, and minor Indian princes could contract alliances with more important powers regardless of whether they were related to them as kin.

Whatever the doubts of some social scientists about typifying the postclassical Indian sociohistorical context as feudal, the characterization makes sense from our religiohistorical perspective. For of the three traits of feudal societies in general offered by Wolpert to justify the use of the term "feudal" for postclassical India, all are conducive to worldly attitudes with curious religious parallels. These traits are (1) political decentralization, (2) local economic self-sufficiency, and (3) the nobles' holding of land conditionally in return for military service.[8] In a world of political decentralization and local economic self-sufficiency, respect for power manifests in personal loyalty to an individual at hand, just the type of attitude taken by the devotee toward the spiritually powerful holy man. To maintain the bounty bestowed on him by his guru, moreover, the devotee—like the vassal of the lord—is ideally supposed to render him some kind of service: physical if appropriate, or perhaps monetary, but sometimes just the loyal practice of the guru's teachings as a contribution to his hidden spiritual work.

A religious individual whose primary spiritual responsibility is toward an individual guru of his own will not always take too seriously the socioreligious norms of the larger community. At the same time, any potentially iconoclastic aspects of his piety are likely to be fostered by the internal nature of the practice given by his guru: for someone seeking salvation through the subtle body as microcosm, the performance of outer communal ritual may not seem so essential. Consequently, the inner tantric practices that began to burgeon during the early postclassical era not only added new dimensions to established religious traditions, but also provided license for traditions clearly outside the religious establishment. Thus, the authority vested by *tantrika*s in the living, possibly idiosyncratic guru, the internal nature of much tantric practice, and the self-sufficiency of tantric scriptures all helped give rise to a number of individualistic religious developments that had little use for Brahmanic orthodoxy.

By the ninth and tenth centuries we find Buddhist *siddha*s and *nāth* yogis, later followed by the *sant* traditions of Maharashtra and the Hindi-speaking north. The relatively high degree of religious autonomy the individual finds in these traditions parallels the highly decentralized power found in the political arena. And like many of the new princely houses—some of which were probably established by recent invaders or were of indigenous non-Aryan origin—these traditions found themselves at a distance from the time-honored sources of religiocultural legitimation.

Both the new political movements and the new religious developments derived such internal coherence as they had, as well as links to the respectable past, through models taken from the strongly patriarchal Aryan kinship system. Practical relationships among individuals were grounded in traceable bonds of lineage, while more or less mythical genealogies provided loosely knit clan-traditions with a bridge to an ancient heritage.

Large kinship units, whether mythical or historical, are described with little terminological consistency in Indian anthropology, where we find mention by different authors of "tribes" and "families" as well as "lineages" and "clans."[9] Our usage here will reflect specifically religiohistorical concerns, though it seems to be consonant enough with a standard anthropological usage described by Graburn: "Generally speaking lineages are descent groups leading back to a known ancestor, whereas clans are groups descending from a common *mythical* ancestor."[10] In this study "clan" will be used to refer to a consciousness of kinship through broad, historically untraceable, generic relationships. "Lineage" will refer to a sense of kinship that identifies definite relationships to specific persons.

"Clan" and "lineage" certainly had different meanings in politics and religion. Humble and pious *sant*s usually had little in common—and little to do—with local princes. But the spiritual power of one and the political power of the other were seen to manifest themselves in similar ways. Thus the internal order of *sant* tradition bears comparison with that of the Rajputs, the dominant Hindu political power in the postclassical north.

Illustrating how "power was widely diffused" in Rajputana among rival, kinship-based political entities, Susanne Rudolph describes their "cultural and ethnic unity":

> A common caste culture, expressed through bardic literature and the shared chivalric ethic, and a feeling that all Rajputs were peers, created a common psychological climate even if it led to no political unity.[11]

This description, with a few appropriate changes in vocabulary, provides a nice account of the coherence of *sant* tradition:

> A common *religious* culture, expressed through the *sant bani* and a shared devotional ethic, and a *feeling that all true sants were peers,* created a common spiritual climate even if it led to no institutional unity.

Among both *sants* and Rajputs, such structure as there was to tradition was provided by notions of clan and lineage and their purity, personal power and contract. A general notion of clan provides *sants* and Rajputs alike with a sense of their tradition as a whole, an orientation to the wider Indian heritage, and some broad internal discriminative categories. A consciousness of the *sants* as all finally one with the divine *satguru* parallels the Rajputs' seeing themselves as all "sons of rajas," descended finally from the heroes of the Hindu epics. This group derivation gives the Rajputs a link to the respectable past that the *sants* can find—when they want to—by citing Kabir's (probably nonhistorical) connection to Ramananda and orthodox Vaishnava *bhakti*. At the same time, both *sants* and Rajputs discriminate as to just who they accept as their own: as Rajputs distinguish locally ranked subclans when giving and taking women in marriage, so followers of *sant* tradition sometimes distinguish different groups among those spiritually akin to them when giving and accepting invitations to religious gatherings.

In both politics and religion concrete relationships between individuals are informed by the same concepts of lineage that connect the members of the extended Indian family; they exhibit, moreover, the same familiarity and the same tensions that these imply. Thus the normal Hindi word for fellow disciple is *guru bhāī,* guru-brother, or *guru bahan,* guru-sister—and in certain Kabirpanthi groups marriages between guru-brothers and guru-sisters have been forbidden as incestuous.[12] Similarly, the term *chāchā guru,* "father's-younger-brother-guru," is sometimes used to refer to a respected (though junior) qualified brother-disciple of one's own guru. Like the sons of a raja, qualified disciples of the same guru can branch out and establish centers of their own—often identified in terms of their localities as well as their founders—while one disciple may inherit the master's *gaddī*. And like the sons of a raja, guru-brothers can find themselves at odds with each other, especially, as we shall see in chapter 6, over matters of succession.

Parallels between the religious and political norms also extend to the contractual aspect of the relationship between the Rajput and his lord: the disciple, offering obedient service, and the guru, pledging eternal protection, are often understood to be entering into a set of voluntary mutual obligations. And in religion as well as politics such relationships are seen to exist between specific persons. Allegiance is generally held to be due to one's immediate master and to no one else, including figures in the lineage senior even to him. To illustrate this point,

Soamiji Maharaj, the source of the Radhasoami lineage, tells the story of a *faqīr* stranded on a raft in the sea. He refuses first the proffered hand of Muhammad, then that of God, and then that of his guru's guru, whereupon "the Guru Himself came, embraced the disciple and took him immediately to his house."[13]

While the same model of kinship was adapted by both Rajputs and *sant*s, the practical realities of politics and religion made different elements crucial in the two versions of the model. Thus, a notion of purity was certainly fundamental in ideas of legitimacy of power among both *sant*s and Rajputs. But in spiritual kinship the crucial and debatable issues of purity came up in regard to lineage: was the disciple indeed a true spiritual son of the master? The lineage of the Rajput, however, while politically important, was not generally a matter of controversy. Debatable issues of purity for Rajputs came up with regard to the caste of prospective marriage partners, when attention was paid to the relative status of the groups constituting the Rajput "clan."

Practical structures of spiritual and political kinship differ as well in the dynamic between relationships of equality and subordination. Among the Rajputs these relationships are sometimes in tension: the raja is normally a lineage brother to many of his nobles, yet still very much the first among them. Among the *sant*s, relationships of equality and subordination do not normally take place among the same individuals: the disciple is in a relationship of relative spiritual equality with his guru-brothers but enters into one of subordination with his guru.

The different religious traditions that burgeoned during postclassical times present varying patterns of spiritual kinship. The structure of *sant* tradition outlined above is roughly paradigmatic for the loosely organized, practically oriented traditions of holy men who flourished during the era. These would probably include the early *siddha*s and *nāth*s, so far as we can tell, as well as more conventional yogis within Hinduism and Buddhism and the Chishti Sufis of Indian Islam. But the patterns so far seen among the *sant*s appear drastically altered in traditions with a dominant singular-personality focus and strong eternal-heritage elements. These factors occur not only in Vaishnava sectarian lineages, often known as *sampradāyas,* but also in the sectarianized forms of *sant* tradition itself, which are generally called *sant panth*s.

A good example of the different ways in which a lineage of gurus can develop is found in Sikh tradition. The word "Sikh" derives from the Sanskrit *shishya,* "disciple," and the original Sikhs were simply the disciples of Guru Nanak; even today the Sikhs are sometimes called

Nanakpanthis. In its earliest phases, Sikh tradition appears as a fairly conventional *sant* lineage, with a succession of spiritually qualified gurus and disciples. Among the later Sikh gurus, however, the succession became hereditary—a regular occurrence in Indian religious traditions. Less common, though not without parallel among *sant*s,[14] is the emergence of a heritage featuring some military ideals, a heritage that developed among the Sikhs in a widely expanded community suffering persecution. What does seem unique to Sikh tradition, however, is the way in which this military heritage found a focus in the later Sikh gurus to produce a lineage having political ramifications as well as spiritual and biological bases.

The tenth Sikh guru, Gobind Singh, had no heirs, and the lineage ended. Today, men acknowledge their identity as Sikhs through wearing five symbolic objects that Guru Gobind Singh is said to have named at the founding of the *khālsā,* a new form of Sikh community. Yet even as a special mediating personality founding a community, Guru Gobind Singh, through a dramatic hoax,[15] demanded the ultimate test of loyalty to his person as holy man. The origin of the Sikhs in a holy-man tradition remains also in the basis of salvation to which they turn: while that basis is principally a scriptural heritage, it is one composed largely of verses by gurus in the Sikh lineage. Thus if Sikh tradition today appears as a heritage with no active focus in a holy man, it keeps alive at least the *ideas* of guru and lineage.

The importance of the ideas of guru and lineage for postclassical Indian religious institutions have been noted by Joachim Wach. In contrasting the medieval Hindu *sampradāya* in its many variations to the 'separating' Christian sect, Wach stresses the *sampradāya*'s "positive connotation." It is able to preserve the heritage of an "outstanding religious personality" through his "physical or spiritual descendant."[16] Among the many Vaishnava *sampradāya*s that emerged in the north during postclassical times, the largest outside Bengal was the one started by Vallabhacharya, whose path is sometimes called the *puṣṭimārg,* "the sustaining way." While today predominant in the western areas, particularly Gujarat, it developed in the more central northern regions and used for many liturgical purposes the Hindi literary language called Vraj *bhāṣā,* the dialect of Krishna's birthplace. In studying the patterns of North Indian religion we will be returning to the Krishna devotion of the Vallabha *sampradāya* to see some dynamics of tradition oriented toward a singular personality in contrast to those of traditions of holy men. Below, however, we will be looking at the verses of Sur Das—an important Hindi poet whose verses are canonical in the *puṣṭimārg*—together with those of some *sants*, to see how they reflect a common idiom of North Indian devotion.

Religiocultural Contexts: A Continuous Universe, Channels of Grace

The parallels we have seen between the organizations of secular and religious power reflect a common South Asian world view that takes the varied orders of the created universe as forming a continuous, substantial whole. Different modes of substance interpenetrate, and those seen to be immediately continuous with one another are also understood to have similar properties. Moreover, it is not only the great orders of the universe that interpenetrate, but also living beings, who can combine in their persons properties derived from many different types of universal, substantial order—biological and psychological as well as political and spiritual. When two substantial beings come in close contact with one another, some transference of properties between them is normally seen to take place. If one of them is better organized and more powerful, the more telling effect of the transference is generally on the other. Thus the powerful guru is usually understood to be able to transform a yielding disciple.

A number of analogies have been given to describe the transformative powers of the guru in *sant* literature: the guru is likened to the sandalwood tree, which gives its sweet smell to those who remain around it; or to the philosopher's stone, turning the disciples he touches into gold.[17] One of the most striking of these analogies is that of the *bhrangī* and *kīṭ,* the "bumblebee" and "bug" of ordinary Hindi, which in *sant* lore, however, turn into most extraordinary insects indeed. Standard sources agree that the *bhrangī* "makes the *kīṭ* like himself,"[18] though different accounts are given of how this takes place. In Radhasoami tradition attention is frequently drawn to the flying *bhrangī*'s noisy buzz, which suggests the spiritual sounds (*shabda, nāda*) accompanying the experience of ascension in Radhasoami practice. One modern guru explained the process of transformation this way: when the *bhrangī* approaches the *kīṭ* he buzzes loudly in his ear, causing him great anxiety. The *kīṭ* then retreats into himself, leaving his outside to harden while his inside softens. Eventually the *kīṭ* becomes soft and light enough to fly away from within, leaving an outer shell behind. The author of the following song, probably Kabir, describes the transformation in somewhat different terms, stressing the universal effectiveness of the *bhrangī*-guru's transforming power:

My guru's a great *bhrangī*
When *kīṭ*s come near, that *bhrangī*
Gives them colors like himself. [Refrain]

Their legs become different, their wings become different,
He colors them a different color.
He doesn't look at rank or origins
For the devotee is an outcaste. (1)
When it flows into a crossing channel
The Ganges water itself is called a little stream
But someone who has thus become the river
No longer has to jump across it. (2)
He stopped the crooked
Movements of my mind
To show that beyond the essence in essentials
And the companion in companionship. (3)
He unbound my bonds
And tore through what was pressing me;
He gave Kabir an access to the Lord beyond all reach
And dyed him in Ram's colors.[19] (4)

The guru, then, appears as a powerful transformative force able to qualify his devotees for knowledge of the formless divine. But as these verses of Radhasoami Maharaj demonstrate, in *sant* tradition the guru—frequently referred to as the *satguru,* "the true guru"—can also appear as a powerful attractive force:

A glance intensified my guru-love
And drew my soul to his sweet feet. (1)
My gaze stays in the vision of Hari,
My love increasing every moment. (2)
I make myself an offering to the *satguru*
The *satguru,* destroyer of my senses. (3)
He took me up with arms outstretched
And gave me firm devotion. (4)
I now perform his worship,
Surrendering to him all my body, mind, and wealth. (5)
Other than the guru, there's no one I obey;
Other than the *nām* I know no resting place . . .[20] (6)

In these verses we see both the guru's glance exerting force on the devotee—it "drew" him—and the devotee's efforts at conscious subordination ("Other than the guru, there's no one I obey"). The willful surrender of one's body, mind, and wealth (*tan, man, dhan*) to the guru in verse 5 above is a stock phrase in the songs of the *sant*s, to be seen again soon below.[21] While this phrase does also come into Vaishnava homiletics, it is less often found among the poets of Krishna devotion, who delight in presenting the attractive force of the Lord as needing no complementary efforts from the devotee. In the following song of Sur Das the pull of the Lord appears distinctly more involuntary than that in the song of Radhasoami Maharaj above. While in that song the love of the devotee for the guru increases as he looks at him, here the milkmaid complains that she has lost control of her eyes, always intent on Krishna. In both songs the guru's power is described in a language of control and obedience that recalls the realities of medieval social and political life.

My eyes do not obey me. [Refrain]

I've given up; I'm silent.
  Even when they're near me they won't heed my call. (1)
They seem no longer mine
  Now that they've seen the face of Hari.
It pains me when I think of how
  They take their time in coming back to me. (2)
And when they do return
  We're always fighting.
My eyes use force to drag me toward him;
  They've turned into his messengers. (3)
They've no respect for scripture, world, or family pride—
  So useless they've become.
Sur wonders at the magic power to steal in Shyama
  He took the milkmaid's eyes and keeps them as his slaves.[22] (4)

This song is one of many by Sur describing a milkmaid's eyes as subtle extensions of her person now attracted to her Lord. While, as we have seen, a link to the guru through gaze and vision is described in *sant* poetry, more fundamental there is a link to the divine through subtle sound, a factor also found in the Krishnaite poetry in the figure of Krishna's flute. Thus, we recall, the *bhrangī* guru is frequently seen to transform his disciple in part through his *buzz,* and a group of songs devoted to *shabda mahimā,* "the glory of sound," comes near the beginning of many collections of *sant* poetry, often following immediately after an initial group of songs glorifying the guru. The following verses, attributed to Kabir, affirm that it is the *shabda,* "sound," through which the disciple becomes one with his guru and the uncreated divine:

Sadhu, concentrate on *shabda!*
  Grasp the sound through which all else came forth. [Refrain]

Just to comprehend the *shabd* a little
  Turns the disciple into the guru who is *shabda.*
It's the glory of the guru and disciple,
  And makes the inner path appear . . .[23]

North Indian devotion, then, presents holy men and singular personalities as substantial beings who manifest channels of grace in the world. The devotee has access to these channels by merging his own substantial being into that of his Lord, at least in part through subtle senses of sight and hearing. The climax of devotion is then sometimes described as dissolution into a great divine sea at the end of these channels. Thus, Sur writes:

My eyes are mine no longer. [Refrain]

Gazing intently on beautiful Shyama
  They've spilled out and flow like water. (1)
My eyes behave like water
  Rushing downstream madly.
The water finally merges with the sea;
  My eyes become attached to every part of Krishna. (2)
The sea has no bottom, one cannot pass through it—
  Nor can one find the end of Krishna's beauty.
Says Sur, the milkmaid's eyes became converging sacred rivers
  And mixed into the endless sea of Shyam.[24] (3)

The old Hindi word for "attached" (*rāynā*) at the end of verse 1 of this poem derives from a Sanskrit root (*ranj*) that gains a similar meaning of attraction and gladness, but which has a primary sense of "being colored." The colors (*rang*) that we have seen Kabir's *bhrangī*-guru imparting to his disciples above also derive from the same root, and occur as well in conjunction with water imagery. In the following song, attributed to Kabir, we similarly see colors, attachment, and flowing waters coming together to describe the experience of devotion. Yet while the experience of devotion described in this poem is just as transformative as that to the *bhrangī*-guru, it is more intensely blissful—though more constant and steady than the intensely rushing torrents of Sur's milkmaids. The guru is a dyer (*rangrej*), slowly drawing the devotee's spotted cloth (*chunrī*) through his sweet, liquid colors:

The *satguru*'s a dyer—
He's dyed my spotted cloth. [Refrain]

He got out all the black
And colored it vermillion.
Washing by itself won't do the job;
Still, every day the color of my cloth gets better. (1)
In the reservoir of feeling, in the water of affection,
He drew my cloth through colors of love.
Applying good, thick starch he shook it out,
All brightly colored. (2)
The *satguru* has dyed my cloth,
The *satguru,* so clever and so wise.
To him I offer everything—
My mind and body, wealth and life. (3)
So says Kabir: the dyer-guru has shown mercy toward me
I put on my cool cloth and lose myself in bliss.[25] (4)

The milkmaid's eyes spilling out madly toward Shyama, the Ganges' water itself turning into little streams, and the dyer-guru's sweet colored reservoirs all present poetically creative permutations of a stock devotional image: as small bodies of water flow into large ones, so can human beings unite with divinities. Recently, a number of anthropologists have explored some of the more mundane implications of the general Indian perception of a fluid, substantial universe, and some of their formulations will become important later in our discussion. Of course, many cultures—including much of the premodern West—have naively, and not so naively, taken the universe as a preeminently substantial reality. The Indian vision of the universe stands out less through its positing a substantial universe than through its presenting one that is fluid and continuous.[26] But this characteristic Indian vision is not confined to Hindus alone. Similar perceptions are found in the tantric Buddhism of the postclassical period and in mystical Indian Islam. The typical Buddhist and Sufi variations on the Indian vision of a continuous universe will be explored in chapter 7, as we examine the

Indian holy man in some greater religious contexts. The *sant*s, however, flourished in a predominantly Hindu world where the popular religion was becoming increasingly oriented toward Vaishnava deities—a world which knew a version of the fluid cultural reality that is reflected in the songs cited earlier. We will now turn to the configurations taken by the immanent foci within that world to form complex channels of grace and power.

Configurations of Foci Within North Indian Contexts

Less obvious than the flowering of the *sant*s in a general Hindu environment is just what it means for a tradition to be Hindu. For in addition to sharing elements of a common Indic world view, different Hindu, Buddhist, and Islamic traditions also drew on common forms of religious practice. *Maṇḍala* and *abhiṣeka* figure prominently in the tantric ritual of both Hindus and Buddhists; certain shrines in many rural areas are frequented by Muslims and Hindus alike. What makes Hindu traditions different? From the vantage point of the immanent foci we can call traditions Hindu when they link the religious resources they offer to the eternal heritage of the Vedas. In practice, a link to the Vedas gives some spiritual legitimacy both to the Brahmans, sanctified as Vedic specialists, and to the caste hierarchy, which the Brahmans head. Hindu traditions so defined thus usually manage to justify the eternal socioreligious order. Yet the link to the Vedas can also take highly unorthodox forms. Local, popular traditions often find a connection to the Vedic heritage that appears tenuous, or even crude: local and regional gods are understood as manifestations of the great Hindu deities; a village fortune teller is said to know the *sukṣma veda,* the subtle Veda. At the same time, many educated, respectably born Hindus recognize their mythic and ritual heritage in a pan-Indian lettered tradition.

Thus, though all Hindu traditions give a place to the Vedic heritage, many in fact subordinate it to other foci. The ways in which the traditions of great Sanskritic Hinduism have interacted with smaller, local ones have been examined at length in the past decades.[27] From our perspective, the pan-Indian tradition of Sanskrit texts and the locally divergent forms of ritual popular in towns and villages appear as two complementary dimensions of the heritage focus that Hinduism presents as a greater religious context. To understand the meanings this context gives to the immanent foci we will first sketch out their roles in traditions highlighting Sanksrit texts and popular ritual. What happens when one of these manifestations of the Hindu heritage actually dominates tradition? Then, against the configurations surrounding the singular personality in the Vallabha *sampradāya* and the holy man in tantric yoga, we will finally locate the image of the *sant.*

Many traditionally educated Brahmans continue to find the practical grounds of their faith in the great heritage of Sanskrit texts, which can drastically subordinate gods and holy men. Remaining unattached to any Hindu sectarian development, they take their hereditary status seriously, and rigorously follow the sanctioned customs that will maintain it. Sometimes they identify themselves as *smārta* Brahmans, because they follow the *smṛiti*s, the "remembered" texts. Though often compiled later, the codes of behavior specifically known as *smṛiti* (like the Manu *smṛiti*) generally recall an earlier period of Indian religion, that of the *brāhmaṇa*s. These texts present the Vedic sacrifice as a ritual heritage developed to such an extent that it dwarfed potential singular personalities. The gods of the sacrifice, the *deva*s, derive their meaning from a complex ritual context: they can thus be called upon when needed and ritually manipulated at will. Even as the great gods of Hinduism gain importance in the postclassical period, *smārta* brahmans continue to give more weight to the gods' worship, revealed in ancient texts, than to any hidden communion with the deities' magnificent personalities. The holy man, too, remains well subordinated to the bases of salvation and community offered by the eternal Vedic heritage. To the individual, he offers knowledge of a lettered tradition; for the community, his authority is in his hereditary qualification as ritual officiant.

Popular Hinduism, on the other hand, gives freer reign to foci other than the heritage, and the Brahman and his codified texts may in fact have little role to play at all. Here the Hindu heritage consists of local mythological resources and ritual practices not so rigorously tied to prescribed forms. While much religious ritual is performed, there are fewer norms for what constitutes it as exactly right. Help for practical problems is sought both in local systems of esoteric knowledge and, more often, in the grace of regional deities. Thus, as singular personalities, regional deities can command the devotion of the faithful and become the dominant elements in personal religion. Shamanistic links to regional deities are then offered by holy men, who may also, as wandering *sādhū*s, become revered objects of worship in their own right. Besides these more charismatic roles, the holy man in popular religion is likely to serve in village rituals that demand a sanctifying presence, but not the formal education that the professional *smārta* Brahman is expected to have. In transmitting a local heritage, then, the holy man is likely to serve not as a literate teacher intent on preserving the norms of written texts, but as an accessible preacher and knowledgeable storyteller. Yet in this role his practical influence may be weighty.

Sectarian traditions focused on a singular personality have sometimes emerged when a strong holy man brings together vital aspects of great and little versions of Hinduism. A teacher with both personal charisma and a Brahmanic education can transform a local tradition from one that has focused on a regional manifestation of a pan-Indian deity into a well-defined, enduring *sampradāya.* Means to salvation are revealed less in the diffuse scriptures of the heritage as a whole than in the few books written—or commented on—by the gifted teacher, now taken as a very special personage. The hidden saving power of the Lord is accessible through the *mantra* imparted by the special personage, and the ceremonial initiation into the *mantra* through the generations becomes an important revealed basis of community. Thus, the *puṣṭimārgī*s say that Krishna appeared to Vallabha at Gokula and gave him access to a *mantra.* As a religious institution, the *puṣṭimārgīya sampradāya* keeps access to this *mantra* available through an initiation called *brahma sambandha,* "the link with brahma," and has elaborated its founder's philosophical teachings and ritual practice at length.

Both regional and Sanskritic heritages have contributed to the development of Vallabha's *sampradāya.*[28] At temples Krishna is worshipped to the accompaniment of the vernacular songs of Surdas and a group of seven other poets who wrote in the regional language of Vraj, all known collectively as the *aṣṭachhāpa,* the eight seals. At the same time, Vedantic texts have been written in Sanskrit to justify both the *puṣṭimārgīya* style of worship and the worship of Krishna to the exclusion of other deities. Thus emerging as a very imposing singular personality, Krishna offers grace which can eventually flow to all. Nevertheless, no one of base substance should be allowed to approach his image on earth: only the spiritually pure are allowed access to it. Needing to discriminate among indefinitely large numbers of people in a matter-of-fact way, the *puṣṭimārgīs* developed criteria for purity out of the publicly recognized norms of the Hindu heritage. The major temples have been traditionally open only to Hindus of clean caste, and meals for the deity prepared only by Brahmans of the *girnāra* and *sanchora* subcastes.

Responsible for the temple service, if in many cases not always performing it himself, is the *gosāīṃ,* the hereditary guru of the sect. He is revered not only as the inheritor of a specific sanctified image of the deity, but also, and more importantly, as the physical continuation of Vallabha, a very special person giving access to Krishna. Thus linked to the divine both through his descent from Vallabha and through the image of Krishna with which he is entrusted, the *gosāīṃ* is sometimes treated as an incarnation of the deity.

As a holy man, however, the *gosāīṃ* has a status that differs considerably from that of the yogi, also sometimes seen by his disciples as the incarnation of a deity, usually Shiva. While the *gosāīṃ*'s links to Krishna through his pedigree and the image he inherits are hereditary, the yogi is usually seen to have achieved the state of Shiva through his own meditative powers. The *gosāīṃ* gives access to the hidden power of a single crucial *mantra* that has come down to him, and presides over the revealed ritual worship of Krishna. The yogi as guru in tantric tradition has power over many *mantra*s, and his hidden form in meditation can itself appear as the Supreme Lord. Like the *gosāīṃ,* the tantric yogi is able to find support for his role as holy man in the revealed textual tradition of the Vedic heritage. Indeed, both *tantrika*s and Vaishnavas admit in principle the Hindu idea of a sociospiritual hierarchy, though their particular styles of piety give them different perspectives towards spiritual rank, purity and pollution.

For the *puṣṭimārgīya* Vaishnava, becoming one with Krishna's pure substance demands a strict avoidance of pollution. As the *puṣṭimārgīya* worship is a very public affair, elaborate and well orchestrated, open to all respectable Hindus, so the laws of purity demanded of worshippers are also largely formal and externalized. As Brahmans, Vallabha and his descendants had little trouble with the traditional Sanskritic norms, but now membership in a sectarian community becomes another factor of socioreligious rank, and purity is measured in terms of access to the divine image. At the main *puṣṭimārgīya* shrine in Nathdwara, Rajasthan, only the presiding *gosāīṃ* (known as the *tilkāyit*), his sons, and a few special people he appoints are allowed inside the *nij mandir,* the small inner temple of Krishna. They must bathe in their own separate bathrooms before entering the *nij mandir;* and they become polluted again if they touch anyone outside their own ritual category, urinate, have a runny nose, or emit gas.[29] Their helpers are bound by somewhat less strict rules of purity, and more menial workers in the temple complex by even less strict ones.

Meditative yogis, on the other hand, speak of purifying the mind-stuff (*chit shuddhi*), and are usually more relaxed about observing a commonly prescribed set of ritual norms—though they may be very rigorous about following some idiosyncratic rules (*niyams*) of their own. While the developed tantric philosophies normally do take the traditional sociospiritual hierarchy as a divinely given world order, they tend to advocate an attitude more daring and adventurous than the Vaishnavas toward worldly objects. Some tantras put the virtues of the hero (*vīra*) close to that of the divine (*divya*): the spiritually strong man should be able to withstand the dangerous force of the vital energies of the universe, indeed even to transmute them. Thus the way is open for the ritual inversion of caste norms and the sexual *sādhanā* at worship circles (*chakra pūjā*) attended by some—but not most—tantric yogis.

Elements of both a virile yogic attitude toward spiritual life and a sweet Vaishnava devotion also appear in *sant* tradition. But the early *sant*s seem to have presented internalized forms of both yoga and devotion that depended on no neat system of ritual or vision of sociospiritual hierarchy. Thus they neither accepted the traditional Hindu norms nor ritually inverted them, but often rejected them entirely. Coming largely from low castes themselves, many early *sant*s mocked the hypocrisy they found in accepted Hindu and Islamic religious attitudes.

It was not, then, the ritual and philosophies of lettered traditions that provided the *sant*s with terms in which to speak of their experience, but everyday life and proverbial sayings. The singular personalities of Hinduism, imbued with the aura of Vedic sanctified tradition, were, by Kabir, stripped of their characteristic attributes. Many devotees were then left to find a source of the divine in the holy man alone. Revealed externally as a living guru with a physical body, the *sant* could give his disciple counsel and help him by means of his own psychic power. The disciple, moreover, could also recognize hidden links to the guru, knowing the guru as a being who manifested within him—a being finally one with the Formless Lord. The *sant* could then stand as a channel of grace independent of both Hindu and Islamic heritages, for neither the living holy man, nor the projection of the guru within the disciple or onto the Lord above, needed any further basis of legitimacy.

2

Three Foci for North Indian Hindus

While individual *sants* could and sometimes did attempt to stand independent of any sanctified heritage, the *sant* tradition as a whole developed within a greater religious context dominated largely by Vaishnava Hinduism, and in fact assimilated many Vaishnava norms. Later, exploring the development of tradition among the *sants*, we will see how these forms are adapted and modified; but first we need to examine the ways in which the Hindu forms have flourished on their own grounds.

To this end three traditions of North Indian worship will be presented, each clearly dominated by one of the immanent foci. The elaborate iconic worship at Nathdwara, the main *puṣṭimārgīya* shrine, exalts Krishna as a magnificent divine personality. Not far from Nathdwara lies Pushkar lake, a shrine of both regional and pan-Indian importance. One of the few places particularly sacred to Brahma—revered by all today as the creator but with no important sectarian tradition of his own—the scene at Pushkar encapsulates some dynamics of tradition within the eternal heritage known to Hindus generally. The modes by which devotees interact with one another and the divine at these two pilgrimage sites will then be compared to the interactions focused around the Radhasoami holy man as moving center, a living destination for devotees.

Focus in Space: The Distribution of Grace and the Shape of Community

Late in the year 1671, Tilkayit Damodar Lal, the sixth successor to the *puṣṭimārgīya* founder Vallabha, arrived at the village of Sinhad, north of Udaipur, in southern Rajasthan. He brought with him an imposing stone image of Krishna with his hand stretched up, palm upwards, a pose conventionally suggesting one of Krishna's youthful exploits: as a child, he had lifted up Mount Govardhan over Vraj country to shield his homeland against Indra's wrath. The ritual worship of the *puṣṭimārgīs* had developed at Govardhan around this image of Krishna, which many saw as embodying the very person of the Lord. Devotees could thus know the image itself as a god, whom they called Shri Govardhan Nath, "The Master of Govardhan," or simply Shrinathji, "The Master"—of Govardhan, the *gopīs*, and all his devotees. But Aurangzeb's active distaste for graven images had made Govardhan, in Vraj Country, close to the center of Mughal power, unsafe for Shrinathji; it was thought best that he flee.

With his retinue, Damodar Lal had accompanied Shrinathji from Vraj via a long circle through Jodhpur, where they had stayed for a while. The Jodhpur Raja, unfortunately—fearing, perhaps, the wrath of Aurangzeb—had not remained hospitable. But the wife of the Raja of Udaipur was said to be a staunch Vaishnava, and there was talk that her husband would provide a hundred thousand troops for Shrinathji's safety.

Sinhad itself, at any rate, seemed like a secure place. It was not very close to any important centers of power, as Shrinathji's previous home had been: the cities of Udaipur and Chittor—traditionally the objects of Mughal attack—lay considerable distances away. True, the land around Sinhad was rockier and drier than Vraj country, but the hills and jungle that surrounded the village could themselves provide some protection. At Sinhad the *tilkāyit* built a temple to Shrinathji and a small palace for himself adjoining it. Both temple and palace prospered: the village grew into the town known as Nathdwara, "the portal of Shrinathji," and became both the spiritual and administrative center of the *puṣṭimārgīya* Vaishnavas.

From Gujarat and Bombay came well-to-do *puṣṭimārgīya* pilgrims, and the traditions that developed around the town reflected their origin as well as that of Shrinathji.[1] While the dry bed of the river Banas nearby was referred to as the Yamuna, a river which runs through Vraj country, inside the town well-kept Gujarati restaurants did a thriving business. Soon people no longer talked about the practical circumstances accompanying Shrinathji's shift from Vraj to Nathdwara. They knew better: Shrinathji had come, of course, because he was fond of playing chess with a certain young lady named Ajab Kunwar who lived in the area. She had invited him to make his residence near her instead of wearing himself out through frequent comings and goings. Shrinathji, unfortunately for Ajab Kunwar, couldn't change his residence just when she asked, but he promised to do so later. His coming to Nathdwara with Tilkayit Damodar Lal in 1671 was the fulfillment of that promise. Certainly it was Shrinathji who told the *tilkāyit* just where to stop on the journey. The wheel of the heavy cart in which he was riding got stuck in the mud at the village of Sinhad. Clearly, Shrinathji himself chose the site where his temple was to be built.[2]

About a hundred miles north by northwest, and uncountable years earlier, Brahma settled on Pushkar as the site for an impressive Vedic sacrifice. Brahma couldn't quite decide just where to perform his sacrifice, and as he was trying to make up his mind, a lotus he was holding—*puṣkara* in Sanskrit—dropped from his hand. Falling to earth, it formed Pushkar lake, and Brahma decided to perform his sacrifice there. The spot was indeed well suited for the enactment of a great religious event. While not far from places where large numbers of people live, Pushkar remains a beautiful little lake. Even today its waters are clear, visibly efficacious for purifying baths.

Brahma invited all the gods to come attend his sacrifice, which they did. One goddess, however, was not immediately visible among the divine throngs—Brahma's wife, Savitri. Now the eternal Vedic ritual prescribes a necessary role for the wife of the person sponsoring a great sacrifice, and Brahma, tired of waiting, hastily married another woman. When Savitri finally appeared and learned of Brahma's second marriage she was furious and left in a huff, stopping at a hill to the north of the lake. At Pushkar today a temple to Savitri remains on that hill, while temples to all the other gods are clustered along half the lake's shore. If Brahma himself no longer inspires much devotion, many of the other gods certainly do, and Pushkar continues to be a vital place of pilgrimage.

Indeed, in an earlier era Pushkar may have been even more important as an all-India center than it is now. It is extolled at length in the Mahabharata, and appears there as the first stop in a grand tour of the sacred fords.[3] A long song of praise to Pushkar, moreover, the *Puṣkara Mahātmya,* finds it ways into some recensions of the Padma Purana.[4] Today, Pushkar functions primarily as a regional pilgrimage center for Rajasthan, and for people in its immediate vicinity it remains most sacred indeed: many pilgrims in Ajmer district, where Pushkar is located, consider a pilgrimage to the Ganges "useless" (*bekār*) unless it is concluded with a dip in the lake. The town, moreover, has its own role to play in the worldly life of the region. Around the full moon of the Hindu month of Kartik, when the waters of the lake are most potent, a great cattle fair is held at Pushkar. Different caste communities maintain separate temples there, which during the fair are usually filled to overflowing. Streets are jam-packed as people of highly diverse caste communities attempt to drive hard bargains at the market, move to eat and sleep in their own living places, and then go to bathe in the same holy lake.

Way on the other side of Rajasthan, in a village not far from the Punjab, a gentleman farmer is taking a stroll with a small group of attentive people. They have come from places all over North India to spend time with the gentleman they surround, a guru in the Radhasoami lineage with a fairly small, but devoted following. These devotees have managed to leave their normal occupations for a few weeks, perhaps using up their yearly vacation time, and value their days spent with their guru. Now and then one of them will recognize remarks in the guru's discourse and signs in his activity meant especially for him, but most of the time the guru seems to be talking to the devotees around him as a group, and as a group they receive his *darshan.* Almost everyone among them finds the atmosphere at the ashram highly charged, and the daily routine of meditation and audience with the guru productive of both ecstasy and psychic strain.[5]

Not very long before, the ashram resembled an ordinary farm. Most of the people visiting the guru now, if they had heard of him then at all, knew him only as a pious devotee of his own revered master. But when that master passed on, some disciples recognized him as the successor. There were detractors too, of course, recognizing other successors. Still, the guru accepted those who wanted to come to him, and finally found it necessary to build some accommodation for them. When his spiritual work on earth was done and he himself passed on, people would probably stop visiting this remote spot.

In towns in the Punjab and outside them, near busy streets in the middle of Agra and Delhi, on the outskirts of Gwalior city, Radhasoami ashrams have grown up under similar circumstances, differing according to the guru's personal style and the size of his following. Some have remained small, and offer most disciples a chance for some personal interaction with their guru: an interaction often as chastening as it is blissful, spoken of alternatively as *gaṛhat,* stern "fashioning" of the disciple, and *vilās,* or *līlā*—words Hindus use to talk about divine play.

At other, larger and more established ashrams, some of which have passed through several generations of gurus, the chance for individual play with the master diminishes. Most disciples must be content to listen to the master's public discourses and get a glimpse of him from afar. Yet in the last chapter we saw how visual contact with the guru, as with the god, can be both powerful and appealing: "A glance intensified my guru-love and drew my soul toward his sweet feet."[6] People come, then, just to be near the holy presence of the guru, even if they do not expect to be able to interact with him personally. The guru's presence can, moreover, sanctify the places and objects with which he comes into contact. As Vraj country is holy through Krishna's continuing presence there, and Nathdwara, Shrinathji's new residence, is holy like Vraj, so is the place where the guru resides holy. But while the various sites of Vraj (and their replications in Nathdwara) are thought of in definite mythological terms, the places and things sanctified by the guru have less specific mythological character of their own. They are usually perceived as ordinary and mundane in themselves, yet having an aura of sanctity acquired through the guru's touch: thus are seen the guru's house, his chair, the food distributed in his name.

Indeed, food that the guru has sanctified probably offers the most concrete way of assimilating his grace. In his power to sanctify food the guru seems to differ little from a god. In most Hindu religious traditions the devotee offers—depending on his degree of purity—prepared food, grains, or money to his chosen deity; he will then frequently receive some of this back, or other food touched by the deity, as *prasād,* or "sanctified leavings." In verses of the sort sung regularly before the image of Shrinathji, Sur Das presents parallels between mixing in the divine waters, the *darshan* of the divine being, and feeding and being fed by him.

My gaze has fallen into the sweet juice of Shyama.
All the gods are found there:
  Shiva, Brahma, Sanaka, and Narada the sage.
So many ways my gaze enjoys this taste:
  It eats it up, it offers to be eaten, it pours out the sweet juice . . .[7]

Yet Shrinathji, the Radhasoami master, and Pushkar Raj appear to focus the divine in their characteristic ways, each offering different dynamics for partaking of divine waters, *darshan* and *prasād.*

Devotees and Deities Who Travel and Take Food

At Shrinathji's city of Nathdwara the flow of grace through *darshan* and *prasād* is well focused and moves through a relatively homogeneous constituency. While only a sizable minority of pilgrims to Nathdwara are *puṣṭimārgī*s like the administrators of the temple there, most would identify themselves, at least for the moment, as Vaishnavas. Predominantly Brahmans and *baniyā*s, "traders," more come from Gujarat and Bombay than from the surrounding areas of Rajasthan.[8] A good number of the more affluent, of whom there are surprisingly many, choose to eat at modern-style restaurants serving rich, delicately prepared, pure vegetarian food. Some would rather join the majority who eat from leaf-trays of food sold as *prasād* by the temple authorities in the bazaar that has grown up around the temple. In addition to mealtime *prasād,* the temple authorities also sell more durable *prasād* made from flour, sugar, and *ghī,* which can be taken home to be saved or distributed.

Life for the pilgrim at Nathdwara revolves visibly around the major temple situated near the center of the town and the daily cycle of *darshan*s Krishna gives there, a cycle following the events of the day at which an important person might be pleased to be attended by servants and grant audience. The inner temple is open at fixed hours only, and notification signs are posted at the major rest-houses. Pilgrims converge on the temple at the appropriate times, experience a rather elaborately orchestrated *darshan,* and disperse, perhaps with *prasād.*

The meals that Shrinathji leaves as *prasād* can be lavish indeed. "The Deity is served with sixteen vegetables, nineteen types of *bhāt,* eight types of *khīr,* seven types of *khichṛī,* three types of *thulī,* three types of *halwā,* sixty-four varieties of curry, twenty-six types of soup vegetables and a large variety of other items . . ."[9] On a feast day at Nathdwara called Annakuta, "mountains of food," Shrinathji receives fifty-six kinds of sweets. In 1970–71 the annual expense of service to Shrinathji was well over twelve lakh rupees (about $150,000), about ninety percent of the total expenditure of the temple. Of this nearly a third was spent on butter and oil alone.[10] This *prasād,* of course, is distributed to temple workers living in Nathdwara; residents of the town, moreover, will say that all food served there is *prasād.* It is indeed difficult for the pilgrim to procure some simply made everyday food items in Nathdwara. Tea in the bazaar is normally boiled in milk alone (not, as usual, in a mixture of milk and water) and is sold in disposable clay mugs, not cups, to avoid possibility of pollution. Certainly, the purity and richness of the food at Nathdwara can be seen by the devout to embody the purity and richness of Shrinathji's substance. Yet in general, those alone can partake of Shrinathji's *prasād* who keep themselves not only relatively pure, but also relatively rich.

The attitudes toward *darshan* and *prasād* evident in Nathdwara are reflected in the practice of *puṣṭimārgīs* in their homes throughout India. Pious *puṣṭimārgīs* keep an image of Krishna in a small family shrine and serve him regularly. Meals are normally offered to the deity first and are then consumed as *prasād.* An ideal that all food consumed should be *prasād* can give *puṣṭimārgīs* a particular devotional perspective on practices in fact followed by many high-caste Hindus. Like many other pious Hindu householders, the pious *puṣṭimārgī* will refrain from eating outside the home; like the others, the *puṣṭimārgī* may see food from outside as ritually unclean, but he also wants to eat the food that has first been offered to his family image. Shrinathji, like the most pious Hindu, is not only vegetarian, but also avoids onion and garlic; *puṣṭimārgīs* follow the example of both. At the same time, in reflecting the value given to a specific tradition over against a complex sanctified hierarchy, *puṣṭimārgīya* practice can differ from that prescribed by the Hindu heritage generally. Thus, most Hindus will normally accept the *prasād* of any reasonably respectable deity, provided they have no qualms about the status of the hand giving it to them. Devout *puṣṭimārgīs*, on the other hand, will take *prasād* only from their own temples.

While *puṣṭimārgīs* attempt to model the ways of their own homes around that of the court of Shrinathji, pilgrims to Pushkar adhere to the ways of their own communities after they arrive there. Most important Rajasthani communities have their own *dharamshālās* at Pushkar; in fact most of the many small temples dotting the shore of the lake were originally started as rest-houses for particular castes. At the temples, groups of pilgrims often cook their own food. There are certainly sound economic reasons for this practice, but there is also no general provision at Pushkar for ritually clean *prasād,* as there is at Nathdwara. Villagers on a short pilgrimage will frequently bring a few days' supply of durable breads with them: *pūṛīs*, *parāṭhās*, or *sakarbaṛī*—the latter a specially prepared wayfarer's bread. Thus, while people take durable, ritually pure food away from Nathdwara, they bring it to Pushkar.

The food brought to Pushkar or cooked at one of the temples there can, of course, be turned into *prasād* by offering it to the deity at hand. For at many Hindu temples—but not at that of Shrinathji—the *darshan* of the deity can be had at most times by anyone ready to leave an offering. Similarly, officiants ready to perform Pushkar *pūjās* can be found at most hours, and a solitary ritual dip can be taken at any time if the traditionally auspicious early morning hours are inconvenient. Thus, while the religious life of visitors to Shrinathji's court is governed by Shrinathji's predictable schedule, that of visitors to Pushkar runs pretty much according to their own convenience.

When someone goes to visit his guru, however, he usually receives *darshan* at the guru's convenience, which may not be easy to predict at all. At a large annual gathering such as the birthday celebration of a reigning Radhasoami master, one might see crowds of devotees standing outside his residence. They may have heard rumors that he is to appear soon, but they have no hope of knowing just when. As at Nathdwara, many of these people regularly come across regions, and most are middle-class. But their caste origins cover a wider spectrum of Hindu society than those of the Nathdwara *baniyās* and Brahmans. And unlike pilgrims to Nathdwara, who often come in small family groups, or those to Pushkar, who may come with their extended family or groups from the village, someone visiting his guru may well have come alone. At the ashram, then, visitors may be happy to meet with old guru-brothers and guru-sisters.

While the devotee is thus likely to find some welcome community at the guru's ashram, it may not be spontaneous and unbounded. The guru, as long as he is well, normally retains control of his immediate domain, and has around him a group of people practiced at carrying out his wishes. Alternative norms of authority develop, not always explicit, based on length of discipleship and relative access to the guru as focus of community. Around the periphery, the bonds of relationship through a shared guru among fellow disciples may have trouble competing with the distinctions of caste and class retained from the world outside.

The ambiguous attitude toward the everyday realities of the Hindu cultural world evident when the disciple visits the guru's home is also seen when the guru visits the disciple's. Unlike Shrinathji, who chose to stop indefinitely at Nathdwara, or Pushkar *rāj,* set forever in the Aravalli hills, the living guru is usually free to travel—and most Radhasoami masters regularly do. Attempting to serve the guru in one's own familiar surroundings adds new dimensions to everyday life. First of all, it intensifies it. Routine tasks elicit anxious concern: a local disciple brings milk and a new cup to the station where his guru's train is scheduled to stop for an hour. Will the guru take it? What if the milk curdles? Unexpected coincidence becomes miraculous personal affirmation: the guru's nephew will, alas, not accept the outside milk for his uncle, the guru; then, suddenly, he finds his own milk has curdled, and there's a problem with the guru's cup too! The devotional efforts of the disciple—the future Sahibji Maharaj of Dayalbagh—are justified.[11]

But everyday life around the guru is not only more intense; it is also more perplexing. Higher spiritual powers upset expected social rules, but neither completely nor predictably. Thus the Radhasoamis, stressing the interiority of spiritual life, reject in principle the religious value of caste distinctions: at gatherings at the ashrams, all devotees normally eat together, though back in the world they might adopt some of the world's more traditional standards. Still, the disciple did not really expect the guru to refuse his milk because he feared ritual pollution. Why, then, did the guru's nephew refuse to take it? Was it traditional Hindu ideas about the value of food prepared and served within the family? Was it that the guru had now begun to take on the awe-inspiring characteristics of a singular personality like Shrinathji, approachable only by a very special elect? Or was it through some specific fault, perhaps one of pride, in the nephew? Or in the disciple? Revealed rules of the Hindu heritage cannot be counted on to work dependably around the guru, nor is his hidden spiritual status clear. Maybe the whole incident was to be a mysterious lesson in humility for the disciple and the nephew in turn. At any rate, everyday physical accident around the guru can often seem shrouded in mystery—mystery which appears in a world where basic Indian cultural concepts remain, but traditional Hindu hierarchical patterns are taken less seriously and altered, while never quite suspended.

Mystery and Community

Not only around gurus do normal Hindu patterns of socioreligious interaction frequently appear ambiguous, but also around gods. Brahma, we recall, had invited the gods to a sacrifice at Pushkar and was waiting for his wife Savitri to come. He was annoyed with her for not coming on time, and the jar of *amrita* that was to be held on her head was beginning to weigh heavy on his. Finally he sent Indra out to find another woman for him to marry. The only girl Indra could find, however, was a Gujarin—a member of a cowherding caste usually thought of as ritually clean but not particularly distinguished. Brahma managed the situation by passing the Gujarin through a cow—into the cow's mouth and out the other end.[12] And since, as Brahma said, cows are really the same as brahmans, the woman just born (so to speak) of a cow had become fit to be his wife. Because she emerged from a cow—*go* in Sanskrit, *gāy* in Hindi—she was called Gayatri.

While Brahma was anxious to follow the correct code of conduct in regard to ritual, caste, and family, he could adjust them to his own convenience. Hindu mortals have less power to maneuver, and when it comes down to matters of family and ceremonial obligation, they usually do what they must. Wives will generally be prompt enough about performing ritual duties, and if they aren't their husbands will just have to wait. To become a Brahman a Gujarin will have to tend her cows dutifully in anticipation of a better birth some day. And if she is not a Brahman, she can hardly expect to find a Brahman husband. Indeed, looking to the Hindu heritage as one's primary basis of religious community means learning to live with the caste and family obligations attendant on one's place in a vast and complex society. The society will eventually accommodate most individuals and groups who choose to accept the role it gives them: different caste communities continue to build their own temples at Pushkar, just as latecoming gods could join the rest at Brahma's sacrifice. But as foci within a Hindu context the great god, who can alter traditional rules, and the guru, whose authority may attenuate them, are each able to provide a base for a religious community with its own internal structure. Among the *puṣṭimārgī*s and the Radhasoamis, moreover, we can see how the shape of religious community is consonant with the mystery of its source.

As sources of grace both Sur's Krishna and the Radhasoami guru present combinations of human and divine qualities. But these are clearly different combinations—each a paradox, but with its own devotional and socioreligious implications. For Sur the human and divine come together in the image of the child-god, helpless but all-powerful. In this song, a favorite of both Indian and Western scholars, the contrast between the stumbling child Krishna and the creator and destroyer of the worlds is striking indeed:

Watching Krishna walk gives joy to Mother Yashoda [Refrain]

On all fours now, close to the floor, Krishna flounders;
  His mother sees the scene and points it out to all.
He makes it to the doorway then
  comes back the other way again.
He trips and he falls, doesn't manage to cross—
  Which makes the sages wonder:
    Ten-millions of worlds he creates in a flash
      And can destroy them just as fast;
    But he's picked up by Nanda's wife, who sets him down, plays games with him,
      Then with her hand supports him while he steps outside the door.
When they see Sur's Lord, gods, men, and sages
  Lose track of their minds.[13]

Yet less than a third of the thousand or so child-poems of Sur are what Kenneth Bryant calls " 'epiphanies': poems of revelation and ironic contrast, poems that play the child against the god."[14] In the following song the play between baby Krishna's childlike and divine qualities is presented sooner through suggestion than through striking contrast. The image of crawling Krishna reflected countless times in the inlaid jewels of Nanda's courtyard recalls the vision of a many-armed, many-headed deity—who then goes to his mother's breast to suck:

Kanha's coming: crawling, crying joyfully. [Refrain]

In the courtyard of Nanda, golden and jewel-studded,
  Hari hurries to catch his reflection.
Now and then Hari, seeing his shadow,
  Gives it a grasp with his hands.
Then gleefully gurgles: two little teeth shine.
  Hari repeatedly seizes his image.
    Hand-shadows, foot-shadows, on the golden ground
      Together all shine forth.
    As if each hand and foot in every jewel on the earth
      Had come together in a lotus-throne adorning Krishna.
Yashoda seeing the sweetness of childhood,
  Calls out to Nanda again and again.
Then hiding her son in the folds of her sari,
  Suckles Sur's Lord at her breast.[15]

In most of his songs, however, Sur merely describes in detail Krishna's antics with his loving family and friends, leaving it to his audience to remember that the child is also God. The following song, like the other two, is one of several collected under the headings *dhuturoṃ chalnā* and *pāvoṃ chalnā,* songs describing baby Krishna crawling and taking his first steps. This one, however, is probably more representative of the type:

Yashoda, his mother, is teaching him to walk. [Refrain]

He stumbles and then grabs her hand
  Unsteady, his feet have found the floor. (1)
At times she looks at his beautiful face
  And prays for his well-being. (2)
At times she beseeches her family gods:
  "Let my boy Krishna have long life." (3)

At times she gives a shout to Balram:
"Come play here with your brother in the yard." (4)
Sur Das knows that this great glory of the Lord's play
Gives delight to Raja Nanda.[16] (5)

There is certainly some nice irony in Yashoda's praying to her family gods for the long life of Lord Krishna, but there is no vivid portrayal of Krishna's divine attributes, and only in the last line a rather conventional reference to his *līlā,* divine play. The religious force of the *puṣṭimārgīya* liturgy, elaborately enacted at Nathdwara, can be understood in part through its vivid evocation of Krishna's divine attributes as well as his childlike ones: when descriptions of Krishna the lovable child are sung as accompaniment to a lavish and majestic worship of a most unchildlike image, both sides of the devotional paradox come together.

It is not difficult to see how *puṣṭimārgīya* piety could have an especial appeal to members of the merchant castes. As prosperous family people they could both appreciate the child-god's antics and maintain his elaborate worship. Indeed, Weber gives the "Vallabhacharis" as an example of the "religion of the mercantile classes."[17] As a fairly homogeneous merchant group, moreover, the *puṣṭimārgīs* have at times been able to wield real economic power. Thus, contributions were raised for the temples on the basis of a small levy on goods traded by *puṣṭimārgīya* merchants. This seems an appropriate and even equitable way of meeting the religious expenditures of a mercantile community; but when that community had control over certain essential commodities, as it did in Bombay toward the beginning of the last century, the levy could be seen in effect as a direct tax on the populace at large.[18]

Still, for all the sweet majesty he commands, the image of the Lord worshipped by the *puṣṭimārgīs* remains an image. His world is centered in the heavens of the inner vision, where divine qualities take conventional human shapes. The outer earthly body of the image is very stable, of clay or stone, and its public worship, as we have seen, will normally follow a predictable liturgy designed to evoke the heavenly world within. The private worship of the Lord as a divine child can similarly follow a prescribed attitude of Vaishnava devotion and lead to an archetypalization of everyday life. In contrast, the mystery of the Lord as living person revealed in the Radhasoami guru derives from the conjunction of the formless (*nirguṇ*) divine and a most concrete human form, a conjunction that to the devotee may appear tense and unstable. The earthly embodiment of the guru known to close disciples is a living, changing person whose behavior may seem continually paradoxical, and his outer worship is performed through practical service that is often unpredictable and almost always most mundane.

Paltu Sahib, an eighteenth-century *sant* with whom we will become better acquainted in the next chapter, portrays the living guru in a series of sharp contrasts:

At times his words are humble;
  At times he sits up proud.
At times he sings out Hari's play;
  At times he says the name of Ram within.
At times he says the world is true;
  At times he holds it false.
At times he talks about the Lord with Form;
  At times he shows the Formless.
At times he talks about the dualistic path;
  At times he becomes non-dual . . .

This series of contrasts in fact extends for a total of about thirty lines. It is preceded, moreover, with an admonition to disciples: the *sant* is not the same as the ordinary man in the world; don't judge him as one.

These, says Paltu, are the *sant*'s distinctive signs:
  To hoard and to renounce are nothing for him;
He sets out things according to his destiny
  Without acquiring any blame.
Give up all your explanations,
  Don't use logic now:
The doer here is someone else,
  Why not find satisfaction in him?
The one who wants real happiness, says Paltu,
  Should give up calculations;
Doubt is the name of the world,
  In death and old age—pain.[19]

The doubt and pain of attempting to fathom the mysteries of the guru are the subject of this song by Babu Shyam Lal, known as Guru Data Dayal, in the Radhasoami line:

So hard the path of *guru-bhakti*—
  Let the guru make it easy. [Refrain]

As a man the guru seems to men,
  Yet as a man he's known to someone who knows nothing.
    How can one ever rest? (1)

The guru sometimes acts just like
An unaffected child
And the soul is struck with wonder. (2)
The satguru gives proofs within the body
And a little faith begins to grow
But later must be sacrificed.
Again and again the mind becomes fickle; (3)
Again and again the fool becomes trapped in illusions
And loses his way. (4)
The fool doesn't know where his welfare resides
Or the will of the Lord (5)
And acts to his own disadvantage.
Again and again he will hear holy words, and again and again will forget them.
He won't recognize the satguru
Or know his greatness. (6)
Let that great Lord we know as Dhara Sindhu Pratap
Watch over us, protect us in all ways
And give the gift of *bhakti.*[20] (7)

Disciples, however, eventually learn to live with doubts and shifting understandings of the guru. Thus, to a devotee at a good-sized Radhasoami center I once explained that I had come to "study perceptions of the guru." Her first response was laughter, after which she said that her perceptions of the guru in fact "change all the time."

Not only do the perceptions of the living guru outside change; so do those of the guru seen within. As Babu Shyam Lal notes in the song above, it is when the disciple sees "proofs within the body" that his "faith begins to grow." The disciple sees proof of the hidden, but substantial link that the guru has forged with him through subtle visual and auditory signs that he experiences. Some disciples will, moreover, speak of the occurrence of inner sights and sounds at the time of initiation as positive proof of their guru's qualifications to give initiation.

As spiritual practice progresses the disciple experiences the guru within in different ways: the sights and sounds that lead to the divine can present themselves as an endless variety of images and voices. But perhaps the most central experience of the hidden guru within is the physical image of the living guru himself. Tying the disciple's spiritual experience to the person of the living guru, it impresses on him the power of the guru's grace. Linking subjective experience inside to an objective guide without, the image of the guru marks crucial stages of spiritual progress. The following passage by a prominent disciple of

Sant Sawan Singh of Beas describes the changing forms of the guru from the "Third Eye," where an important stage of spiritual experience begins, to Sat Lok, the entrance to the highest division of the heavens:

> The Guru or Master remains with the disciple all through the journey from the Third Eye to Sat Lok, but his form does not remain like that of a man throughout the whole path. At the Third Eye his form is the same as his human form, outside in the physical world; but later, in higher transcendent stages, his form (as of all souls there) is different in different planes. However, in Sach Khand or Sat Lok, his form is again of man, as it is at the Third Eye or outside in the physical world . . . It is not that the same form becomes more and more radiant or effulgent; *the very form changes from* stage to stage . . .[21]

Thus, the image of the guru in his "human form" as it exists "outside in the physical world" appears to the disciple when he is able to stop identifying with his own physical body at the Third Eye. It appears to him again when he is finally able to merge with the Formless Lord at Sat Lok.

Neither in his inner, hidden aspect, leading the disciple to the Formless Lord, nor in his outer, revealed aspect, providing psychic force and spiritual counsel, does the guru appear able to offer the basis for a religious community at once extensive and coherent. Only a limited number of disciples can have regular contact with the living guru outside, although those who have learned to live with his changing attitudes and teachings might indeed constitute a close, coherent community. The gurus who do give initiation to large numbers of people usually offer along with their hidden inner presence some form of fixed revealed knowledge: a set of precepts to follow or the elements of a consistent teaching. Thus, the image of the guru provides a link to the divine that bypasses customary ritual, and his teachings present the Hindu socioreligious hierarchy in a very dubious light; but neither image nor teachings offer any full-scale social bonds to replace them.

We can find, then, among the Radhasoamis both small, loyal groups focused around the guru's living person, and far-flung, disparate communities, whose members know primarily the guru's divine image within. Neither type of group resembles the extensive and potentially powerful community focused around the *puṣṭimārgīya* Krishna, in whom the human and divine form a more unified, if less physically substantial, whole.

Focus in Time: Seed, Continuity, and Creation

The characteristic socioreligious structures that have evolved within the communities focusing on the Radhasoami Guru and Vallabha's Krishna demonstrate both continuity and change over time. As alternative types of dominant focus, however, the Radhasoami Guru and Krishna present different bases for continuity and contrasting patterns of change. Despite their spiritual lineages' different roots, both Radhasoamis and *puṣṭimārgī*s see them evolving along lines suggested by the growth of an extended Indian family lineage. The organic development of both types of lineage, moreover, should ideally follow regular patterns of growth. For traditional South Asians not only know all aspects of their world to be ultimately grounded in a single continuous substance, but they also know their world to be guided by a single comprehensive order.

In the Indic religiophilosophical language this order is spoken of as *dharma*—a word which derives from a root meaning "support" and which has come to refer at once to the fundamental nature of an object, the activity natural to a person, and to general laws of correct behavior. In a number of analytical studies, Barnett, Marriott, Inden, Nicholas, and other anthropologists have spoken of the interdependence of the substantial world with the order pervading it as coded substance. "Code" in this formulation derives from *dharma* as "code for conduct."

Perhaps the most powerful image of coded substance in its temporal potentiality is that of the seed, *bīja* or *bindu,* the latter term having particular reference to human semen. The image of the seed appears in many contexts. Conscious acts can produce seeds that bear inescapable "fruit"; Patanjali refers to the *samādhi* from which one need not return as "seedless," *nirbīja.* But yogis also talk about seeds in more positive ways: semen, biological seed, becomes the source of vital power that is transmuted in yoga, and specific seed *mantra*s (*bīja mantra*s) can eventually blossom in the lotuses of the subtle physical body. South Asians, then, know definite analogies between the spiritual and physical potentialities of seed. Both aspects of the potentiality of seed can govern the continuity of Hindu religious traditions, where a parallel is drawn between *nād paramparā* and *bindu paramparā:* succession through the sound (*nād*) of *mantra* and succession through physical seed; spiritual and biological lineage.[22]

Spiritual succession to the Brahmanic heritage is normally dependent on biological factors. Ritual access to the Vedic *mantra*s is limited to those born Brahman by caste. Indeed, the model of the Vedic sacrifice that lies behind the origin myth of the multi-community pilgrimage site of Pushkar also lies behind a famous myth giving the origins of the basic caste divisions of Hindu society. Rig Veda 10.90, called the *puruṣa sūkta,* describes the sacrifice of *puruṣa,* the cosmic person whom Inden describes as the code-man embodying the *dharma* of the universe.[23] The myth presents the four basic caste divisions as arising from the different parts of *puruṣa*'s body: the *shūdra*s, servants, emerge from his feet, the *vaishya*s, common people, from his thighs, and the *kṣatriya*s, warriors, from his arms.

The Brahmans, deriving from *puruṣa*'s mouth, fulfill their *dharma* through Vedic mantra: its recitation, preservation, and transmission. But the Brahmans themselves know a biological continuity. The Vedic *mantra*s, then, the powerful source of tradition, are preserved through biological seed.

As Brahmans derive from the mouth of the sacrificed *puruṣa,* so Vallabha is the incarnation of the mouth of Krishna (his *mukhāvatāra*). But Krishna's mouth is both the source of cosmic sound and the receptacle of divine sacrificial fire (*adhidaivika agni*). Thus the words of Vallabha are said to have the power of the eternal Vedic truths. According to one modern scholar writing from within *puṣṭimārgīya* tradition, an *āchārya,* "teacher"—like Vallabhacharya—"will never describe any heavenly (*alaukika*) thing whose root is not present in the Vedas." A tradition founded in this way by an *āchārya* is called a *sampradāya.* Some "great men of knowledge and devotion," however, "like Dadu, Nanak, and Kabir,"[24] were not able to find roots in the Vedas. The traditions they founded are called *panth*s. The Vallabha *sampradāya,* then, is here distinguished from the *sant panth* as Brahmanic from non-Brahmanic, a distinction that would probably be accepted, though with a different valuation, by many in *sant* tradition. For while our Vallabhite scholar can find a continuity for his tradition with eternal orthodox truths through the idea of "Vedic" *āchārya*s, the follower of *sant* tradition can look to an eternal spiritual "clan" of *sant*s, whose knowledge is understood to surpass the Veda.

"Clan," as we recall from our discussion of the North Indian sociohistorical context, is used in this study to refer to felt bonds of kinship among large classes of people with a common mythical origin. As illustrated in the myth of *puruṣa,* where great classes of men derive from different parts of *puruṣa*'s body, notions of clan are fundamental to the major caste divisions of Hindu society. These notions are also basic to the continuity of sociospiritual prerogatives within that society:

an effective knowledge of Vedic *mantra* is transmitted by Brahmans, and its scope is limited to them.

Though Vallabha was a Brahman, the *mantra* that was revealed to him at Gokul was not the prerogative of Brahmans alone. Indeed, the Lord told him that all should repeat the phrase "Shri Krishna *sharanaṃ mama,* " "Shri Krishna is my refuge" although the scope of this *mantra* has been generally restricted to respectably born Hindus. At the same time, the right to transmit this *mantra* is limited to Brahmans springing from the biological seed of Vallabha, who are often referred to in conversation as his *aṃsa,* a "part" of him. Thus, while the spiritual power of the mantra can transcend certain, but not all, biological factors of caste and clan, spiritual succession depends on descent through individuals, a consciousness of kinship we have referred to as lineage.

Among the Radhasoamis, too, succession is a matter of lineage, but the lineage here is a spiritual one. The right to give initiation into the Lord's name (*nām*) is normally passed from a guru to a disciple who is not a physical relation, though sometimes it does fall to sons and grandsons. The spiritual scope of *nām,* moreover, transcends distinctions of caste both in theory and in practice.

The practical dynamic of continuity, too, differs in the *sant* and *puṣṭimārgīya* lineages. As examples from the end of chapter six will show us in detail, a successor to a *sant* can radically and explicitly alter such tradition as he has inherited. The *gosāīṃ*s, on the other hand, inherit an explicitly revealed philosophical teaching and an elaborately codified ritual tradition. Change in tradition is thus more subtle and guarded. At minor shrines, prescribed ritual can be presented in a simplified form: booksellers report that the authoritative manual of *puṣṭimārgīya* ritual (called *Sevā Vidhi,* "The Means of Service") is not even available in Hindi, only in Gujarati. Persons at Nathdwara conversant with modern tradition, moreover, remark that some important *gosāīṃ*s develop noticeably individual liturgical styles.

The different degrees of flexibility within the two traditions are reflected in the different political models to which they seem to turn. *Puṣṭimārgīya* norms of authority resemble those of established kingdoms, a resemblance that may owe something both to the Mughal imperial patterns developing concurrently with the *puṣṭimārg* and to its predominant Western Indian environment. Indeed, the courts of the more important *gosāīṃ*s recall those of minor Rajput lords in Rajasthan. Each of Vallabha's seven grandsons through Vitthalnath was given a specially sanctified image of Krishna (like Shrinathji, but less exalted) around which an elaborate temple complex was eventually built. The *gosāīṃs*, frequently called *mahārāj*es, often had luxurious courts there and lived in grand style. Principal succession was to one of these image-court complexes, and had to fall to a male descendent of Vallabha. Today it normally goes to the eldest son of the reigning *mahārāj,* though the rule is not firm, particularly when the eldest son appears obviously unqualified.

Sant succession patterns, by contrast, sooner resemble those of Rajputs expanding into the Gangetic plain. A number of spiritual "sons," sometimes rivals, could each strike out new territory on their own. There was more mobility; establishments were simpler. The Sikh hagiography frequently shows the early gurus setting up temporary camp-court.[25]

While principles of succession among the *sant*s are left fairly undefined, perceptions of the ultimate source of their tradition are even more so. As an extended clan, the *sant*s are sometimes presented as beginningless and endless. A scattered *sant* clan, diffuse in its manifestation but offering specific, ageless truths, can then appear to present an eternal heritage. But when ideas of lineage are paramount among *sant*s, the source of tradition is often seen as a singular personality—a magnificent figure of the past, who, though gone, has left a lasting fount of grace. Part II will show us the ways in which different versions of *sant* tradition present alternative configurations of immanent foci in a common idiom of lineage, clan, and coded substance.

II

THE LIVING HOLY MAN AND CONTINUING TRADITION AMONG THE *SANTS*

3

The Hindi *Sants* as a Tradition of Holy Men

If *sant* tradition has come to be seen by those within it as something more than a collection of extraordinary holy men, it nevertheless finds its highest ideals in the individual *sant:* a distinct human being in a particular local religious situation. As individuals, moreover, *sant*s had different spiritual capacities. Some were known for their humble devotion; others, for their bold assaults on the hypocrisy they perceived. Not all were gifted poets. Even though Hindi literary scholarship knows the *sant* as a particular type of devotional singer, as a religious tradition, the *sant*s also include many figures who have left no verses extant at all. Of the latter, many of the most notable have been the immediate successors of (or the occasional predecessor to) some famous *sant* poet. But figures coming later in a lineage have also been remembered as important spiritual personalities. Today, we frequently see gurus without poetic gifts of their own giving impressive prose discourses as commentary on the verses of illustrious figures of the past—a practice common in many traditions and with likely precedent among earlier *sant*s.

The most illustrious *sant* poet by far has been Kabir, and on both the literary and religious sides of the tradition his figure looms large indeed. As one of the principal figures in both Hindi literature and North Indian religion, Kabir has been the subject of considerable scholarship—in the West as well as in India. Monographs have been written about him, critical editions of his works attempted, and translations of his verses made.[1] This book will not add much to the Kabirian scholarship per se; it will, however, treat the formative influence of the figure of Kabir on the Hindi *sant* tradition as a whole. To look at the way the tradition developed in the wake of Kabir—and to a certain extent in spite of him—we will first compare Kabir to Namdev, his famous Marathi predecessor; the diverging styles of piety represented by these two figures will then be examined in Paltu Sahib and Charandas, two contrasting eighteenth-century *sant*s. But in the eighteenth century these diverging styles of piety presented themselves differently, in a tradition having undergone considerable transformation.

The Formative Beginnings: Namdev and Kabir

Little record remains of the *sant* piety that existed in North India before Kabir made his mark on it, but there are signs that some form of oral *sant* tradition had begun to take root in the north well before Kabir's time. The Adigranth of the Sikhs, compiled about 150 years after Kabir's probable floruit in the first half of the fifteenth century, preserves some verses of several *bhagat*s, "devotees," from diverse northern regions.[2] Of these, Beni and Sadhna are obscure figures who may well have antedated Kabir. Others are understood in tradition to be in the same lineage as him: Ramananda is said to have been Kabir's guru; Sena, Dhanna, Pipa, and Raidas, his guru-brothers.

There is probably some basis to Ramananda's reputation as a liberal Vaishnava saint, a reputation which accounts for these mostly low-caste *sant* disciples attributed to him by posterity. Like Kabir, he is traditionally taken as having flourished around Banaras; but it is historically improbable that he survived there through Kabir's time. Sena, Dhanna, and the rest might indeed have been roughly contemporaneous with Kabir, though most were probably of a younger generation. They came, moreover, from disparate regions: the figure of Sena appears in the local legends of the kings of Bandhogarh—modern Rewa, central India;[3] there is little doubt that Dhanna was from Rajasthan. The regional diversity of these early *sant*s does seem to indicate an oral tradition that had spread throughout the north by Kabir's age. The eventual perception of these figures as guru-brothers of Kabir indicates the lofty stature that Kabir grew to have among later devotees, who wanted their gurus to share in his glory.

The only reliable verses we have for a number of the early *sant*s are the ones Guru Arjan compiled in the Adigranth. Certainly all these verses were selected in a tradition that had already experienced the impact of Kabir. Nevertheless, some do seem to indicate a precedent in the north for the yogic language and iconoclastic tone for which Kabir is famous.[4] Some verses attributed to Namdev are also found in the Adigranth, though Namdev appears as a much more important figure in his home region of Maharashtra, which knew a *sant* tradition of its own. And it is Namdev and his Marathi fellows who have provided the only extensive body of *sant* literature now known to us that may also have had some impact on Kabir.

In studying Namdev, as in studying Kabir, we confront a highly varied corpus of texts attributed to a particular historical personality. No amount of textual scholarship will establish the definite authorship of verses long preserved through popular oral tradition. Our ultimate literary personae in fact turn out to be bodies of verses integrated through principles of language, theme, and recension in ways that do not always reveal organic wholes. Marathi scholars can then speak of three separate Namdevs: two that are integral primarily through principles of theme, the last through principles of language and recension. Thus we have: (1) Namdev the devotee of the incarnate Lord, whose descriptions of the Lord's play recall those of Sur; (2) Namdev the iconoclastic *sant,* the inspiration of Kabir; and (3) the Hindi Namdev of the Adigranth. Hindi scholarship on Kabir speaks instead of two great regional traditions—which show some language variation—found in three sectarian recensions, showing definite thematic differences. In the east we have the voice of the Kabirpanthi *Bījak,* often scathing and metaphysically obscure; in the west, first the Kabir of the Dadupanthi collections, frequently rapturous and ecstatic, and then the Kabir of the Adigranth, more sober, speaking often of guru-devotion.[5]

Both the composite Namdev and the composite Kabir sing of a Lord at once beyond all and pervading all, one to be approached at times through devotional rapture, at times through yogic insight, and often through both at once. But even in their compositeness Namdev and Kabir reveal differences in personality, differences that can be understood, in part, through an understanding of the local religious environments in which the two *sant*s lived.

The popular devotion prevalent in Maharashtra during Namdev's time was oriented toward the shrine of Vitthala at Pandharpur. Vitthala, like Krishna, is understood as an incarnation of Vishnu, and many of Namdev's songs present vivid descriptions of Krishna's play, bringing to mind those sung at *puṣṭimārgīya* temples. In the following song, for example, Krishna is revealed as the Lord of Govardhan, the same whose image is enshrined at Nathdwara:

The sky is overcast with roaring clouds,
Lightning flashes;
Clouds burst continuous heavy rains.
The son of Devaki saves us from this:

The cowherds call him Kanha,
Govardhan hill was lifted by his own hands.
Nama says he saves.[6]

But in other places, Namdev, like the Hindi *sant*s, uses a Vaishnava name to stand for the Lord existing beyond all forms and encompassing them all:

The being is Vitthal, the soul is Vitthal
God is Vitthal, Vitthal.
Father is Vitthal, Mother is Vitthal
Relations are Vitthal.
This world is Vitthal, the other world is Vitthal
The eternal saviour is Vitthal.
Name is Vitthal, Form is Vitthal,
The saviour of the fallen is Vitthal.[7]

Both scholars and devotees sometimes explain the two types of songs in the Namdev corpus by speaking of two distinct stages in the life of Namdev the person. According to this account, Namdev was first an ardent devotee of Vitthala and later in his life learned the truth of the Formless Lord as well. Thus the British scholar Nicol Macnicol writes:

> The chief religious interest in Namdev's life lies in tracing a change or development in his thought which his *abhanga*s reveal. At first he is purely the emotional *bhakta,* all tears and cries and raptures. Later in his life, however, he seems to have passed through an experience which greatly altered his outlook on the world . . .[8]

Devotees, however, are more interested in recounting the story of this experience than giving a scholarly interpretation of it. Convinced by other famous *sant*s that he needed a guru, they say, the *bhakta* Namdev sought out a holy man named Visoba Khechara. He finally found Visoba lying asleep in front of a temple, with his feet on a Shivalingam—the holy emblem of Lord Shiva. Namdev was shocked at this insult to the image of the Lord and woke up Visoba with a reproachful shout. Visoba, smiling, asked Namdev to please move his feet someplace where no Shivalingam stood. But wherever Namdev put Visoba's feet, another Shivalingam emerged. In this way, according to one popular narrator of the story, Namdev "experienced both nirguna and saguna (impersonal and personal) aspects of God."[9]

The piety of Namdev, then, is seen to bring together two important types of religion *within* Hinduism: the worship of the *nirguṇa* and *saguṇa* divine, of the Formless Lord and His image. Kabir, however, lived a century later in a region to the north which had already seen considerable Muslim impact. In scoffing at the worship of any image of the Lord, Kabir appears to transcend the norms of Hinduism and Islam both. Popular legend has Kabir the abandoned son of a Brahman widow raised by Muslim parents. Seen to combine the attributes of both Hindus and Muslims through the story of his birth and adoption, he mocks the empty rituals of both communities at the time of his death. Kabir's Hindu disciples, the story goes, wanted to follow their custom and cremate his body; his Muslim disciples to follow theirs and bury it. But no body at all was to be found when they lifted the funeral shrouds, only a bed of flowers.

The mockery of empty religious forms that the legendary Kabir effected at his death is perhaps exceeded in some of the songs of the Kabirian corpus. Songs of Namdev, too, decry religious hypocrisy:

Shaven-headed commits sin;
  The poor body is still demanding:
This is no *sannyāsa* . . .
. . . .
Nama says by changing the dress
  The inner shame is not hidden.[10]

But no song of Namdev is as ruthless as the most virulent of Kabir. Where Namdev's weak *sādhū* is simply not able to change his character as he adopts robes of *sannyāsa,* renunciation, Kabir presents a hypocritical *nāth* who is truly vicious, using the accoutrements of *sannyāsa* to delude "like a cloak furled." Linda Hess captures the power of Kabir's acerbic wit in her translation of this *shabda* from the *Bījak:*

How will you cross, Nath,
how will you cross,
so full of crookedness?
Look how he meditates,
serves and prays.
Look: the white plumage,
the crane's sly ways.
Mood of a snake, look:
utterly lewd,
utterly quarrelsome,
utterly shrewd.

Look: a hawk's
face, and the thoughts
of a cat.
Schools of philosophy
like a cloak furled.
Look: the witch vanity
gulps down the world.[11]

Yet it is the vanity and hypocrisy to which the *nāth* yogi is prone that Kabir decries in this song, not the truths accessible through his internal practice. Indeed, the technical vocabulary of the *nāth*s is found in profusion in Kabir's songs, though it is often embedded in a context highlighting the *sant*'s love for the divine. Internal yogic practice often comes together with devotion in songs describing the play of *holī* between the guru and the disciple. *Holī* is a festival marking the beginning of the new year in the spring, and as a popular holiday is celebrated through a relaxation of normal social and personal boundaries. At *holī* people traditionally are free to act out an unrestrained exchange of substance, throwing ceremonial red powder at one another, or more raucously, cow dung and muck from the street. The most traditional substance to throw at someone at *holī,* however, is colored water, which is frequently squirted through large syringes. As a stock image, seen in chapter 1, merging waters of potentially different colors may refer to the dissolution of the devotee into the Lord. The *sant*s can then easily use the idealized play of *holī* as a metaphor to describe the merging of disciple and guru as yoga progresses. The following song is from the western, more devotional recension of Kabir:[12]

Play *holī* with the *satguru*
  And birth and death and wandering will pass. [Refrain]

He's made meditative means his syringe
  And squirts it with forgiveness
Who's begun to sport with *ātmā* and with *brahma*
  In the middle of the city of the body. (1)
He plays *holī* in the narrow lane of knowledge
  And revels in the muck of love.
Both greed and attachment are cut down and flee
  When they hear the endless *shabda*. (2)
In the hall of *trikuṭī* an instrument is playing:
  Thirty-six ragas are heard.

Where sister *surat* sees the show
She showers the *saṭguru* with *holī*'s red powder. (3)
He mixes with her, gives her *holī*'s play
And tells her of the path.
Kabir says: that one knows the truth—
Released while still alive. (4)

In this song the meditative means (*dhyāna jukti*), the city of the body (*kāyā nagar*), and the endless *shabda* all make reference to elements of yogic practice. *Trikuṭī,* "the place of three points" between the eyes is a frequently recurring term, one of the several yogic expressions adapted from the *nāth*s that have become a standard part of *sant* esoteric jargon. Songs of the Marathi *sant*s too, of course, often show a technical yogic vocabulary, and the earliest of the Marathi *sant*s are seen as the successors to legendary *nāth*s. Indeed, Namdev himself can find a *nāth* lineage: Visoba Khechara, the guru who displayed to him the Shivalinga-*māyā,* was a disciple of Jnanadev; the latter, they say, was initiated by his older brother Nivrittinath, who had received initiation from Gahinanath, a disciple of the great *nāth,* Gorakh. Nevertheless, in Kabir the yogic references are considerably more frequent. For while the religious context in which the Marathi tradition developed was the popular Vaishnavism of Pandharpur, the local religion that Kabir knew was probably some form of popular *nāth*ism itself.

Prominent scholars in the East and West have suggested that *nāth* traditions were vital in Kabir's caste—the *julāhas,* weavers recently converted to Islam. But the route by which the traditions of *nāth* yogis reached the *julāha*s remains unclear. Vaudeville writes about a general popular "Nathism," drawing on tantric elements from both Hindu and Buddhist sources, as an important component in the religion of large segments of the Indian masses. H. P. Dvivedi treats the *julāha*s more specifically as a caste of householder *nāth*s, yogis who were "fallen from their proper state" (*āshrama-bhraṣṭa*) and had become Muslim. Fallen or not, castes of householder *nāth*s and yogis are certainly evident in India today. Briggs, writing in the 1930s, describes the customs of these castes in various regions of the north. Many are popularly believed to have access to magical powers; some maintain a tradition of oral epic and song.[13]

In 1980, Ann Grodzins Gold led me to a community of householder *nāth*s in rural Rajasthan. Members of many of the clean cultivating castes look to gurus among them for magical protection, especially against pestilence. These *nāth*s, too, maintain a tradition of oral religious performance, a tradition which, as it turns out, includes the singing of *nirguṇ bhajans* similar to those of the *sant*s. The *bhajans* are sung throughout complex and extended funeral rites, as well as at more informal and open gatherings. In the last line of each song, which conventionally contains its author's "signature" (*chhāp*), the name of Gorakh is often heard, or perhaps that of the performer himself. But at least as often as either of these may be heard the name of Kabir.

Just what the relationship of these householder *nāth*s is to the *nāth sādhū*s of old, and the relationship of both to Kabir and the *sant*s, has been treated in part in another study.[14] Yet it is clear not only that an early form of popular *nāth*ism profoundly informed Kabir's experience, but also that the *nirguṇ bhakti* epitomized in the figure of Kabir has a prominent place in the religion of many householder *nāth*s today.

At the same time, the image of Kabir, aloof and iconoclastic, together with the extended Kabirian corpus—comprising more than could be attributed to an ordinary mortal—has remained formative among Hindi *sant*s through Radhasoami Maharaj in the nineteenth century and his successors in the present day. Nevertheless, the model of Kabir was not one that all *sant*s cared to follow to its strident extremes. The two other most important of the earlier *sant*s, Nanak and Dadu, were notably less scathing in their iconoclasm. By Soamiji's day, moreover, the tradition had seen considerable diversity not only in its devotional style, but also in its sociological roots.

The early *sant*s were largely, but not exclusively, from very low social strata: Kabir was known as a weaver, Sena a barber, and Raidas a tanner; but Dhanna was a *jāṭ,* a member of a clean cultivating caste, and Pipa was famous as a raja. Later movements of the disenfranchised classes did and still do sometimes rally around a *sant* banner,[15] but people well established within the Hindu heritage have also claimed the famous *sant*s as their own and assimilated *sant* piety. Thus Nabhaji, writing probably in the beginning of the seventeenth century, described several of the early *sant*s in his important encyclopedia of Vaishnava devotees.[16] As the *sant* tradition became more reputable, it increasingly attracted the attention of respectable Hindus. Thus, alongside *sant*s from traditionally unclean and Muslim castes, we begin to see a few Brahmans and an occasional landlord. By the eighteenth century we find a preponderance of *sant*s among members of the middle Hindu castes: those of traders and clean cultivators, most of the former identifying with the *vaishya*s, "merchants," of classical times, and some of the latter with the *kṣatriya*s, "warriors."

Sant Tradition and the Hindu Heritage in the Eighteenth Century: Paltu Sahib and Charandas

Of the important eighteenth-century sants, the one most strongly influenced by the Kabirian model was Paltu Sahib of Ayodhya. Like Kabir he lived in a popular Hindu pilgrimage place and used vivid, startling language to speak out against ritual pilgrimage. He, too, wrote *ulaṭbāṃsis*, songs in the enigmatic, "turned around" (*ulṭā*) language for which Kabir was particularly famous. Indeed, Paltu's name derives from a verbal form (*palaṭnā*) which itself means "to be inverted or changed" and which often appears together with *ulṭā* as a popular colloquialism: *ulaṭ-palaṭ*—mixed up, backwards, turned around. Paltu Sahib, then, is "Master Turned-Around," not only in his use of startling and occasionally enigmatic language, but in his spiritual direction: turned around inwardly, with his gaze facing the Lord.[17] One of the better-known *sant* poets, skillful and vigorous, Paltu is sometimes referred to as "the second Kabir."

The textual corpus attributed to Paltu is more compact than that attributed to Kabir,[18] but as with Kabir, we know with confidence only the barest essentials of Paltu's life. There is little reason to doubt the tradition that Paltu was a Kandu *baniyā,* a caste traditionally engaged in shopkeeping. References to his traditional caste and occupation can be found in his songs, and he is still particularly revered in communities of *baniyā*s in the localities around Ayodhya. He was thus probably of local origins. Indeed, Paltu is commonly thought to have been born in a village to the south of Ayodhya, where a temple to Paltu exists today; commentators on Paltu, moreover, cite references to this village in verses from otherwise unpublished texts.[19]

It is difficult to date Paltu from his corpus alone, but one of his disciples, Hulas Das, writes of his own initiation in the *saṃvat* year corresponding to A.D. 1769.[20] So it is very probable that Paltu had reached adulthood by then, and likely that he had reached a spiritual maturity toward the middle of his years. The time and place of Paltu's death remain a mystery. He aroused the animosity of the religious hypocrites of Ayodhya to such an extent, the story goes, that they locked him in his house and set it on fire. Some say that Paltu was then burned to death. But another ending to the story is popular among the Paltu-*panthīs* of Ayodhya. According to one respected *sādhū,* as Paltu's house burned down, Paltu himself went up with the smoke and landed inside the great temple to Jagannath at Puri. The *mahant,* the "priest in charge," at the Paltu Akhara, gave a more sober account:

Paltu escaped to Puri after the fire, came back when passions had quietened, and then died of old age at Ayodhya. Paltu's remains, most local *sādhūs* affirm, are under the *samādhi,* the "memorial tomb," at the Akhara in Ayodhya, though there are some who claim that the true *samādhi* of Paltu is located in a village at some distance, in the Bhojpuri area.[21]

Whatever the historicity of Paltu's visit to Puri, the popular account of his sojourn there does reveal the role that established divine images can play in a later, Hinduized *sant* tradition, though we will see them figure in a different way in the verses of Paltu himself. When the priests of Jagannath opened the temple doors in the morning to find Paltu sleeping in the inner sanctum they were both puzzled and angry: puzzled, because the temple doors were locked at night; angry because some unknown vagrant was defiling the image of the Lord. The temple priests proceeded to abuse Paltu violently, and finally threw him into the sea. Meanwhile, the raja of Puri, who was very pious, had a dream. As he was sleeping, the Lord told him that within his kingdom a devotee was being abused. "As long as my devotee remains in distress," the Lord said, "I will remain hidden from your sight; for my devotee is certainly my own true nature."[22] The raja awoke with a start and proceeded immediately to the temple of Jagannath, the spiritual center of his kingdom. There he found the priests struggling in vain to open the doors of the temple, which had magically sealed themselves shut. The priests confessed to what they had done, and all went together to the sea in search of Paltu. Paltu was all apologies when they found him, asking to be pardoned for sleeping in the temple. They returned to the temple, and Paltu was able to open its doors with a touch of his stick. For the Lord shows the hypocrite the power of the true devotee, who is always humble, and who always forgives.

The respect paid to Jagannath in the story above no doubt reflects a sentiment that developed among Paltu-panthis after Paltu's time. One of Paltu's poems, in fact, mentions Jagannath with distinct disdain.[23] Nevertheless, in Paltu's songs we sometimes see a rhetorical strategy similar to that at work in the story above: the use of traditionally hallowed Hindu symbols to say something about certain evils *sant*s see in traditional Hinduism itself. While Kabir, the low-caste *julāha,* ridicules the established forms of Hinduism and Islam from a standpoint outside both, Paltu, the eighteenth-century *baniyā,* works from inside the Hinduism he knows.

Now a poet can work from inside the Hindu mythological tradition without attempting to evoke intense adoration for a divine image in the fashion of Sur Das and other poets of Krishna devotion. Krishnaite poets attempt to arouse our attraction for the Lord by developing a sustained and concrete image of him. In the first song below, however, Paltu mentions three separate incidents involving epic heroes and their low-born devotees; but he dwells on no one incident long enough to evoke a concrete fascination with the hero's divine person. The effect of the three incidents taken together is instead to contrast the power of sincere devotion with the pretentiousness of empty piety:

What counts in the court of the Master
  Is only devotion and love. [Refrain]

Only devotion and love—
  The Master is pleased with devotion:
He left the well-cooked fare to take
  Some greens from the slave-girl's son. (1)
While many did austerities,
  Were strict in all their vows
He ate the berries Shivri gave:
  The *ṛiṣi*s and the *muni*s died of shame. (2)
King Yudhishthir bade all his people
  Feast at a great sacrifice;
The pride of all was humbled, though,
  When no bell rang without Supach. (3)
Let no one pride himself
  On caste, says Paltu:
What counts in the court of the Master
  Is only devotion and love.[24] (4)

The song begins with an allusion to Krishna going to meet Duryodhana in an attempt to avert war: he stops first at the house of Vidura, who, the son of a sage and a slave girl, is at once wise and humble. Paltu then recalls Shabari, a low-caste woman who gives berries to Rama when he is wandering in the forest. Finally Paltu mentions the *ashvamedha* sacrifice performed by the victorious Pandavas at the end of the Mahabharata war: the bell needed to begin it wouldn't ring until the arrival of Swapacha, a low-caste devotee who was not at first invited.[25]

These incidents are well known, and are recalled by other devotional poets: a familiarity with the Hindu lore necessary to appreciate the song, then, could certainly be expected of the pious Vaishnava; it could not, however, be so easily assumed in the disenfranchised, sometimes nominally Muslim castes in which many of the earlier *sant*s arose and had their followings. Today, the song is frequently anthologized and commented on by the Radhasoami gurus.[26] Its very popularity attests to the diffusion of *sant* tradition among members of respectable Hindu castes.

While Paltu denounces caste pride, he can idealize and spiritualize traditional caste virtues: some traditional Hindu models, when understood correctly, *should* be emulated. While the aggressive, iconoclastic virility sometimes found in the Kabirian corpus may reflect Indian Sufi models, Paltu in the following poem invokes some similar values by internalizing the virtues of the Rajput: the warrior prince by caste, the Rajput sets the norms for Hindu authority in postclassical times. Here Paltu describes the spiritual Rajput, who by boldly burning the citadel-body and mercilessly massacring the passions sets them free.

The persistent, concentrated assault of Paltu the spiritual warrior is reflected in the verse form for which he is most famous, used here as in the last poem. Called the *kuṇḍalilyā,* it presents a pithy refrain that is developed throughout the rest of the song. The second half of the refrain is repeated at the beginning of the first line; and at the end of the song, according to one devotee, the whole refrain "comes down like a hammer to drive the point home."[27]

The one who can set free the citadel-body
  Is really a Rajput [Refrain]

Really a Rajput:
  He sets fire to the stronghold,
And frees entrenched enemy lines
  In a flash. (1)
Inside the citadel-body he goes
  To take residence there.
Mind's a thug and tries to grab him
  But falls dead on the spot (2)
Killing anger and passion
  He cuts off the heads of Sir Ego,
Of Envy, of Greed:
  The blood flows in a stream. (3)
The *avadhūt* dwells
  In the eighth of the heavens, says Paltu
He sets free the citadel-body
  For he's really a Rajput.[28] (4)

The Rajput ideal internalized by Paltu appears as that of the more mobile, less established warriors moving into the Gangetic plain. The vigorous, independent authority it implies is consonant with the Kabirian model of the *sant,* and as it happens, the Gangetic Rajputs were, for Paltu, the local variety. But in the eighteenth century it was possible for a *sant* not only to internalize vigorous Rajput ideals, but also to live in the fashion of an established prince of Rajputana. The image we have of Charandas, born in Rajasthan but living most of his life in Delhi, seems to reflect the royal, if not imperial, models found in the cultures of these two environments. In fact, in an important sectarian biography of Charandas we find a chapter entitled "Shri Maharaj Ji Lives in Delhi Like a Prince."[29] His court does indeed recall that of a *puṣṭimārgīya maharāj,* and he comes closer to accepting the widespread Vaishnava norms than perhaps any other Hindi *sant,* certainly closer than any to be treated in this book. Since his biography has been chronicled with more care than that of other *sant*s of his age, it is possible to make some conjectures about his development as an individual holy man. And when the story that emerges is contrasted to what we know of Paltu, we see the diversity of styles among *sant*s in the eighteenth century.

At the end of a short work by Charandas called *Jñānasvarōdaya* is found the following short declaration:

My birth was in Dehra;
  They called me Ranjit.
Murlidhar's son and
  A Dhusar by caste,
To Delhi I came
  As a child.
Roaming about I met Shukdev
  Who called me Charandas.[30]

These essential details of Charandas' life are elaborated in hagiographies written in Hindi verse by two of his disciples: Ramrupji's *Guru Bhakti Prakāsh,* "The Light of Guru-Devotion," oriented toward doctrinal matters; and Jogjit's *Līlā Sāgar,* "The Sea of Play," longer and more anecdotal. We learn that Dehra, Charandas' birthplace, is near Alwar, in Rajasthan, and that the boy was known there as Ranjit. Jogjit and Sahajo Bai—who was a female disciple and cousin of Charandas—both give the same date of birth for him in 1703.[31] While he was still a young child, his father, Murlidhar, died. Murlidhar had a habit of going off to the forest to meditate, they say, and one day he never came back. Soon after, Ranjit's mother took him with her to live with her parents in Delhi, where the latter had recently moved from a town near Alwar. Charandas did some traveling, as holy men in India often do, but for the most part lived out the rest of his life in Delhi, where he died a well-known *sant* in 1782.

Thus, many of the points that Charandas mentions in the passage above soon become clear. His caste status, however, and even more, the identity of his guru Shukdev, remain ambiguous. These ambiguities, as we shall see, are closely related to Charandas' dual espousal of *sant* tradition and a Vaishnava heritage.

Charandas refers to himself above as a "Dhusar by caste," a fact nobody seems to dispute. While Charandas is unquestionably a Dhusar, he is also sometimes spoken of as a Bhargava, one coming from the line of Bhrigu, the Vedic seer. The caste status of Bhargavas has long been problematic. Apparent redactors of the Mahabharata, Bhargavas of the past made their ancestors appear as ambivalently pure Brahmans, caught up in the passions of life and war. Today, the redactoral talents of the Bhargavas often translate into success in the book business—both as publishers and booksellers. The ambivalent socioreligious identity of the group thus presently hovers between Brahman and *vaishya,* the third of the classical Hindu *varṇas,* which has come to be associated with trade. Since many Bhargavas are active in the Charandasi *panth* today, most people concerned with the *panth* have an opinion about the status of the Bhargavas as a caste. One respected Charandasi *sādhū* in Jaipur, when questioned, explained that Bhargavas were Brahmans, but did the work of *vaishya*s. A second made distinctions among Bhargava groups: some were Brahmans, others were *vaishya*s. Yet whatever the doubts of the orthodox, many Jaipur Bhargavas are commonly known as Brahmans.[32]

Among Charandasis today there are many who insist that Charandas was in this latter category of Bhargava Brahmans—although all the early scholarly authorities speak of Charandas matter-of-factly as a Dhusar *baniyā,* that is, a member of a trading caste, by *varṇa* a *vaishya.*[33] The disinterested voice of the *Hindi Shabdsāgar* affirms both the identity of the Bhargavas with Charandas' Dhusar caste and the ambiguous Brahman/*vaishya* status that many Charandasis see them to have. Under Bhargava it tells us that "the people of this caste call themselves Brahmans, but their vocational inclinations (*vṛitti*) are very much like *vaishya*s. Some people call them Dhusar *baniyās.*" Thus Charandas, like Paltu, came from a trading caste, but one that took pride in its Vedic ancestor. It is not surprising, then, to find that Charandas looked for a guru in the heritage of the Vedic past, and ultimately recognized a very different kind of spiritual being than did Paltu.

There seems little reason to doubt the tradition that Paltu had a living guru named Govind Sahib, an illustrious figure in his own day who appeared in a line of noteworthy *sant*s. Lineages that take a source in Paltu, Govind Sahib, and others in this line are still alive—if not exactly flourishing—in districts of eastern Uttar Pradesh, and preserve accounts of spiritual succession that appear accurate enough at least back to Paltu's generation.[34] In some editions of Paltu's verses, moreover, we find references to Govind, and even Guru Govind, though not very many.[35]

Charandas, on the other hand, mentions his Guru Shukdev often indeed, but it is not clear whether this Shukdev was ever a living person. According to Charandas himself, his guru was none other than Shukdev the perpetually twelve-year-old son of Vyasa, the sage who divided the Vedas, first recited the Mahabharata, and composed all of the *purāṇa*s. Shukdev is the eternally innocent son of an all too prolific father, traditionally seen to have access to heavenly realms that Vyasa, subject to human instincts, cannot reach.[36] As we have seen, stories from the Mahabharata told by Vyasa to Shukdev also help Paltu to make his point; but in acknowledging Govind Sahib as his guru, Paltu recognized a religious heritage in which Vedic tradition ultimately counted for little. For Charandas to affirm Shukdev the son of Vyasa to be his guru, on the other hand, is to affirm his links as a Bhargava to the Mahabharata, and ultimately to the Veda. In Shukdev, Charandas finds a direct line to the origins of the Hindu heritage through an appealing and unsullied source.

The reverence of Charandas for the Hindu heritage is immediately evident in *Bhaktisāgar,* "The Sea of Devotion"—the principal collection of his works. A number of the pieces in it are in fact popular adaptations of classical texts. Charandas offers, for example, Hindi adaptations of five Upanishads "from the *Atharvaveda.*" He also tells the story of Nasiketa from the *Brahmāṇḍa Puraṇa* (found in an earlier form in the *Kaṭhopanishad*), which gives him a context in which to present in detail the horrors of the Hindu hells.[37] *Haṭha* yoga practices are described at length, as well as the eternal sphere of Mathura.

But in *Bhaktisāgar* we also find a long collection of short verses that put together yoga and devotion in the characteristic *sant* style. The following song, like the one of Kabir seen earlier,[38] alludes to the spiritual meaning of *holī,* the spring festival:

Sister, I have found beloved Hari
And my portion is now full. [Refrain]

In a sea of happiness, in bliss
I play *holī* with him always. (1)
Sister, love's the sandal paste
I rub on knowledge-tresses;
With the subtle scent of flowers
I anoint his limbs. (2)
I fill up my jug
With the colorless one's colors
And go then to the empty hall of *shunya*
To pour them on my lover. (3)
When the festive red powder got me proud, sister,
Off went my beloved far away.
The satguru then gave me a dark powder for my eyes
And my lover came in person to my sight. (4)
How he clapped in time to love
And played the *anhad nād;*
I found my all-bewitching Lord
And sing of bliss and fortune. (5)
Sister I've been ground and mixed together with my lover
So I count my portion twice.
Charandas, through Shukdev's grace,
Found married bliss forever.[39] (6)

In this song we see references to divine sounds ("Sister, how he clapped his hands in time to love," verse 5) and direct mention of *anhad nād,* as the audible *shabda* is sometimes called. The Sanskrit *shunya* (frequently found in Hindi as *sunna*) is a word meaning "empty" used in a technical sense by many *sant*s to refer to a "void" region of the heavens. But as a poetic image Charandas' empty hall of *shunya* contrasts with Kabir's "narrow lane of knowledge"—also probably a yogic reference, to the central subtle artery yogis call the *suṣumna.* Kabir's *holī* is slightly rowdy street revelry, with "muck" and a "show"; the *holī* of Charandas, the princely *sant* of Delhi, is more elegant and refined: it takes place in an empty hall, with the subtle scent of flowers.

In the works of Charandas, then, we see some rather elegant treatments of *sant* genres found in Kabir together with a very un-Kabirian respect for the Vedic heritage. Scholars sometimes explain the presence of both *sant* and traditional Hindu themes in the corpus of Charandas the same way they do the presence of both in the corpus of Namdev—through a reference to different stages in the life of a holy man. But where Namdev, we recall, is seen as a passionate *bhakta* of Vitthala who later learns the truths of the Formless Lord, for Charandas the progression is reversed: he appears as a *sant* who later embraced a more complete Vaishnava Hinduism. For Charandas, if not for Namdev, this progression seems to have entailed no radical conversion demanding drastic modification of previously held beliefs: the elaborate metaphors in the song above suggest comfortable familiarity with both *sant* experience and ritual Hinduism at once. Indeed, what we can construct of Charandas' biography indicates that he purposefully attempted to integrate elements of Hindu tradition into *sant* experience. The traditional Hindu elements that appealed to Charandas can be understood in part from accounts of his travels; his purpose can be understood from his situation in Delhi.

The biographers of Charandas describe a number of journeys he made after he had reached adulthood. At Panipat, north of Delhi, he apparently lived for several months as the respected guest of some local gentry ("*rājās*"). As an established guru he toured near and far to visit both holy places and groups of disciples.[40] These tours may have given Charandas exposure to diverse aspects of Hindu tradition, but judging from our earlier examination of Sahibji Maharaj on tour,[41] Charandas' tours were probably more spiritually exciting for his disciples than for him. A journey more crucial for Charandas himself, however, was one he made sometime in the middle of his life to Vraj country, the fount of Krishna devotion. There, they say, he composed his description of the true nature of Vraj, and had a vision of Lord Krishna.[42]

But probably more decisive for Charandas' spiritual development than any later journey was his experience as a young man of initiation from a guru he knew as Shukdev. Shukdev, in some Hindu traditions, is included with his father Vyasa, Sanaka, Dattatreya and others as among those perfected sages who are continually active on earth. Having become perfect (*siddha*), they can reveal themselves to the devout through the subtle senses like gods, but they are also understood to be present on earth in a more densely physical way—eternally embodied: in the Himalayas, perhaps, or wandering in the jungle; maybe hidden as an ascetic in an ashram. The *nāth* yogis, too, have a related tradition of eternally present *siddha*s, a tradition probably as well known in Charandas' time as it is today: Gorakh, some say, may now be living hidden in Dattatreya's ashram.[43]

As a physically embodied being who can also reveal himself through visions, Shukdev appears in the hagiographies in forms that can be variously interpreted. On two occasions Shukdev seems to have come to Charandas in subtle form: he came as a *sādhū* to Charandas the child at Dehra, but the elders couldn't see him; at Vrindavan he appeared after Charandas had had a vision of Krishna.[44] Yet Charandas' initiation, all the hagiographers agree, was given by Shukdev at a specific place and time: on the first day of the bright half of the Hindu month of *chaitra,* in the *saṃvat* year 1789, Shukdev initiated Charandas at Sukra Tal, where he had earlier, according to Ramrupji, "explained the story [of the Mahabharata] to Raja Parikshit."[45] Charandas was nineteen years old.

Western scholars who have had occasion to treat Charandas in passing usually see the Shukdev of this story as representing some living person: "a holy man named Sukdeo Das," "Sukh [happiness] Deva" or "Baba Sukhdeva Das."[46] Certainly, in describing Charandas' initiation, the sectarian hagiographers emphasize the fact that Shukdev appeared in a physical body. When, after searching for a guru for three years, Charandas is in despair, Shukdev appears to him in a vision, as he had before. But this time Shukdev tells Charandas to go to Sukra Tal to meet him face to face. On their meeting, Shukdev initiates Charandas in traditional Hindu style—with a bath, a mark on the forehead, and a *mantra.*

A description of Charandas' proper Vaishnava initiation would certainly provide a charter for later Vaishnava practices among the Charandasis, a fact which in itself warrants its presentation in the narrative. Thus, Charandas' experience of initiation from Shukdev may well have been a vision, like the rest of his encounters with him. He may then have had no living guru; he certainly acknowledges no ordinary one. But according to Ramrupji, of Charandas' disciples the one with the strongest Vaishnava predilections, following the initiation Shukdev gave Charandas instruction in yoga as well as devotion. Soon after, Charandas retired to a cave outside Delhi, where he engaged in ascetic practice for fourteen years. Ramrupji tells us that Charandas performed Patanjali's eight-limbed yoga, *rāja* yoga, *bhakti* yoga, and *sankhyā* yoga, but describes most of the practices Charandas performed in the *sant* vocabulary used by Charandas himself: he talks of *surat* and *nirat,* and the *anhad shabda.*[47]

For the ardent Krishna-*bhakta* to portray his guru as having experienced a long period of non-Vaishnava ascesis certainly suggests that Charandas is remembered in tradition as having undergone a distinct change in spiritual direction. This, together with the ambiguous physical character of Shukdev and the concrete circumstances of the story of Charandas' initiation, makes the explanation offered by the early Western scholars seem plausible: Charandas had a brief but crucial encounter with a living guru, whose name, perhaps, was something like Shukdev; as Charandas' perceptions changed he began to understand his guru of the past as the legendary son of Vyasa. Judging from Ramrupji's account of Charandas' ascetic practice, Charandas probably learned from his guru some elements of a tradition at least as yogic as it was devotional; and judging from the language with which Charandas described his practice, this tradition may well have been that of the *sant*s.

Yet whatever the source of Charandas' knowledge of spiritual practice—a single guru, several gurus, or general oral tradition—the *Bhaktisāgar* both abounds in songs composed in a recognizably *sant* style and reveals a reverence for the Hindu heritage not found in most *sant*s. To understand the reasons behind Charandas' attempt to bring together popular and Sanskritic traditions it may help to look more closely at his sociohistorical situation as a Bhargava in eighteenth-century Delhi.

The Bhargavas, we recall, often regarded themselves as Brahmans, but were usually merchants by profession—not, as Brahmans traditionally are, teachers and priests. However people of other communities actually regarded their ritual status, most Bhargavas probably taught their sons at least as much about business ledgers as about the intricacies of Sanskrit writings. Charandas himself seems to have been noticeably uninterested in studies, Brahmanic or otherwise. His biographers describe brief periods of childhood education for him, first at Dehra, with a *paṇḍit,* and later with mullahs in Delhi.[48] But Charandas, absorbed in the Lord's name, was not impressed with either Hindu or Muslim learning. He became bored quickly:

The mullah called on him to read;
  The *bhaktirāja* heard him but said nothing.
He kept on thinking in his mind:
  I've read enough—no more![49]

The religious lore Charandas knew, then, was popular and devotional, not priestly, and was probably learned for the most part through the vernacular. No doubt open early to an iconoclastic influence from the mullahs in Delhi—with whom he is shown to have parted on good terms—Charandas might easily have at first been more attracted to the Hindi *sants*' worship of the Formless Lord than to more iconic forms of popular Hinduism. At the same time, as a descendant of Bhrigu, he felt qualified to give Vedic authority to the message he preached. And the socioreligious situation in eighteenth-century Delhi may have given him some immediate reasons to do so.

Treatments of Charandas in Hindi, both devotional and academic, frequently begin with a discussion of the troubled times in which he lived.[50] The political power that the emperor at Delhi wielded over his domains was disintegrating visibly. There was external threat as well: the danger from the Europeans had not yet made itself evident, but older enemies from the West had wrought some terrible havoc. In 1739 Nadir Shah swept down from Persia to eventually, one morning, slaughter tens of thousands of the inhabitants of Delhi in a fit of revenge; from the survivors he then exacted an onerous tribute. In later years came further Iranian invasions, followed by attacks from Afghani chiefs. Driven by circumstances, the nobles of Delhi—mostly Muslim, like its invaders—were generally forced to profit from each new situation as they could, and the successful managed to maintain a lifestyle as luxurious and dissolute as ever.

Against such a backdrop, it is easy to see how Charandas might appear to later Hindu writers as a fount of saving Vedic truth in a world of Mughal depredation. His disciples, moreover, also saw him as a potent focus of spiritual power, one which could rival the authority of the Mughal emperor, indeed, even that of the ravaging Persian.

One day when Charandas was sitting in meditation, say the *sant*'s hagiographers,[51] he had a terrible vision. It jolted him, and he got up and started writing. In six months' time, he wrote, Nadir Shah will invade Delhi, but he won't stay for long. He recorded the dates of both Nadir Shah's invasion and his departure, and gave the note to a Muslim noble to keep. Once Nadir Shah had taken possession of the capital, the noble showed the letter to the Mughal emperor, who showed it to Nadir Shah himself. Impressed, Nadir Shah summoned Charandas, but Charandas declined to come. Then, believing Charandas to be a dangerous magician, Nadir Shah had him captured and thrown into prison. But when Nadir Shah came the next day to mete out punishment to him, Charandas had vanished from his cell. They didn't have to search very hard for him, though: he was soon found sitting quietly at home. Again, Charandas was taken and thrown into prison, this time bound in chains. But that night Charandas, bound in chains, appeared to Nadir Shah as he lay in his private chamber, and gave him a kick on the head. With this Nadir Shah implored Charandas' forgiveness. He had him taken home in royal style forthwith, and a few days later himself paid court to the holy man. "Don't understand him as a Hindu or a Muslim," Ramrupji has Nadir Shah say about Charandas, "but of the race of God."[52]

Like Paltu, then, Charandas is seen as a holy man of Hindu culture who nevertheless stands independent of the ritual forms of the Hindu heritage—who is ultimately "of the race of God." But Paltu, addressing observant Hindus at a traditional pilgrimage center, inveighed against the foolishness of empty Brahmanic forms; Charandas, living in a cosmopolitan city during difficult times, loosened Brahmanic injunctions to reach a wide range of devotees. If Paltu tended to reduce the divine unity he saw to the one Formless Lord who recognized no ritual, Charandas integrated aspects of Hindu ritual into a unity encompassing "endless" divine forms. In the following verses from a work called *Bhakti Padārath,* "The Material of Devotion," Charandas attempts to describe the indescribably full Lord, the One who is more than both his *saguṇ* aspect, "with forms," and his *nirguṇ,* "formless" one.

In him there are countless forms,
 Profound and without bounds.
Look how he has manifest
 In shapes and names and sounds.

I'll tell you the names of the seeds and the trees
 And show all their manifestations:
For he who comprehends the seedless
 Knows the *nirguṇ* truth;
But when he understands the truth in all its forms
 He sees the marks of branches, roots, and fruit.
In this way is *brahm* complete,
 Not in formless *nirguṇ.*
Not *nirguṇ* and not *saguṇ:*
 They're thought-up names—not him.
But what I say is nonsense,
 For no one can tell the untellable tale.
When someone tries to tell it, pay attention,
 But don't think what he's said's the final truth.
Says Charandas: great *ṛiṣi*s, *muni*s,
 Heavy *paṇḍit*s—all have searched and failed.

He's *nirguṇ* and he's *saguṇ,*
 He's different from them both.

Who he was I never knew
  However much I pondered.
Endless power, endless play,
  Virtues of all kinds,
A spectacle of endless shapes
  To which Charandas gives offerings.
Endless names, distinctions, actions,
  Endless *avatārs*;
Of *avatārs*, though, Shukdev thinks that
  Twenty four stand out,
Then Ram and Krishna, both complete,
  Two in twenty four:
From *nirguṇ* he is *saguṇ,*
  For *bhakta*s to adore.[53]

If Paltu is called the second Kabir because of his rejection of ritual form, Charandas here recalls Namdev, in whose collected works and legends the conjunction of the *saguṇ* and the *nirguṇ* also appears striking. Namdev, too, wrote of the Lord's fullness: "Father is Vitthal, Mother is Vitthal/ Relations are Vitthal . . ." But Namdev remained an author of expressive, sometimes esoteric religious lyrics. Charandas here comes closer to the didactic, abstracting preacher. He begins with an attempt at analogy ("I'll tell you the names of the seeds and the trees") and builds to a conclusion a popular audience might easily follow: devotion to Rama and Krishna.

Thus, the lasting image of Charandas as a fount of accessible Hindu spiritual power in a world overshadowed by a collapsing, predominantly Muslim political culture may well have reflected something of Charandas' own religious purposes. As a popular preacher, Charandas saw himself explaining the essence of the Vedas in Hindi:

In making *The Material of Bhakti*
  I present the Vedas' witness.
Merge now with their secrets,
  Which Charandas will tell in common language.
Through guru Shukdev's glory
  I'll tell the Vedas' sayings,
Formed first in the Sanskrit language,
  Ageless and eternal witnesses.
From Narada and Narayan
  And Brahma's mind-born sons
Shukdev heard and told to Parikshit
  What I tell now. So listen![54]

The early years of the present century have seen a parallel invocation of a pristine Vedic heritage by religious and nationalist leaders living in an environment similarly recognized as corrupt through an influence from the West. In providing a basis for Hindu renewal, Charandas, like many of these leaders, saw the need for the development of some social liberalism. Charandas too has a song like Paltu's above, in which he makes allusion to Shabari, the low-caste woman who gave berries to Rama, and to the bell that didn't ring at the Pandavas' sacrifice.[55] In his version of this song, Charandas further shows explicit solidarity with *sant* tradition, praising the glory of the low-born *sant*s of yore: "Kabir the *julāha*" and "Raidas the *chamār*." Even more revolutionary than his attitudes about the spiritual limitations of caste appear Charandas' ideas about the spiritual capacities of women—perhaps because he was able to put these ideas into practice. Two of his best-known disciples were women, Sahajo Bai and Daya Bai, both poets whose verses have been published; Sahajo Bai, moreover, became an important guru in her own right.

Yet as a *sant,* Charandas emphasizes the interiority of religious experience considerably more than do the twentieth-century social reformers. In offering the "Vedas' witness" he presents *yogic* Upanishads, and uses them to expound problems of inner experience, sometimes with *shabda.* In evoking devotion to Krishna he stresses the deity's hidden, interior nature:

Krishna always lives in Vraj
  But doesn't meet me.
. . . .
He hides from worldly vision
  But will meet the one with fixed attention.
  The sphere of Mathura is nowhere manifest,
  If it's manifest it isn't Mathura.
To see the sphere of Mathura,
  One needs the inner eye.[56]

Thus, while Charandas may have seen his age ripe for the reassertion of a Hindu heritage, the synthesis he evolved was a *sant*'s Hinduism—some similar, more recent versions of which we will see at the end of chapter 6. Like the synthesis of Charandas, none of them make many ritual or sectarian demands, and all retain something of a *sant*'s lingering iconoclasm and popular tone.

4

The Forms of *Sant* Tradition: The Development of Lineages and the Perception of Clan

Through the appearance of charismatic figures like Charandas, with large popular followings during their lifetimes, *sant* tradition was continually revitalized; but the tradition maintained itself largely through lineages of the great gurus' disciples. Thus, after Charandas' death, several of his disciples were able to attract substantial followings of their own. The different ways in which Charandas' chief disciples approached him during his life illustrate the varieties of guru-disciple relationship possible in postclassical Indian religion. The animosity with which these disciples interacted with one another after their guru's death illustrates the crisis of authority that may occur with the passing of an established holy man. As we examine the beginnings and eventual fate of the lineage of Charandas, we will be introduced to the basic forms in which *sant* tradition appears as it evolves socioreligious institutions. These forms can then offer points of reference for understanding the diverse directions in which *sant*s and their lineages have developed.

By the time of Charandas' death his many disciples could be found in Rajasthan and the Punjab, and far into the Gangetic plain. A considerable number were qualified to give initiation, and continued the lineage from their own seats. The lists that are preserved of these qualified disciples present us with numbers more traditionally auspicious than verifiable. A list of fifty-two is very common; another tradition gives us a hundred and eight, with fifty-two major disciples; still another list adds an odd thirty-one to the auspicious fifty-two.[1]

Most of the persons mentioned in the extended lists are known to us now only as names. But among the disciples of Charandas there were about a dozen or so well remembered in legend, and a few distinguished through their verse. Of these, three well-remembered poets were to become the principal successors to Charandas at Delhi. Coming to their guru through different routes, all common in postclassical times, the three had different relationships with him. These different relationships were no doubt crucial factors in their spiritual development, but we can only guess just how they informed the distinct spiritual personality that each presents.

Of the three successors to Charandas at Delhi, Ramrupji, whom we have met as the biographer of his guru, knew Charandas at once most personally and from the greatest mythic distance: he came to Charandas while still a boy and was raised by him; but more than most of Charandas' disciples, his guru-devotion seems to have been colored by, if not encompassed within, his Krishna worship. Known as a *bhakta* to tradition, he puts the story of his guru disproportionately in Krishna country. Of the two hundred forty pages of his biography of Charandas, fifty-eight present scenes situated in Vrindavan, as opposed to twenty-four of Jogjit's three-hundred-fifty-four-page biography. Indeed, Ramrupji was fond of presenting the facts of his lineage, as well as doctrines of everyday morality, in epic terms. In addition to the songs he produced in the *sant* style, Ramrupji also composed a long poem on the birth of Shukdev, and related two epic situations in didactic Hindi verse.

Sarasmadhuri, an important guru in Ramrupji's lineage who flourished at the turn of the present century, offers some details of Ramrupji's life that seem plausible; the core of the story he recounts is also found in Jogjit's biography of Charandas,[2] and many Charandasis still tell it today. Ramrupji lost his mother as an infant, we are told, and his father left him with a wet-nurse in Delhi while he went off toward the east to look for work. His father sent money to the wet nurse for a while, but then stopped and was not heard from again; some say he had perished. The wet nurse, childless, then adopted Ramrupji as her own. When Ramrupji was ten, she also died, but, fortunately, her brother was a devotee of Charandas. He took him to the *sant,* who raised him himself.

For a well-established holy man to adopt a young child was a common practice in medieval India and still takes place today. Ideally, the boy serves his guru dutifully, and the guru sees to his young disciple's education. If, at maturity, the boy decides he does not want to be a *sādhū,* he is free to leave. If he remains, he may be a prime candidate to inherit his guru's property and authority. In addition to the attitudes of adoration and awe toward the guru's divinity that we have seen in the *sant* poetry, disciples who grow up in their guru's home often experience both the affection and the tension that are common in most family relationships. Ramrupji certainly did demonstrate an adoring and affectionate attitude toward the personal Lord. But the personal Lord to which he gave much of his attention was the image of Krishna, and he tended to portray his guru in Krishna's mythic light.

Did Ramrupji's turning toward the personal Lord in his mythic aspect derive at all from tensions he might have experienced in his close personal relationship with his guru? Or, perhaps, from an overfamiliarity with his guru's humanness? Certainly, other psychic factors came into play that we will never know. But both Ramrupji's situation vis-à-vis his guru and the type of devotion that he developed contrasts with those experienced by Sahajo Bai, another important successor to Charandas. She was related by blood to Charandas but not raised by him—and she seems to have found in the person of her illustrious relative a most inspiring focus of the divine.

A Dhusar from Charandas' home region of Mewat, Sahajo was definitely of Charandas' immediate biological clan. Many say she was also a member of his closer extended family. According to Ganga Das, the respected and scholarly past *mahant* of her seat in Delhi, she was his first cousin, the daughter of his father's sister. Legend makes much of Sahajo's family ties, both to her immediate relations and to her distinguished cousin. We are told that as the final preparations were being made for Sahajo's wedding, Charandas, invited as an important relative, admonished her with these words:

Sahajo, why beautify your face
  For just a moment's married bliss;
Death will come, you won't remain—
  Everyone departs.[3]

Sahajo, bedecked in her wedding finery, at once recognized her calling. She announced to all that she refused to get married, but would live her life in devotion to the Lord. While Sahajo's family members were trying in vain to dissuade her from this new resolve, the bridegroom's party approached with great fanfare. During the festive procession a firecracker was lit, startling the bridegroom's horse, which tripped over a branch and fell. The bridegroom perished. Seeing the inevitability of his daughter's religious vocation, Sahajo's father not only gave his blessing, but also himself became a prominent devotee and led his other children to Charandas' holy feet.[4] Thus, Charandas' biological relations came to have a spiritual relationship with him as well.

As a devotee, Sahajo seems to have looked considerably less to the Krishna mythology to find an image of the divine than to the person of the living guru himself: her verses present the subtleties of the guru-disciple relationship. One of her best-known couplets presents a typology of gurus:

Gurus are of four kinds,
  Each one its own:
Bhrangī, lamp, and sandalwood tree,
  As well as philosopher's stone.[5]

In further couplets, these traditional analogies are expanded. In addition to reflecting intellectually on the transformative power of the guru, Sahajo treats practical problems of guru-devotion at length: obeying the guru's orders, disobeying them, and grasping the "guru's word."

Sahajo's guru-devotion is, indeed, legendary. There was once a period, they say, when Sahajo had imposed on herself a rule of not taking her own meals until Charandas had eaten. She ran into problems, however, when her guru went on a short tour to Shahjahanpur, not too far away. Having fasted for several days, Sahajo became distraught. But Charandas could see her plight from afar, and had compassion on her. He came to her as she was sitting for her nightly meditation.

—You have come far, Maharaj, she said, and must be hungry. Let me bring you some food.
—But it's the middle of the night, answered Charandas. How can you have anything ready?
—There are some sweetmeats downstairs.
—All right, go get them.

After himself taking some sweetmeats, Charandas offered them to Sahajo Bai, who gratefully accepted. He then took off his bracelet, gave it to her, and told her to call everyone in the house to have his *darshan.* When they arrived, however, Charandas had vanished, though his bracelet remained. People began to laugh at Sahajo Bai and call her crazy; but later they came to know that the very same night at Shahjahanpur Charandas had publicly announced that Sahajo Bai was

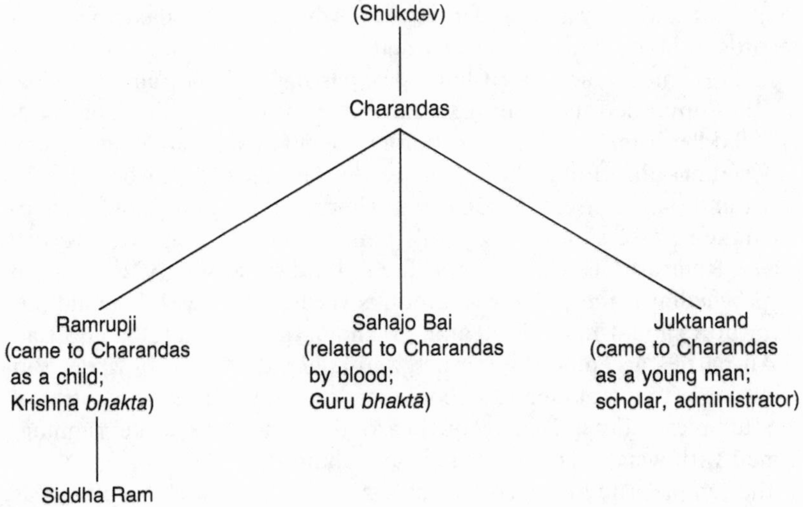

Fig. 1. The chief successors to Charandas.

so devoted to him that she should have his bracelet.[6] Mad with guru-devotion or not, Sahajo Bai, as a woman *sant* in eighteenth-century India, must have demonstrated the strength and independence of soul that we have seen to be characteristic of "holy men."

Juktanand, who finally emerged as the most important of the three successors, while perhaps the most distinguished, is the least remarkable. Unlike Sahajo Bai, related to Charandas by blood, or Ramrupji, adopted by him as a child, Juktanand apparently came to Charandas as a young man in search of the truth—if not the commonest route to a guru, then certainly the most idealized. Without ties to his guru through blood or childhood affections, Juktanand seems to have found in him a spiritual teacher alone, one whom he served primarily through his scholarship and practical competency. Jogjit refers to Juktanand as a *dvija,*[7] a twice-born Hindu, and Juktanand was certainly comfortable with Sanskrit: he translated the very extensive Bhagavat Purana into Hindi verse. A capable administrator, during his tenure as *mahant* he also saw to the maintenance of a number of far-flung land grants. Well versed in the *shāstra*s and with a head for practical details, Juktanand seems a sensible choice as director of Charandas' temple and material holdings. But many were not happy with Juktanand's succession. When Charandas passed away, some say, Ramrupji was away in Rohtak; who knows just how Juktanand received his *vasiyat nāma,* the title to succession? Shyam Sundar Shukla, who has examined the court records in Delhi, tells us what ensued.[8]

In 1791, nine years after Charandas' passing, Siddha Ram, a disciple of Ramrupji, filed suit against Juktanand in the court of Shah Nizamuddin. Siddha Ram was a scholar, but he was no bookish weakling; in the proceedings that followed he was to display his strength both in the court and on the street. Siddha Ram charged that Juktanand had himself taken possession of his guru's papers and had forged the *vasiyat nāma.* Ramrupji, he claimed, was the rightful successor. After a month of proceedings, the judge rendered his verdict: neither Juktanand nor Ramrupji should have the temple; it should go instead to Sahajo Bai.

All parties accepted this verdict, and adhered to it, for a while. But after some time Juktanand's people made a move to regain control of the temple. Siddha Ram soon heard the news and came running, armed with a staff. The incident upset Sahajo Bai, who had been living at the temple; she filed a complaint against both parties. The place was closed for a while, then arrangements were made for Sahajo Bai to return. Now, however, she had to come and go through a side entrance; no one was allowed to use the main gate.

Unfortunately, this compromise pleased no one, and finally the judge decreed that Sahajo Bai, too, should live in a separate house, like Juktanand and Ramrupji. The custodianship of the temple was to rotate among the three of them in turn.

The temple of Charandas still stands today, on a side street called Charandas lane in the Hauz Qazi section of Old Delhi. The spiritual descendants of Swami Juktanand live in a house across the street, those of Ramrupji and Sahajo Bai live a few buildings away on either side. Each *mahant* maintains a separate temple in his own house, has his own disciples (whose families have often been Charandasis for generations), and gives his own feasts. The relations among the three seats have varied over the years: records show that sometimes members of one sublineage go to the feast given by another, sometimes not.

Today, living in the middle of a rapidly modernizing city and having lost most of their land grants, the Delhi *mahant*s have accepted the authority of Juktanand's seat, and for the most part cooperate to preserve their mutual interests. When a new *mahant* is installed at one of the Charandasi temples scattered in towns and villages in Haryana, Punjab, and Rajasthan the successors to the three main lines all attend, alongside *mahant*s from other Charandasi seats outside Delhi. Together, they keep the lineage alive, though as we shall see, they continue to change its form.

Sants, *Panths*, and *Paramparās*

The various forms that the Charandasis and other *sant* lineages have taken over time reveal present spiritual authority in different relationships to the charisma of a past *sant.* In general, we can speak of three phases in the life of a *sant* lineage, in each of which the living guru's authority takes on particular dimensions.

The lineage typically begins with a solitary figure like Charandas or Kabir who stands out as an original and independent holy man. Many of these figures, we shall eventually argue, probably did have gurus of some kind, though their gurus' identities usually remain mysteries to the critical historian. But whether or not they had living gurus was not a decisive issue as far as their stature as holy men during their lifetimes was concerned: their authority, as Weber might say, derived from their own personal charisma. These holy men, who sometimes produce no successors at all, can be referred to as "solitary *sants*."

Lineages are usually continued by figures who were noteworthy *sants* in their own right, but who acknowledge definite gurus remembered by others: for example, Paltu, Sahajo Bai and Juktanand, both Ramrupji and his disciple Siddha Ram. In practice, the fact that these *sants* were disciples of great gurus was a significant element in their spiritual credentials, but their demonstrated personal characteristics were probably in most cases at least as important. These figures can be said to be within a specific *sant paramparā.* In Hindi, the term *paramparā* can mean "tradition" in many of its imprecise English senses, but it can also refer more specifically to an extended lineage of gurus and disciples. In this study a *sant* lineage will be called a *paramparā* as long as the dominant focus of spiritual power within it resides in the figure of the living holy man, and not in ritual forms recalling a *sant* of the past.

We shall reserve the term *panth* for the final phase of a *sant* lineage, when it has become a sectarian institution similar in many ways to the *sampradāya* of Vallabha described in part I. The *panths* are seen to disseminate the teachings and spiritual power of a past *sant;* the *mahant* occupying the past *sant*'s *gaddī* normally acts as an officiant—his charisma is clearly derived. Thus, the present successor to Juktanand has described his duties as looking after *panth* affairs, seeing that the ritual service to Krishna is performed regularly, and transmitting a *mantra* understood to come ultimately from Shukdev through Charandas.

People finding a focus of the divine within each of these stages of a lineage tradition grasp the coherence of *sant* tradition as a whole in different ways. For while a solitary *sant* may see himself as part of a *sant* clan, as his *paramparā* develops into a *panth* the identity of the lineage itself, not of the clan, is likely to become increasingly more important for his devotees.

Solitary *Sants* in a *Sant* Clan

The solitary *sants*, whose predecessors in a lineage remain vague, themselves usually do maintain some perception of an extended *sant* clan. Their verse reflects this perception in two ways. First, they frequently sing of the glory of the pious holy man, which outshines even that of the gods. They use different terms to refer to powerful devotees: *sādhū, avadhūt, harijan.* Among later figures, the term *sant* is particularly common. In the following verses of Tulsi Sahib, the term "*sant*" is used to refer to those devotees who have attained the highest divine realm:

Now we find one separate nameless Lord
  Beyond the void and great void.
That Lord is beloved of the *sants*;
  Sants make their court at his abode.
No one knows its secrets,
  Though Nanak and Kabir Das tell us,
And Dadu, Dariya, and Raidas;
  For Nabha and Mira inapproachable enjoyment.
And many other *sants* have sung about the inapproachable path
  After having reached its rank.[9]

In this passage Tulsi Sahib cites a number of illustrious figures as having realized "the inapproachable path." Indeed, a reference to the names of earlier figures in the tradition as "witness" is the second way solitary *sants* express in verse their identity with a larger *sant* clan. In these verses, we find first the names of five *sants* definitely associated with the *nirguṇ* tradition: "Nanak and Kabir Das . . . Dadu, Dariya, and Raidas." Then we find two figures usually taken as *saguṇ bhaktas*, Nabha and Mira, for whom the highest divine appears in an aspect more associated with Vaishnava tradition: "inapproachable enjoyment." At the end of the last chapter we noted how Charandas, more relaxed about mixing *sant* and Vaishnava traditions, presents figures from both in a song praising the glory of low-caste devotees. One of his disciples, Daya Bai, has written a veritable litany of *nirguṇ* and *saguṇ bhaktas* which extends for one hundred and five verses.[10] Other *sants* have been more discriminating. In the following verses, Dhanna, a solitary sixteenth-century *sant* from the cultivating *jāṭ* caste praises the devotion of only a few illustrious low-caste figures, all from the *nirguṇ* tradition—Namdev, Kabir, Raidas, and Sena:

To Govind, Govind, Govind
  Namdev takes his mind,
And even though a little cotton-printer,
  He's become a millionaire. [Refrain]

With love for the Lord Kabir
  Abandoned all his weaving:
Even he a low *julāha*
  Is virtuous and deep. [1]
Ravidas the tanner
  Gave up tanning *māyā*
And present with the holy men
  Found Hari's *darshan.* [2]
The barber Sena loved the Lord:
  In every house they've heard of him.
Pārbrahm settled in his heart,
  They count him as a *bhakta.* [3]
On hearing of them all
  This *jāṭ* began to know devotion;
Dhanna of great fortune
  Met the Master face to face.[11] [4]

Clan and Lineage in *Sant Paramparā*s

A solitary *sant* such as Dhanna sings of his good fortune to have met the Lord face to face: he, too, became spiritually transformed, like others in the *sant* clan. A figure within a *paramparā,* on the other hand, is likely to sing of the grace of *sant*s and the transforming power of the guru. In the following song, Paltu, who stands in an illustrious *paramparā,* sings, like Dhanna, of the virtues of *sant*s generally. But for Paltu here the *sant* is preeminently the guru, and he develops some of the analogies to the guru's transformative power that we have seen formulated by Sahajo.

So fortunate, I found the company of *sant*s
  And bashed *Kāl,* the ensnarer; on the head. [Refrain]

The *sant*s give grace
  And naturally Ram's *māyā* stops. (1)
The *sant*'s a *bhrangī;* I'm a *kīṭ:*
  He makes me like himself with slaps and blows. (2)

The *sant*'s a sandal-tree; I'm wood:
He makes me like himself through his magnificence. (3)
The *sant*'s a philosopher's stone; I'm iron:
With just a touch I shine within the world. (4)
The *sant*'s a flower; I'm sesame oil:
With just a touch I've got sweet scent. (5)
Says Paltu, when you're dead release is useless:
The *sant*'s protection lives—find it and cross![12] (6)

That the *sant* can make his disciple "like himself" is an understanding central to the perception of a lineage as a vital *paramparā*. The *sant*s of the lineage in which Paltu stands seem, moreover, to have in fact been able to produce other spiritually gifted individuals: an unusual number of them were remarkable poets. Scholars of Hindi literature speak of these poets as forming the *paramparā* of Bauri Sahiba, "Madam Mad Woman." Little is known of Bauri herself. She is said to have had a spiritual pedigree that reached back through three generations to a guru named Ramananda—through a different Ramananda, some say, from Kabir's traditional guru.[13] The authenticity of the few verses ascribed to her and her successor, Biru, remain doubtful; indeed, all we know of the figures in the lineage through Biru is based on sketchy—and, one suspects, contrived—traditions of the later *paramparā*.

With the traditional successor to Biru, a Muslim named Yari Sahib, we can begin to discern a genuine historical figure. Yari, whose full name is given as Yar Muhammad, left a small corpus of songs and, they say, five qualified disciples—three with Muslim names, and two with Hindu ones; works of Yari's two Hindu disciples are preserved in *sant* tradition. Paltu is connected to Yari through four generations of gurus, all poets whose verses have been published. A diagram outlining the relationships among the *sant*s from the lineage of Bauri to be discussed here is given in the Appendix.

The *sant* poets of the Bauri *paramparā* not only demonstrate individual personalities but come from different places and various caste communities. Thus, in studying the stories of the meetings between the successive gurus and disciples in the *paramparā* we can learn something about the continuity of a lineage not only over time, but also over space and society. For while what is miraculous in these stories is credible only to the believer, much of what is prosaic in them appears plausible indeed. Even if we cannot be sure that these stories do in fact reflect something of historical event—which they certainly may—we can surely assume that they reflect what those within *sant* tradition believe to be in the realm of everyday reality.

The most important disciple of Yari in Delhi was Bulla, from what is now eastern Uttar Pradesh, the populous Indian state in the Gangetic plain. He was, they say, a servant of Gulal, a landlord with considerable holdings near Gazipur. Bulla was a *kunbī,* a member of a clean, though not particularly distinguished, cultivating caste; Gulal was a Rajput. Gulal became embroiled in a dispute over his land, an occurrence that was probably as common in Gulal's time as it is today. To pursue his case, Gulal went to Delhi, taking with him his trusted servant, Bulla. The case dragged on, and Bulla found time to visit Yari Sahib, the famous disciple of Biru. Though Yari Sahib was a Muslim from Delhi, his lineage, it seems, was destined to flourish among Hindus to the east.

Yari initiated Bulla into the secrets of spiritual practice. Bulla, absorbed in his practice, abandoned Gulal, who finally left Delhi for home when his business was completed. But Gulal, they say, remained anxious about Bulla; and when Bulla eventually showed up at his old village, Gulal coaxed him back into service.

But Bulla by now was no longer the farm worker he once was. He would lose himself in divine revery while doing his chores, and Gulal began to get annoyed. One day, seeing Bulla rapt in meditation next to his plow, Gulal became angry and gave him a hard blow. As Bulla broke his meditation, curds came streaming from his hand. He had been out of his body feeding some distant *sādhūs*, he explained, and was just about to offer them curd when he was interrupted. With this, Gulal recognized Bulla's greatness and rushed to embrace his feet. As followers of his present-day successors point out, Gulal thus had the distinction of becoming the servant of his own servant.

Capable of such humility, Gulal, too, became a great devotee and attracted a large number of disciples. Among them was a Brahman named Bhikha, who was to be his most important successor. Gulal the landlord had material as well as spiritual wealth to pass on, and the former, at least, is still impressive. At Bhurkura in Gazipur district—where Gulal had his land and Bulla, Gulal, and Bhikha sat as gurus—a large religious establishment remains today and continues as an important local religious center.

The mobility over space and between communities in the legendary history of this lineage is the sort that occurs matter-of-factly in the lives of respectable Indians. Movement over space is entailed by business interests; relationships among caste communities in the lineage correspond to the mixing among Hindus of clean castes and reputable Muslims that often takes place in Indian social—but not ritual—life. Indeed, the succession here presents a progression from lower to higher Hindu status, thus offering a parallel to the increasing respectability of *sant* tradition over time: Yari the Muslim, Bulla the *kunbī,* Gulal the *kṣatriya,* Bhikha the Brahman. While each of these *sant*s had no qualms about going to a guru of lower ritual rank, as gurus themselves they seem to have maintained a sense of caste propriety. Or such, at least would be inferred from the following traditional recounting by a Brahman *mahant* of Bhikha's meeting with Govind, Bhikha's qualified disciple and Paltu's guru.[14]

Govind, we are told, was a Brahman from Paltu's village near Ayodhya. A bright child, he was sent to Banaras to study Sanskrit. He was a good speaker, and on his return to his village became popular as a teller of tales from the Bhagavat Purana, popularly known in Hindi as the Bhagvat. One of his most avid listeners was the young man Paltu, whose family Govind served as a *purohit,* a Brahman carrying out traditional rituals. After some time, however, Paltu stopped attending Govind's performances from the Bhagvat. Govind noticed and asked why. Paltu explained that mere verbal knowledge led nowhere, as far as he could tell; he would instead try to *act* on the Bhagvat's words.

Govind was deeply impressed by Paltu's answer and the two made an agreement: each would go off in a different direction, and whoever found truth first would tell the other his secret. At this point, according to our narrator, Paltu protested. What if he were first to find the truth? How could he, a *baniyā,* give spiritual secrets to a Brahman who had, moreover, taught him the Bhagvat and been his family *purohit?* Govind assured him that it didn't matter; caste had no place in spiritual initiations. He was soon to find, however, that matters were not so simple.

Paltu and Govind separated. Paltu went north to Ayodhya; Govind proceeded southeast toward Puri. Stopping in Banaras, Govind heard about the greatness of Gulal and his disciple Bhikha. He decided it would be worth his while to visit them. At Bhurkura he first met Bhikha, was impressed, and asked for initiation. But Bhikha thought that the proper course was to refer Govind to his own guru, Gulal. Gulal, however, told Govind that it would be better for him to be initiated by Bhikha; for both Govind and Bhikha were Brahmans, and Gulal was only a *kṣatriya.* Still, Bhikha was adamant: how could he be so presumptuous as to give someone initiation when his guru was alive and easily accessible? He persisted in his refusal. Govind then went back to Gulal and tried to humble himself before him, even going so far as to eat his leavings. Gulal disapproved. "Look," he said, "you're a Brahman who left home on pilgrimage to Puri. First complete your pilgrimage, come back, and then we'll see about initiation." But when Govind returned from Puri he found that Gulal had passed on and Bhikha had inherited his seat. Govind took initiation from Bhikha, and according to his agreement with Paltu told the secrets he had learned from Bhikha to him. Ultimately he settled at a place near his native village, which was eventually called Govind Sahib after the illustrious *sant.* The shrine at Govind Sahib remains well known in Faizabad and Azamgarh districts, and every winter for two weeks, his successor there presides over a fair of considerable local economic importance.

Today, the local shrines in the lineage of Gulal, Bhikha, Govind, and Paltu may not only serve economic functions, but can also play a role in the religious allegiance of regional caste groups. Discussing Paltu, we noted that many of the *baniyā*s of places near Ayodhya find a spiritual identity in the tradition of that *sant.* Similarly, a qualified disciple of Bhikha named Harlal Sahib was a Kaushik *kṣatriya,* and the successors to his seat at Chitbaragaon command the allegiance of many of the Kaushiks of the *das parganā* area of Ballia. Chitbaragaon, Bhurkura, Ayodhya, and Govind Sahib remain the major centers of the tradition today. In addition, there are a number of small *maṭh*s in villages within a number of districts of eastern Uttar Pradesh,[15] at most of which annual gatherings are held (called *melā*s, "fairs").

While *sādhū*s normally regard a particular establishment as "home," they recognize each other as spiritual relations, interdining with each other and going to one another's fairs. Those conversant with the tradition also speak of the branch of the lineage at Delhi, though few have anything to do with it. One venerable *sādhū,* a Brahman, said that he had once gone to Delhi and visited the tomb of Yari Sahib. But it was tended by Muslims, he noted, and very run down. He merely paid his respects to Yari Sahib and left, without revealing himself as a distant spiritual relation: "The Muslim *faqīrs* maintain their prejudices," he said.

Today in eastern Uttar Pradesh the lineage functions as an established *panth.* Nevertheless, many of the routinized religious forms that have developed reflect the lineage's past as a vital and disparate *paramparā.* Thus, the spiritual focus of the tradition is diffused among a number of important *sant*s, none clearly dominant. Since Bhurkura, the seat of Gulal, is its largest center, most of the *sādhū*s in the lineage refer to it as the Gulal *panth,* the name by which we will later refer to the tradition when discussing some of its current problems. Many householder-devotees, however, while realizing the extended nature of the lineage, and even perhaps going to a distant fair, will call the tradition by the name of the guru to whom they are most attached: a Faizabad *baniyā* calls it the Paltu *panth;* someone initiated by a guru in succession to Govind calls it the Govind *panth.*

Even within a sublineage, respect is given to its individual members. At the older establishments, tombs are usually preserved for each successive *mahant.* At Bhurkura, the seat of Bulla, Gulal, Bhikha, and seven of their successors, lights are waved daily in front of each of their tombs in turn—though to save time a ritual circumambulation is made only around that of Bulla, the first of the *sant*s at Bhurkura, who can represent them all. During the annual fair, moreover, offerings of sweetmeats and curds are made at each tomb, recalling Bulla's miraculous feeding of the *sādhūs*—and Gulal's interruption of it.

The circumambulation of Bulla's tomb alone and the presentation of *his* curds at *all* the tombs certainly reveals the characteristic reverence of a *panth* for a local founder. But the respect still given to all the tombs also reflects a perception of equality among all the *sant*s in the lineage, the same type of equality as found in the idea of a great clan of *sant*s. It is then an easy step for the Gulalpanthis to attempt to adopt Jagjivan Sahib, another member of the *sant* clan, into their own lineage.

Jagjivan Sahib was an eighteenth-century figure who eventually established himself at Kotwa, in Barabanki district, not far to the west of Ayodhya and Govind Sahib. His followers, called Satnamis,[16] remain very numerous in some of the areas where Gulalpanthis have their *maṭh*s. Many local Satnamis, however, have never heard of Bulla, and certainly not as Jagjivan's guru. According to the Satnami *mahant* at Kotwa, Jagjivan's guru was a *mahātmā* named Vishveshvar Puri from Banaras, a statement that sounds plausible enough and that everyone in the tradition seems to take for granted. The Gulalpanthis, however, are forced to resort to a most unconvincing story to make Jagjivan one of their own. Bulla, they say, slowly making his way home after his initiation from Yari, came upon Jagjivan in the forest. And it was from Bulla, according to the Gulalpanthi account, that Jagjivan, at the time still a child, learned the secrets of yoga. Though they did not succeed in winning the Satnamis to the truth of their claim, for the Gulalpanthis themselves the story seems to succeed as a mythic strategy for dealing with powerful rivals. The strategy is certainly a familiar one:

since the Satnamis were too well established to beat, the Gulalpanthis simply joined them—and as the senior partner.

The Development of Lineage and *Sant Panth*s

In the illustriousness of the notable *sant* poets it has produced, the lineage of Bauri is clearly rivaled by that of Dadu, which has given to Hindi letters Rajab and Sundar Das. But in contrast to the relative equality given to Gulal, Paltu, Bhikha, and the rest in their tradition, among the Dadupanthis both Rajab and Sundar Das are considerably dwarfed by the figure of Dadu himself. Of course Dadu, like most early *sant*s, did not intend to initiate a *panth* in the same way that Vallabha apparently intended to start a *sampradāya*. In India today, however, there are a great many *panth*s that exist in the names of past *sant*s: Chaturvedi lists over twenty-five. Most, like the Charandasis and the Gulalpanthis, are fairly small and localized. A few, like the Dadupanthis and the Kabirpanthis, have gained important socioreligious roles. The *panth*s often seem to present even more variety in their development than do the *sant*s themselves, a variety in part due to the richness of the Hindu ritual life on which they draw. In the *panth*s we see how the Hindu forms of singular personality and eternal heritage discussed in chapter 2 in *contrast* to the *sant* as holy man, in fact become integrated into the cumulative *sant* tradition.

The appeal of some of the *sants* who have continued to attract small sectarian followings derives in part from their specific human origins: the followings of Paltu, Harlal, and Charandas consist in good part of their own caste-brothers. These *sant*s are certainly depicted as intense *bhakta*s and powerful yogis, but with respect to their origins, at any rate, they are taken to be essentially the same as many of their devotees. Dadu and Kabir, however, both came from the lowest strata of society, and have acquired large numbers of followers who aspire to a measure of respectability. It makes socioreligious sense, then, that the origins of both Dadu and Kabir have been made wondrous in tradition, where their births are seen in terms of mythical patterns of nearly universal scope.

Like Moses, Perseus, and heroes of myth and legend all over the world, both Dadu and Kabir are said to have been found as infants floating in bodies of water: bereft of human parents, sheltered in the primal source of life. Dadu, they say, was taken from the Sabarmati river near Ahmedabad, Gujarat; Kabir, from a pool called Lahar Tara near Banaras. About Dadu, the tradition continues that he was raised by a Brahman, had initiation from an old *sādhū,* began to preach and compose, and eventually collected disciples.[17] Dadu ultimately became the source of a distinctive religious tradition, but one which stands today in a different relation to the greater Hindu heritage from that of the considerably larger tradition of Kabir.

The Dadupanthis revere at once the Formless Lord and the collection of their founder's sacred utterances, a combination that should be familiar to Western monotheists. Among the Dadupanthis, the book itself serves as the principal icon, and like the scrolls of the Pentateuch, a hand-written copy of the *Dādūbānī* can be elevated to a sacramental object. Fanned by fly-whisks and offered prostrations, the book is served with ritual worship that Dadupanthis call *āratī* or *pūjā,* terms that Hindus use to refer to the ceremonial worship of their gods. Indeed, many temples display near the book a picture or two of Dadu, who thus begins to appear, like Vallabha, as a special personality in Hindu tradition, whose revealed scripture gives salvation. As in many *sant* traditions, the Dadupanthis often speak of the Formless Lord as Ram, a Vaishnava name; and a common Dadupanthi *mantra* (which I saw covering the walls of the Dadupanthi temple at Pushkar) shows an assimilation of the sectarian founder with the Lord in good Hindu fashion: Daduram, Daduram . . .

The adaptation by the Dadupanthis of Hindu forms of religious practice is accompanied today by a lessening of their identity as a distinctive group. Most Dadupanthi *sādhū*s I met reported interfeasting with Vaishnavas as well as other Dadupanthis, and many living in their own small temples in Jaipur referred to themselves matter-of-factly as Vaishnavas. To be sure, the Dadupanthi Nagas, a warrior ascetic group that flourished under the Jaipur Maharajas, were a distinct order, and an important *mahant* revered by all Dadupanthis continues to reign at Naraina, Dadu's resting place and the chief Dadupanthi shrine. In modern times, moreover, a central committee has been set up to look after some common Dadupanthi establishments. But the committee may entrust a minor shrine to a non-Dadupanthi Hindu. During the several times I visited the house of the famous Dadupanthi poet Sundar Das at Assi Ghat, Banaras—admittedly far from the Dadupanthi centers in Rajasthan—no Dadupanthi was living in it. Instead, the house, administered by the distant committee, was being tended by a sympathetic scholarly Brahman interested in the verses of Sundar and Dadu as Hindi religious poetry. The Dadupanthis today, then, certainly preserve a sense of their lineage from Dadu and of the importance of his *bānī,* but their perception of a larger *sant* clan tends to become lost in a greater Hindu, often Vaishnava, identity.

Kabirpanthi groups, on the other hand, not only identify closely with their particular lineages, but maintain a sense of the distinctness of their version of *sant* tradition. Like most Dadupanthis, a Kabirpanthi may say that his tradition and the eternal *dharma* of the Hindus are finally one, but unlike the assimilating Dadupanthi, he may well also insist that it is *his* tradition that is the more fundamental of the two. Thus, when asked whether he was a Vaishnava, one important Kabirpanthi *mahant* replied that not only was he a Vaishnava, but he was a *param*-Vaishnava, an "ultimate Vaishnava," who practiced to the fullest the Vaishnava's precepts of nonviolence. But as super-Hindus the Kabirpanthis have also adopted extensive Indic ritual and mythological forms. Eventually emerging as a complex tradition of its own, the Kabir *panth* is understood by those within it to transcend the Hindu heritage.

Kabir, a well-developed singular personality, thus differs from Dadu, who remains an incipient one. Dadu, though of mysterious origins, is normally referred to only in one incarnation; the corpus of his *bānī* is circumscribed; and other figures in his lineage are commonly recognized as important *sant* poets in their own right. For many Kabirpanthis, Kabir is seen as a being who manifested in earlier ages; long, metaphysical works have become attributed to him;[18] and there is only one other figure in his lineage, Dharam Das, who is sometimes recognized as an important *sant* poet.

Certainly, the image of Kabir varies in the disparate Kabirpanthi groups. Unlike the Dadupanthis, concentrated for the most part in Rajasthan, Kabirpanthis are found throughout the Hindi-speaking areas and well beyond them, as far south as Bangalore. The two most important Kabirpanthi regions, however, are eastern Uttar Pradesh and Bihar on the one hand, and the Chhatisgarh area of Madhya Pradesh on the other. The Kabirpanthi center at Kabir Chaura, Banaras, eastern Uttar Pradesh, commands the respect of those Hindus who take Kabir as part of their own extended heritage; the Chhatisgarhi centers are less highly regarded by literate Hindus than the Kabir Chaura *maṭh,* but together they seem to command a larger sectarian following. The different images of Kabir projected by the two main divisions of Kabirpanthis are reflected in the stories they tell of Kabir's appearance at Lahar Tara.

*Sādhū*s at Kabir Chaura are insistent that Kabir was a Brahman, and the story that he was the abandoned son of a Brahman widow is well known there among Indians at large.[19] Kabir's being a Brahman, of course, would certainly help make him more acceptable to respectable Hindus in caste-conscious Banaras. In Chhatisgarh, a tribal area in large part, Kabir is usually said to have appeared miraculously within a lotus flower in the middle of Lahar Tara pond. Especially at Chhatisgarh, then, Kabir appears as a truly singular personality and provides a focus for an accumulated heritage.

The ritual elements of the Kabirpanthi heritage elaborated in Chhatisgarhi tradition may seem familiar to those conversant with popular Indian religion, but the mythic cosmology that gives them their meaning will probably appear unusual. In our examination of the Kabirpanthi heritage we shall begin with the more familiar—a description of a central ceremony, which shows how Indic ritual is turned to reflect Kabirpanthi truths; we shall then consider briefly the ways in which the ritual elements are understood in tradition.

Like the ordinary Hindu, the Kabirpanthi may employ ritual for nonsoteriological ends: to ask for the birth of a child or assure the peace of deceased relatives. The central rite, however, is that of initiation, of which others can appear as variations. It is therefore to this rite—often a major event in which those already initiated also have a chance to participate—that we shall turn our attention.

The Kabirpanthis sometimes call their ceremony *yajña,* in honor of the Vedic rite; more often, it is called *chaukā āratī,* after common Hindu practice. *Āratī* normally refers to the waving of lights in front of a divine image, one of the most frequent forms of Hindu ceremonial worship. *Chaukā,* in ordinary Hindi, refers to a well-defined "four-sided" place that is made ritually suitable for the preparation of food by being plastered with mud or cow dung. Similarly, among the Kabirpanthis, the place of the *chaukā-āratī* is typically cleaned and plastered, then covered with a cloth. Within the *chaukā* is drawn an elaborate *maṇḍala:* a large, central, seven-petalled lotus eventually sprouts eighty-four smaller buds at the periphery. In the middle of the lotus sits the guru, who utters *mantras* and receives offerings—especially of coconuts. *Āratī* is performed to him, accompanied—as in elaborate *āratī*s all over India—by the sound of a conch and the ringing of bells. If the Dadupanthis' book-worship gives ritual form to the *sant*s' *shabda,* which refers at once to the guru's verses and divine sound, then the Kabirpanthi ceremonial visibly places the *sant*s' guru at the center of ritual worship.

At the annual initiation ceremony I witnessed at the Chhatisgarhi temple at Lahar Tara in 1980, the ritual worship of the guru proceeded on a grand scale. The ceremony began at night after a three-day festival celebrating Kabir's birthday. People assembled under a large tent near Lahar Tara pond; in the middle of a further enclosed square area inside the tent sat the guru. He was flanked by a boy on either side, each wearing a shoulder-sash with the guru's name on it and holding a peacock-fan over him. For more than an hour devotees approached the guru one by one, offering coconuts and usually some money. The guru broke each of the coconuts himself; later, the pieces were distributed as *prasād*. Eventually, the new members were initiated individually with verbal instructions and a *mālā*. New *mahant*s were also invested, who would have the authority to perform this ceremony at their own places and thus become themselves the objects of ritual worship.

In his rich book on Kabirpanthi tradition Kedarnath Dvivedi presents varying interpretations of this and other rituals that were given to him by Kabirpanthis.[20] The guru sitting in the *maṇḍala,* we are told, represents Sat Purush in *sat lok,* the highest heaven, where he sits on a throne in a seven-petalled lotus surrounded by eighty-four thousand islands, the abodes of *haṃsa*-souls. The coconut offered to the guru and broken by him then comes to represent the created being in its many dimensions. The roundness of the coconut, apparently, can at once recall: *brahmāṇḍ,* the finite universe; the human body, which the Kabirpanthis often call *piṇḍ,* "a ball"; and most obviously, the human head—all referents given by Dvivedi. The head is the seat of Niranjan, as Kabirpanthis often call the (negative) principle of "mind," conceived as a demigod. Thus, according to Dvivedi, when the guru breaks the coconut he at once "releases the soul from the bonds of . . . *piṇḍ* . . . *brahmāṇḍ* and Niranjan."[21]

While a later *sant,* Tulsi Sahib, would explicitly reject the ritual performances of the Kabirpanthis, he (like many others) adapted much of their many-levelled cosmology. As we study the *sant* technical vocabulary we will see the terms *sat lok* and Sat Purush, Niranjan, *piṇḍ,* and *brahmāṇḍ* used to refer to places and beings in the inner universe. Some later Radhasoami thinkers, moreover, will continue to give Kabir a particularly exalted cosmological role.[22] Yet while the mythic developments among the Kabirpanthis provided a good deal of what was to become common tradition in the wider "clan" of *sant*s, in their own attitude to the *sant* clan the Kabirpanthis often demonstrate a manifest imperialism. Many modern Kabirpanthis will certainly give a brief nod to the virtues of later *sant*s. In one massive tome dedicated mostly to the exploits of Kabir, the author devotes a substantial section to the glory of several *sant*s not taken to be in Kabir's lineage, the majority from the *paramparā* of Gulal, Bhikha, and Paltu. The author of another massive Kabirpanthi tome, however, displays a more imperialistic attitude toward non-Kabirpanthi *sant*s: he lists ten later holy men—including Tulsi Sahib and Radhasoami Maharaj—as founders of Kabirpanthi "sub-branches" (*upashākhāeṃ*).[23]

The perception of the clan of *sant*s most current among the Kabirpanthis is perhaps best reflected in the order of the evening *āratī* performed at Kabir Chaura. Every evening at the Kabir Chaura *maṭh* the monks assemble to honor five holy presences in turn. First a monk makes a circling motion with an oil lamp in the direction of the memorial tomb to Kabir maintained there. Then he turns to the holy ground within the *maṭh* premises where Kabir is said to have given his discourses. The third *āratī* is to the living guru, and the fourth to the tombs of the other gurus in the lineage. Finally, the officiating monk turns to make *āratī* to his assembled brethren. This *āratī,* it was explained to me, was to honor all the *sant*s—who in that situation are most conspicuously the Kabirpanthi *sādhū*s. Of the five *āratī*s performed by the Kabirpanthis, the first four are explicitly directed to the founder of the lineage and his successors, the objects of faith which clearly dominate in developed *sant panth*s. In the last, however, honoring all the *sant*s, we see the Kabirpanthis continuing to recognize a broader *sant* clan, but one conceived in their own image and subordinate to their own traditions.

Change Within *Sant* Lineages: Processes and Problems

Along with, perhaps, some elements of Kabirpanthi cosmology, followers of smaller *panth*s very often assimilate religious forms from some variant of the Hindu heritage. Charandasis have their Krishna *pūjā;* Gulalpanthis in the village sometimes sport the matted locks of Shaivite ascetics; the current *mahant* at the Paltu Akhara at Ayodhya runs a Sanskrit college. Indeed, many of the Kabirpanthis themselves have become diligent Sanskrit scholars, not only making Sanskrit translations of central Kabirpanthi texts, but also producing original Sanskrit compositions of their own.

Different religious dynamics lie behind the paradoxes presented by the Hinduization of *sant panth*s. An obvious factor is the desire to emulate the practice of high-status communities: Kabirpanthis look to the traditions of Benarasi *paṇḍit*s; the Charandasis, to the Vaishnavism of the respectable trading castes with which some of their most important patrons identify. But the matted locks of Gulalpanthi *sādhūs* represent only a traditional custom of Hindu ascetics, not a high-class practice. And behind some of the easy assimilation of traditional Hindu precepts seems to lie the assertion of a unifying truth known to the wise in all traditions. Thus a young Kabirpanthi naively affirms a false etymology he has learned as a slogan: "A Hindu is someone who keeps violence (*HIṂSā*) far away (*DUr*)." The Kabirpanthi, like the good Hindu, should practice precepts of nonviolence; the real Kabirpanthi is the real Hindu.

Not everyone in the *sant panths*, however, is as complacent about their increasing Hinduization as our young Kabirpanthi, and some wistfully recall a pristine past. One older Charandasi *sādhū,* having indiscreetly revealed to me the *mantra* traditionally imparted at initiation, noted the many references in it to the formless divine, which he took as typical of the old and unsullied *sant* tradition. "My object of devotion is the Formless One," he said with pride. "The *mahants* started all this other worship later." Wilson, writing in the middle of the last century, affirms both the truth of this *sādhū*'s statement and the persistency of his attitude. Even the Charandasis of Wilson's time used divine images, the Tulsi plant and the Salagram stone, in their devotions: "They have, however, they admit, recently adopted them, in order to maintain a friendly intercourse with the followers of Ramananda."[24]

But for some members of *sant panths*, an exploration of the extended Hindu heritage can represent a sincere search after truth. As developed institutions, *panths* can routinely offer an immanent focus of the divine in their own accumulated heritages; but only sometimes can they also offer vital internal practice directed by qualified holy men. Many *sādhūs* come to *panths* as children, with little control over their lifelong religious affiliation. To those whose access to the divine is already primarily through a heritage it can appear sensible to expand their horizons toward the rich traditions in Hinduism. As one young Kabirpanthi more interested in books than in yoga remarked: "One needs to study the philosophies in order to really understand Kabir."

In adopting Sanskritic ways wholesale, of course, *panths* face the danger of disintegration into mainstream Hinduism; Wilson writes of two small *sant panths* that seem now to have disappeared. But as Orr suggests, writing of the Dadupanthis, there is perhaps no need to mourn the disappearance of *panths* that have developed into ritual traditions.[25] The *sants* standing at the source of most *panths* usually had no intention of founding them, and their complete collapse into the Hindu heritage would only mean that the ritual precepts developed in the *panth*s have led those who follow them to a larger tradition where ritual precepts are capable of richer development.

When *panth*s do have a distinct religious role to play, however, they can flourish with or without ritual. The Chhatisgarhi Kabirpanthis, very vital today, propagate a peculiar form of Hinduized tradition among non-Hindu tribal peoples of Madhya Pradesh. Other less vital traditions continue to maintain themselves among their own old constituencies. These *panth*s, adapting to changed circumstances, sometimes undergo considerable transformation.

One of the most crucial transformations a *panth* can undergo is a modification of its principles of succession. Authority in *panth*s today devolves both through *nād paramparā,* "succession through sound"—the *mantra* imparted to the disciple at initiation—(spiritual lineage); and *bindu paramparā,* "succession through seed," (biological lineage). While *nad paramparā* remains the most common form of succession in *sant panth*s, there have long been lineages continuing through the biological successor of an illustrious guru. Among the Gulalpanthis, the seat of Harlal at Chitbaragaon has from its beginnings gone to its founder's biological descendants. Some of the Chhatisgarhi Kabirpanthis, on the other hand, cite two founders for their lineages: a celibate ascetic who founded a seat, and one of his disciples who married and began a *bindu paramparā* there. And about fifty years ago, a branch of one of these Chhatisgarhi lineages, established as a *bindu paramparā,* reverted to a spiritual succession.

Considerable confusion ensued when the *mahant* at one of the most important Chhatisgarhi seats died without issue. His wives eventually installed a young relative of his at the traditional seat. A group of *sādhū*s attached to it, however, assembled and decided to form a new seat,[26] and the new lineage of celibate monks has since played an important part in the revitalization of the Kabirpanth in Chhatisgarh.

However, a change from biological succession (through seed) into spiritual succession (through sound) is fairly rare. More often we see a transformation of principles of sound into those of seed, one which is not easily reversible. To understand this transformation, particularly as it has taken place in modern times, we will have to examine one of the most common institutions through which lineages of gurus and disciples have maintained themselves: succession through adoption, an institution that already begins to make spiritual bonds look very much like biological ones.

As we have seen in the case of Charandas' disciple Ramrupji, a *sādhū* could come to his guru as a child. There are a number of reasons for children to go to live with *sādhū*s, and Ramrupji's situation as an orphan seems more an exception than one of the rules. Parents might give their sons to a *sādhū* to be raised out of economic hardship, devotion to the *sādhū,* or the fulfillment of a vow. A boy from an unhappy home situation may himself prefer to live with a *sādhū* who invites him. Indeed, this may have been the case with those current renunciates who, when asked how they came to their *panth*s, say that they felt a deep revulsion from the world at the age of eleven or so.

A boy can have a happy life if he finds himself living with a considerate *sādhū* who has a sufficiently well-endowed establishment. At one village *maṭh* I met a boy of seven or eight with a name that sounds very incongruous in Hindi: Babuli Das—a common child's nickname with the *sādhū*'s suffix attached. During the day he attended the village school; at home he was expected to serve the *sādhū*s present in small ways like a dutiful child. But he was also indulged like a child, with sweets and fruit. A *sādhū* might speak of a disciple he has raised as his "boy" (*laṛkā*), a term commonly used in Hindi as well as English to mean "son."

Succession through adoption, however, is not a thriving institution in present-day Indian society. In today's world, perhaps, many Indians have less reverence for the celibate ascetic than they once did. Parents are less ready to offer their son to a *sādhū;* boys raised to be *sādhū*s find that they would really rather get married. The inheritance and land-ceiling laws of modern India, moreover, make it easier for a man with a family to retain large holdings than for a single *sādhū* at his *math.* In such circumstances, permitting those who would once have remained celibate to marry becomes a strategy for a *panth*'s preservation. Not only are young men who might otherwise have left the *panth* able to remain actively associated with it, but they can provide it with new members through their children.

In the Dadu *panth* today, most members have been born into the tradition as children of lay devotees, and many boys adopted by *sādhū*s are marrying. Indeed, the reason that the adopted son of one respected Dadupanthi *mahant* gave for his marriage was "to keep the *panth* alive." Nevertheless, the succession to the central Dadupanthi shrine at Naraina remains with celibate monks, and its transformation into a *bindu paramparā* does not appear imminent.

Among the Charandasis, however, not only have the *mahant*s at many of the minor seats openly married, but even the succession to the most important ones is undergoing transformation. At all levels, the process of change is eased through legal fictions, often entailing the adoption of a child.

At the death of one urban, celibate Charandasi *mahant* his most competent devotee was a married lawyer. Not yet ready to install a married man there as one of their number, the Charandasi *mahant*s invested the lawyer's young son with the seat. The son is in fact known as the *mahant,* but the father has always done the *mahant*'s work, looking after the ritual worship at the temple and attending ceremonial functions. Meanwhile, the son, now grown up and married, has begun to claim his rights as *mahant,* a situation leading to tensions at home and to some concern within the larger Charandasi community.

The successor to Ramrupji's seat in Delhi not only is openly married, but has also made his wife the *mahantānī,* the female *mahant.* Juktanand's successor, the head of the order, was not happy with the arrangement, but had to accept it. Perhaps, he suggests, making the lady *mahantānī* was part of the terms of the marriage. It may also have been part of a strategy to have traditional devotees accept the marriage itself. The couple now have a son, and the three went together to the investiture of the new *mahant* at Dehra—in part, no doubt, to demonstrate publicly the order of succession. One son is enough, says the *mahantānī*—any more and the sons would end up fighting.

The fights among the successors to Charandas discussed at the beginning of this chapter continue through the lineage, though now the issues have changed. In 1981, the most important succession battle going on was being argued in terms of marriage and celibacy. The successor to Sahajo Bai's seat, who was a highly respected scholarly monk, had recently died. The Charandasi *mahant*s had ceremonially invested as the new successor his nephew, a young man who was wearing a renunciate's robes when I met him. When questioned, however, he refused to answer whether he had ever "had a wedding," as one normally inquires about someone's marital status in Hindi. He was ready to affirm, though, that at present he had no wife. His investiture is contested by an older monk, whose major contention is that the nephew is a married usurper from the old *mahant*'s family, and that the seat should remain with *sādhū*s. In 1981 the case was still in the courts, and was likely to remain there for some time.

Another case of succession to the seat of an illustrious *sant* was still in the courts in 1981; this case, too, pitted *sādhū* against householder, though caste factors were also a major issue, and the financial stakes and local power involved were greater. The shrine to Govind Sahib in the village of the same name is a well-built-up establishment. There is plenty of room for *sādhūs* to live and for devotees to visit, and a large artificial pond for them to bathe in. The temple authorities support schools and rent out stores to local traders serving nearby villages. The annual fair at Govind Sahib is a major event in the area and draws in considerable revenue for the shrine's administrators.

The old *mahant* had died suddenly and specified no one to the succession. Four persons have made claim to it at some time, though the major factions have finally taken shape around two contenders. Both were *sādhūs*. One, who had been attached to the establishment at the time of the guru's death, was highly-respected by the other *sādhūs* and eventually invested as successor by the other Gulalpanthi *mahants*. The *sādhūs* expected him to be able to continue the firm control over the Govind Sahib establishment that the last few *mahants* had exercised. They spoke of a previous era when some local householders had gained considerable power at the shrine and abused its resources to their own ends.

Govind Sahib was a Brahman, and the succession to his seat had traditionally remained with Brahmans, who are numerous in the area. The *sādhūs*' candidate was, unfortunately, a *kurmī,* a member of a clean cultivating caste that most *sādhūs*, however, would dignify as coming within the *kṣatriya* ("warrior") *varṇa.* Many of the local householders, unhappy with a *kurmī mahant,* turned to another candidate, a Brahman. *Sādhūs* accuse this candidate of reappearing after an absence upon hearing of the old guru's death and promising to return to the householders the control of the temple they had formerly abused.

The case went from court to court, with accusations of casteism and corruption on both sides. "It's the Brahmans against the *kṣatriyas*," said one observer, "and all the judges are Brahmans and *kṣatriyas*, too." At the time I left the scene the case was definitely going against the *sādhūs*. One respected *sādhū* with a history of high blood pressure died of a stroke a few days after receiving news of an unfavorable court decision. At his funeral feast in Ayodhya the other *sādhūs* complained that the householders' candidate was given bigger bribes, and were wondering what they were now going to do.

The issues of caste, money, and marital status involved in succession disputes within well-entrenched *sant panths* differ from those that occur in the disputes closer to the beginning of a *paramparā.* The first successors to Charandas, in fighting over the possession of a temple, were certainly aware of the value of the lands that came with it. But they also sought access to the spiritual power emanating from their guru's holy tomb and the place where he lived and worshipped, as well as the legitimation of their own spiritual authority that possession of the temple would bring. In some succession disputes among the Radhasoamis, moreover, the inheritance of wealth is made distinctly a non-issue. At the passing of one important Radhasoami guru in Delhi several years ago a great many of his disciples turned to his natural son, who probably could have made a good legal case for control of the guru's religious establishment. But he preferred to abandon the establishment property visibly rather than fight over money, and not far away set up a new ashram, which is now flourishing. His concern here seems to have been with keeping his public spiritual authority unsullied by accusations of material gain.

While the issues involved in these succession disputes change as a lineage develops, the basic questions people argue over remain similar: Who is the living guru? What are the qualifications that make him a source of spiritual power? What, finally, is his real spiritual identity? Below we will examine just how the real identity of the guru varies within the different stages of a lineage.

The Problem of the Historical Guru

In most Indian esoteric traditions, the living guru as mediator is usually presented in terms of mystery: the guru, himself identified with the divine, is able to offer something of this identity to the disciple. Different specific esoteric traditions offer their own resolutions to this mystery—each of which, however, the disciple realizes according to his own evolving spiritual experience.

When questioned about the nature of the guru, people in *sant* tradition—and many other Hindi speakers as well—frequently respond with the following couplet attributed to Kabir:

Guru and Govind both stand before me.
  Whose feet should I touch?
The Guru gets the offering:
  He shows the way to Govind.

The guru, then, understood as distinct in some way from the ultimate goal, usually remains an important object of devotion in all forms of *sant* tradition. Nevertheless, the way in which the guru is perceived varies with the particular experience of the devotee and the form of *sant* tradition to which he is attached.

In a *panth,* the past *sant* taken as its source is often revered as the real guru. Most often, the hidden power of this *sant* is understood to be available in a *mantra* passed down to his successor. Some devotees may worship the successor himself as a holy man, but frequently dominating any holy-man focus is the revealed scripture left by a past *sant,* now taken as a singular personality. Thus, the Dadupanthis, as we recall, practice ritual worship of Dadu's sayings and sometimes take as a *mantra* Dadu's name conjoined with that of Ram. When questioned about gurus and *mantra*s, Hariramji, the *mahant* at the important Dadupanthi shrine at Naraina, replied openly that "the only *mantra* is Ram," an answer that certainly does not emphasize the living guru's esoteric power. The real guru, Hariramji continued, was Dadu, while he himself was just carrying on Dadu's teachings as best he could: "Dadu had many disciples; the *mahant*s have just a few each."

Describing the real guru as a very special personality of the past whose verses lace his own discourse, Hariramji presents the *sādhū* in a *panth* as a preacher within an extended, Hinduized heritage. But a good *mahant* may also represent for his disciple a more powerful holy-man focus, a figure to whom lay disciples look for blessings, and initiates, for spiritual secrets. This role of the *mahant* is reflected in the Kabirpanthi guru worship, where the living guru in the person of the *mahant* is homologized to *sat purush,* and offers a *mantra* coming from a past *sant* with well-defined cosmic dimensions. For a member of a *panth,* then, the power of the reigning *mahant* is necessarily understood to derive from that of a past *sant,* who himself may be seen as the real guru; but in individual cases the real guru may be identified with the *mahant* himself, especially if the *mahant* is in fact a charismatic figure and his follower a particularly devoted soul.

While some *mahant*s do in fact have a large popular following, the well-entrenched *panth*s do not seem routinely to generate holy men capable of leading initiates along an inner spiritual path. In practice, the reverence that the follower of a *panth* from birth feels for his local *mahant* may derive less from the *mahant*'s personal piety than from his authority in ritual and, perhaps, his control of substantial economic holdings. The awe felt by a devotee for the person of a guru in the earlier stages of a *paramparā,* on the other hand, is likely to derive not from the guru's role in ritual worship, if any, but—as discussed earlier[27]—from the conjunction of the guru's image within with an experience of his changing, surprisingly human, outer form. The disciple must then learn to act not according to prescribed ceremony, but according to the guru's divine, yet changeable will. Indeed, the Radhasoamis frequently see the guru's spontaneous will as another aspect of the divine *mauj,* a word that in Persian has a primary meaning of "wave" and that in Radhasoami Urdu usage can refer at once to the shifting flow of destiny and to the guru's spontaneously changing intuition. According to Maharaj Sahib, an important Radhasoami guru at Agra, "What the Mauj of the Supreme Being is, is also the Mauj of Sants. It is extremely difficult to realize Their Mauj."[28]

Thus, while a Kabirpanthi can perform ritual devotion to his guru in good faith as long as he believes him to have inherited access to *mantra*s from the divine Kabir, the devotion of the Radhasoami is at once more discriminating and more demanding. The following passage, written in English by Shyam Lal, called Guru Data Dayala, tells us of both the caution that the disciple must take in determining just who is a true guru and the necessity for total devotion to him once he is found:

> Before initiation . . . he should be treated as an elder or friend and not Guru . . . and when the disciple is satisfied that he possesses the supernatural power of evolving and exalting his soul, he must be treated and respected as God. . . . In all cases of failure [in spiritual practice] the main cause was no other than that the disciples either could not get perfect Gurus or did not treat them as God. For success in this matter it is essential that Guru (perfect) must be given, by the disciple in all his affairs, spiritual or temporal, priority over God, until the disciple himself becomes one with Guru and God.[29]

As in the couplet above attributed to Kabir, here too the disciple is instructed to understand the guru to be greater than God. But here the real guru is unmistakably the living master, the "Saint Satguru," not a past *sant* standing at the beginning of a lineage.

In a *panth,* then, the real guru is often identified as the original past *sant* who has become the dominant focus in a lineage tradition; in a *paramparā* the real guru is more likely to be seen as the hidden divinity of the living master. But what of the frequent references to the guru among those who stand as singular *sant*s? What did they mean by the guru? Most seem to have had access to esoteric experience, but few acknowledge a particular spiritual master. This problem has been treated both by scholars dealing with the early *sant*s and by devotees attempting to understand the figure at the source of their lineage. The devotees' arguments are, perhaps, more religiohistorically interesting, but before we examine them it may help first to understand some of the critical issues involved.

Most of the scholarly discussion is found in relation to the problem of Kabir's guru. About the beginning of the seventeenth century, the Vaishnava sectarian writer Nabhaji, probably repeating common lore, presented Ramananda as Kabir's guru—a tradition to which Indian scholars usually give more weight than Western students. Nevertheless, Parashuram Chaturvedi, probably the most important Indian writer on the *sant*s, remains sceptical. He points both to the infinite gratitude to the guru found in some of Kabir's verses and to his reference to the guru as "knowledge," "discrimination," or "*shabda.*" Then, taking seriously the fact that Kabir mentions no one person as his guru, Chaturvedi suggests that in Kabir's usage the guru in fact refers to no one individual, but to the many teachers from whom he has gratefully learned different spiritual truths. This view is shared by Charlotte Vaudeville, Kabir's most influential Western interpreter.[30]

Other Western scholars emphasize the more impersonal qualities of Kabir's guru, identifying him primarily as the divine guru or the "inner voice."[31] Certainly, one could argue that Kabir took the term "guru" from the *nāth*s along with the rest of his esoteric vocabulary and similarly adapted it to his own ends. But the conviction with which Kabir's guru is identified by Western scholars with the "inner voice" sometimes suggests a distinctly Protestant perspective: not only did Kabir reject Hindu gods and ritual worship, he also rejected the established institution of the living guru. Thus McLeod, discussing the predecessors to Nanak in his carefully researched study of that *sant,* has "little doubt that Kabir had no human *guru,* but for him the *Guru* or *Satguru* represented the inner voice, the mystical movement of God in the depths of the individual being . . ."[32] Yet there may be no need to divorce Kabir so completely from his immediate Indian sources. An examination of Indian esoteric traditions can help us understand how for Kabir the guru can be at once an inner voice and a living person. Moreover, the presence of a living guru does seem to be called for by Kabir's devotion, his rhetoric, and his practice.

Particularly in the more ardent, Western recension of Kabir the guru is often presented in distinctly human terms: he is a "hero," "firm and patient."[33] In the following verse, moreover, we find mundane physical distance used to tell of the spiritual unity of guru and disciple:

Though his guru's in Banaras
  And he lives by the sea,
If he's made of worthy stuff
  They never will forget each other.

And when the guru is within close striking distance of his disciple the effect can be palpable indeed.

The satguru, with steady grip,
  Put an arrow in his bow, then let it go.
And I, exposed, was struck. My body
  Like a forest burst in flames.[34]

In addition to Kabir's devotional references to the guru as a being with human attributes, two problems arise when we consider the rhetorical import of Kabir's usage. Most people ready to take Kabir seriously as a spiritual teacher would have felt some kind of inner prompting. So why did Kabir insist on the *necessity* of the guru if the guru referred only to an inner voice? The necessity would seem to be for some sort of objective external guide as well. Kabir was further no doubt aware that singing of the guru as he did would lead many who listened to take him as the "outer" guru whether he liked it or not. So unless we uncharitably understand Kabir as a rank egotist, we should assume that he had some reason for allowing himself to be so taken—the most obvious, of course, being that he had experienced the value of the outer guru himself.

Perhaps the most crucial problems that arise when we deny Kabir a living guru concern the nature of his esoteric experience. Yogic traditions consistently affirm that except for a few rare exceptions everyone on a yogic path needs a living guru to reach the final goal. Some of the grounds behind this assertion are easier to understand in tantric ritual and *haṭha*-yoga practice, where there are obviously specific techniques to learn. But on the subtly physical yogic path, the person of the embodied guru also seems to serve as an important support for the disciple during the final processes of ego-loss: we recall the Radhasoamis' seeing the guru in his physical form at the point of union with the Lord, and note the *tantrika*'s different visions at the top of his head, the guru's "five-fold footstool."[35] Even Sri Aurobindo, who clearly did see himself as offering something different and new, tells of how his first critical *nirvāṇa*-experience came through his relationship with a "temporary guru"—whom he could later characterize as inferior to himself in certain ways.[36]

So if Kabir had no guru, he was either one of the very few exceptions that yogic tradition allows, or he adapted the *nāth* vocabulary in such an idiosyncratic way that it does not refer to yogic experience at all. But the arguments presented above for Kabir apply just as well to other *sant*s whose lineage is not known, and it is difficult to assume that they are all exceptions. Moreover, the content of many *sant bānī,* together with the obvious fact of esoteric practice among the Radhasoamis, makes us believe that there is indeed a yogic basis for *sant* experience. We are, then, led to suspect that Kabir, like most *sant*s and yogis, probably had some sort of living guru—though just who he was will probably never be known.

The arguments we have presented do not imply that all *sant*s had living gurus; there could be exceptions, as yogic tradition allows. But perhaps more likely exceptions than *sant*s like Kabir, who name no guru at all, were those who spoke of legendary figures as their gurus: we have seen Charandas refer to the fabled Shukdev as his guru; another eighteenth-century *sant,* Garibdas of Haryana, referred to his guru as the by then legendary Kabir. Our arguments do not, further, imply that all the yogis and *sant*s who did have gurus had extended relationships with them: we have seen both Aurobindo and Charandas tell of relatively brief but decisive encounters with preceptors. And, perhaps most important, our arguments do not imply that every reference to the guru in the *sant bānī* refers immediately to the living guru. The *sant*s had supposedly realized the mystery of the guru's true identity, and could thus speak of the guru as both Lord and man in ways that reflected their specific traditions, their own particular experience with their masters, and the inspiration of the moment. The "guru," then, could indeed often appear as the "inner voice," but one which the *sant* saw as mysteriously connected to a specific person outside.

The tradition that a guru is needed for success in inner practice by most people but not by all can provide a point of tension for later devotees attempting to understand the *sant* standing at the beginning of their lineage. Did he follow the eternal rule, or was he one of the unique exceptions? For the Radhasoamis today the issue remains a live one, and provides the most obvious doctrinal difference between the two main branches of Radhasoami tradition—the lineages descending through Jaimal Singh of Beas and those that remain centered at Agra.

Beas tradition tells us that Soamiji had a guru in Tulsi Sahib, the late eighteenth-century *sant* of Hathras; Soamiji is accordingly seen as a member of the eternal *sant* clan. L. R. Puri, in his public exposition of this doctrine, tactfully guards his assertion of Soamiji's discipleship, but his opinion is clear: Soamiji, he writes, had an "intimate association" with Tulsi Sahib, to whom he paid "the same sort of love and respect" "as one does to one's spiritual master." Soamiji thus stands as one in the tradition of the *sants*: "*Radha Swami Mat,*" says Puri, "*is Sant Mat pure and simple*" (Puri's emphasis).[37]

The Agra Radhasoamis, on the other hand, generally emphasize the uniqueness of both Soamiji and their own specific tradition. A. P. Mathur stands in both the spiritual and biological lineage of Soamiji's successor Huzur Sahib, whom he sees as important in the "systematization" of the tradition at Agra. In a book entitled, appropriately enough, *Radhasoami Faith,* he characterizes the movement as "a new religion based on *sant* traditions." He is emphatic that Soamiji, as a singular personality, had no living guru, "for if Soamiji was born 'Almighty' . . . there was hardly any need for him to have accepted the discipleship of anyone."[38] Yet whatever the formative influence of Tulsi Sahib and earlier *sants* on Soamiji, there is little doubt that Soamiji himself had a vital spiritual impact on several important disciples. Thus, to understand the place of the Radhasoami lineage in postclassical North Indian religion we can begin by examining the figure of Soamiji as a holy man and what he did with the *sant* tradition that he inherited.

Soamiji and *Sant* Tradition

If Soamiji was not in fact a born *sant,* he was certainly able to imbibe the teachings of the *sants* from an early age. His family belonged to a Punjabi caste, the *khatrīs*, many of whom venerate the teachings of Guru Nanak without adopting the outer marks of the Sikh brotherhood. Soamiji's brother writes that their father and grandfather "used to read with great love and fervour Nanak Saheb's Banis . . . and recited Japji . . . daily." Settled in Agra, "Soamiji Maharaj's father came in contact with Tulsi Saheb of Hathras, who was a perfect Sant. Occasionally, Tulsi Saheb visited Agra also. Because of His Satsang, faith in Sant Mat took deeper roots in Soamiji Maharaj's father." Many of Soamiji's female relatives, too, came to Tulsi Sahib's *satsang,* a word meaning "good company" that is used by Radhasoamis and others to refer to communal gatherings around the guru. We are told that Tulsi Sahib had informed Soamiji's mother of his greatness: a high *sant* had incarnated himself in her family; she was not to regard him as a son.[39]

By the time Tulsi Sahib died Soamiji was already a young man of about twenty-five or twenty-six, certainly old enough to have received a conventional initiation from Tulsi Sahib. Writers from both Agra and Beas, moreover, report his visiting Tulsi Sahib in Hathras, about twenty miles from Agra, during the latter's final illness.[40] But in his own works Soamiji never mentions Tulsi Sahib as his guru, nor did he ever seem to have made an overt claim to be his successor. Indeed, there were some celibate disciples of Tulsi Sahib for whom Soamiji had considerable respect. To one of them, named Girdhari Das, he even gave substantial material support in Agra over several years. Some think that he may also have been sensitive to claims of Girdhari Das to be the local successor to Tulsi Sahib. For while Soamiji had given private discourses to disciples in his home for some years previously, it was not, apparently, until after Girdhari Das had died that Soamiji was persuaded to open his *satsang* to the public.[41]

Vasant panchmi, 1861, the Hindu holiday on which Soamiji opened the *satsang,* is considered by many within the tradition to have marked the beginning of a new religious dispensation. The motives of Soamiji himself for opening the *satsang,* however, are not clear. Some say he was prompted by the urgings of his chief disciple at Agra, Huzur Sahib, who was to become instrumental in the sectarian development of the lineage. His action was not, at any rate, taken out of concern for economic subsistence. For like the communities of Paltu Sahib and Charandas, Soamiji's *khatrī* community has been traditionally engaged in trade, and his family seems to have been fairly prosperous.

Pious as well, the members of Soamiji's family appreciated his devotion to meditation practice enough to eventually stop pressing him to take up employment. Soamiji's parents did manage to get him married, however, to a lady eventually known as Radhaji, but the couple had no children. With Soamiji leaving no biological heir, his youngest brother, Pratap Singh, was to gain eminence in the tradition after Soamiji's passing. Known as Chachaji Maharaj, "His Highness father's-younger-brother," he and a few of his descendents would receive the respect due to pious members of the guru's family.

Soamiji was born and lived practically all his life in Agra. This city knew splendor as a capital of the Mughal empire, but it also came within the ranges of Vraj Country, famous for the sport of Radha and Krishna. We can discern in Soamiji's piety both the Vraj and Mughal aspects of his environment. Like Charandas, Soamiji draws on the idiom of Krishna *bhakti:* the name of Krishna's divine lover Radha was to be incorporated into the name of the Lord for which he was best known; more than any previous *sant* Soamiji developed the poetic convention of the *ārati,* which is built on practices of image worship so common in Vraj. Soamiji's piety, however, was on the whole closer to Paltu's iconoclasm than to the liberality of Charandas. His *āratīs* are an *internalization* of ritual worship, and the Radha he invokes is very clearly not the ardent milkmaid of Vraj, intent on the captivating Krishna, but the loving soul aspiring to dwell with her Formless Lord in an abode described as a "a wonder, a wonder, a wonder."[42]

The word Soamiji uses for "wonder" here is *hairat,* a term from the Sufi vocabulary—which Soamiji, as it happens, knew better than did most *sants*. For Soamiji was well versed in Persian, and he did not hesitate to present the Hinduized *sant* tradition he inherited in the Indo-Muslim terms with which he was also familiar. As the language of the court throughout the Mughal period, Persian was regularly studied among those classes of Hindus who dealt with the administration. Both Soamiji's father and his grandfather had been Persian scholars,[43] and Soamiji had worked briefly in his youth as a tutor in Persian to a nearby Hindu prince. Perso-Arabic vocabulary forms a large component in his Hindustani, which he appears to have normally written in the Arabic-based Urdu script. Subsequent gurus at Agra have continued the tradition of speaking and writing prose in a language probably better characterized as Urdu than Hindi—though their works, aimed at an audience of Hindu origin, have normally been printed in *nāgarī* characters.

While Soamiji quoted Maulana Rumi, told Sufi stories, and even wrote a few Persian ghazals using Sufi jargon,[44] he explained the practice he taught in a technical vocabulary derived from *sant* tradition, which he knew from the songs of Nanak and the sayings of Tulsi Sahib familiar from childhood. But versed in the love mysticism of classical Sufism, and invoking the name of Radha, Soamiji as a holy man himself was distinguished for a particularly sweet and unascetic piety. For the practices of *haṭha* yoga to which even Charandas had paid attention, Soamiji had little patience. Straightforward and demanding a minimum of physical ascesis, the practice Soamiji taught was one that could be taken up by householders if they had the time and the devotion. And while Soamiji did have a sizable following of celibate disciples, the majority were married Hindus from respectable castes. Of these, most seem to have been town-dwellers with a steady income adequate for modest needs—a status which provides one definition of the Indian middle class.

Soamiji, then, as an individual holy man, seems to have reshaped for a particular clientele a version of *sant* tradition that had come down to him. Yet Soamiji cuts a figure very different from that of the illustrious early *sant*s, low-caste and illiterate, traditionally taken as social reformers as well as devotees. The high visibility of Radhasoamis today makes an attempt to understand the relationship of Soamiji and his line to earlier *sant*s particularly worthwhile. For their part, some Radhasoamis claim to be the sole legitimate modern representatives of *sant* tradition. Scholars, on the other hand, can be tempted to extrapolate from Radhasoami practice to earlier traditions that have left few traces. Soamiji's place in *sant* tradition becomes clearer as we see both the ways in which the tradition as a whole had developed by Soamiji's time and some of the elements common to *sant* experience throughout the centuries.

In his birth as well as his style of religion, Soamiji appears in direct continuity with *sant*s who had immediately preceded him. Among the eighteenth-century *sant*s, Soamiji's mercantile, middle-caste origins are unexceptional. His piety, moreover, has explicit roots in an esoteric style of sant tradition that had begun to flourish by the eighteenth century. This *sant* esotericism thrived with particular vigor in the eastern Gangetic plain, which nurtured, among others, Gulalpanthis, Dariyapanthis, and Kabirpanthis. The Gulalpanthis, with their extraordinary lineage of *sant* poets, stand out through the vital tradition of spiritual experience they continued to reveal. The Dariyapanthis presented themselves as a solemn esoteric group and apparently dabbled in magical practice: Dariyapanthi manuscripts regularly begin with threats of childlessness and destruction to all unauthorized persons who should read them.[45] The Kabirpanthis reported elaborate cosmological visions—some of which have reached modern Radhasoamis directly through the *Anurāg Sāgar,* a Kabirpanthi book still recommended by some gurus in Soamiji's lineage.[46] By Soamiji's time, then, *sant* tradition had evolved in a number of esoteric dimensions: experiential, socioreligious, and cosmological.

Along with currents of devotion and reform, these esoteric aspects of tradition find precedent among earlier *sant*s, through the *Bījak* clearly evident even in the narrow Kabirian corpus. In their diversity, what most *sant*s throughout the tradition had in common was less a unity of belief and practice than a vision of the loving Formless Lord—a Lord known through the guru and the *shabda,* in front of whom social distinctions counted for little. While the socioreligious implications of this vision may have loomed particularly large for some of the early *sant*s, by the eighteenth century its esoteric implications had achieved some complex expression in both theology and meditation practice. The teachings Soamiji inherited from Tulsi Sahib clearly came out of this later *sant* milieu, and his followers have succeeded in adapting them to modern ways.

In a tradition as varied as that of the *sants*, each group displays a different aspect of the whole; diverse groups can be seen as modern representatives of the older tradition—as long as we understand the ways in which they do so. Like the Radhasoamis, for example, the Kabirpanthis are both very numerous and see themselves in relationship to a larger heritage of *sants*, if more imperialistically and less vitally than many Radhasoamis do. Revering a figure from the past at once more distant and illustrious than Soamiji, the Kabirpanthis have through the centuries given some *sant* values elaborate ritual expression. The Radhasoamis, by contrast, stand within a few generations from the source of their lineage. Particularly aware of the living guru's personal power, they give complex doctrinal expression to the strong guru-devotion that can arise in the earlier stages of any *sant* lineage. Thus, though the Radhasoamis can legitimately be understood to derive from *sant* tradition, they must also be understood to emerge from the tradition's later, more esoteric developments, and to represent a lineage that still remains close to its immediate source.

The Radhasoami Lineage as a *Paramparā*

On his deathbed Soamiji gave some instructions—which have been interpreted differently by different parties—concerning the roles his leading disciples were to take after his passing. In time a few of these disciples began giving initiation, and were, of course, seen by their devotees as legitimate successors to Soamiji. In Agra, the most important successor was Rai Saligram, known as Huzur Maharaj. The first native Indian head postmaster of the United Provinces, he was clearly a strong and talented individual. ("Anyone who wants to ask something should go to Saligram," Soamiji had instructed.) There was also Chachaji Maharaj Pratap Singh at Soami Bagh, the "garden" retreat Soamiji had built outside Agra ("Pratap will be the master of the garden"). Other successors included a blind *sādhū* named Garib Das who went to Delhi, and Jaimal Singh, an unmarried Sikh soldier who eventually returned to his native Punjab; he was to be the source of the very important Beas sublineage.

At Agra, all was not always harmonious between Huzur Maharaj and Chachaji Maharaj.[47] Eventually, however, they seem to have cooperated with each other: Huzur Maharaj continued the major *satsang;* Chachaji attended it sometimes and did not persist in divisive public claims, but nevertheless permitted a few devotees to be loyal to him personally. Between the Beas gurus and the main Agra center there was no open breach as long as Chachaji Maharaj was alive. Tensions did come to a head, however, after Chachaji passed on, during the time of the principal successor to Huzur Maharaj, known as Maharaj Sahib. Subsequently, at the death of Maharaj Sahib, an important split occurred at the main branch in Agra—which eventually led to the founding of Dayal Bagh, across the street from Soami Bagh.

Meanwhile, other branches sprouted: a devotee of Chachaji Maharaj began to attract followers in Gwalior, south of Agra; a second disciple of Huzur Maharaj, known as Maharishi, a very prolific Urdu writer, built a large establishment at his village of Gopiganj near Banaras; the son of Huzur Maharaj also began to give initiation, and a lineage continues in the family today. A graphic representation of the branching Radhasoami lineage is given in the Appendix.

The personalities of the gurus in the lineage, the circumstances of their succession, and the backgrounds of their disciples all contribute to the diversity of forms within the Radhasoami sublineages. At the same time, these sublineages have much in common. Most Radhasoami gurus continue to cater largely to middle-class, if not always urban, followings and present a piety that includes something of the particularly sweet and iconoclastic devotion characteristic of Soamiji. The inward similarity of the gurus in Soamiji's lineage, though less easily stated, also makes itself apparent. In attempting to understand this similarity we may learn something of the spiritual identity of perfected disciples with their gurus, an identity about which the *sant*s so often sing. The *sant*s themselves, we recall, are fond of speaking about the disciple's assimilation of the guru's qualities in terms of naturalistic analogies: the sandalwood tree gives its smell to nearby wood; the *bhrangī* turns the *kīṭ* into an insect like itself. These analogies from nature, however, may not tell us too much about the *human* spiritual realities involved. To get a better sense of the way in which the inner nature of the disciple becomes like that of the guru, we will examine the continuity of *sant* texts, looking at how the experiences described in the esoteric songs of the *sant*s are transmitted in *sant* lineages. We will begin by examining the technical usage of Soamiji Maharaj, its origins, and its significance for his successors.

5

The Significances of *Sant* Technical Language

The great *sant*s of the past were usually revered as poet-singers, and the dominant scriptural form in the continuing *sant* tradition remained the song, the characteristic literary vehicle for much postclassical Indian religion. Thus, when they wanted to give lasting expression to their visions of reality, *sant*s of even minor poetic gifts were likely to compose verse. Often unpolished and thematically repetitive, the songs of these *sant*s were nevertheless held in great reverence by disciples. For as a record of a guru's experience, the songs presented the truths that he knew—the divine realities and inner worlds that disciples were trying to assimilate. The formal similarities in the description of experience in the songs of *sant*s from the same and different lineages may then provide a basis for understanding the continuities of spiritual life in *sant* tradition.

Within a lineage, the songs of a recognized guru gain their religious value not through any poetic qualities they may have, but through their status as divine revelation—which is not supposed to be continually reworked and polished. Radhasoami gurus today who continue to produce verse usually describe their composition as spontaneous outflow. The songs, they report, are frequently written in spurts during longer or shorter periods of divine inspiration. When asked about how he composed his verses, Dadaji Maharaj of Huzuri Bhavan, Agra, discussed the characteristics of spiritual discourse in general. Of all the Radhasoami gurus, Dadaji Maharaj is perhaps the most acutely aware of spiritual discourse as discourse, for in the world he works as a history professor at Agra College: he contrasted the talks he gives to his devotees at *satsang* with those he gives to his students in class. To prepare his history lectures, he said in English, he has to think a *lot*.

But at *satsang* the words just flow forth. His verses, he says, were similarly unchecked, inspired outpourings, a good many emerging over a single period of several months.

More intense outflows of verse can sometimes be called forth by specific circumstances. Malik Sahib of Gwalior, who traces his lineage to Soamiji through Chachaji Maharaj, used to give yearly feasts on the occasion of the latter's birthday. One year, a well-known *paṇḍit* came to this feast and presented Malik Sahib with a friendly challenge: "I am a man of the *purāṇa*s, immersed in traditional lore; I want to know the secrets of the puranic stories."[1] That night Malik Sahib stayed up late writing songs that revealed some yogic implications in the stories of Krishna, Ram, Hanuman, Ganesh, and others.

Specific occasions can also inspire isolated verses. Most of the gurus who do compose verses have written some to be recited on the important Hindu holidays, verses that reveal the holidays' inner meanings. The early gurus, moreover, are said to have composed verses for individual disciples.[2] Thus, like those of most *sant*s, songs composed by the Radhasoami gurus are taken to be at once spontaneously inspired and directed toward particular rhetorical ends.

Some of the songs, called *chetāvnī*s, "warnings," describe the never-ending frustrations of the world and exhort the devotee to wake up from his attachment to it. Others, called *vintī,* "prayers," recount the devotee's failings and the Lord's power, instilling humility in the listener. Less numerous than these, but perhaps most important for serious practitioners, are songs that seem to have been composed by a guru to communicate his experiences of the inner worlds to an audience that may consist largely of his own devotees. These verses are couched in a technical language of yoga, which, among the Radhasoami gurus, often appears consistent to the point of being conventional. In studying the esoteric songs of the Radhasoamis we shall try to understand what it means to use a learned, conventional language of inner experience in the spontaneous and inspired composition of which the gurus speak.

Short and self-contained, the songs of the Radhasoami gurus, like those of other *sant*s, stand in the tradition of *muktaka kāvya,* "free," unbound poetry. Indeed, the perception of a text as composed of independent, unbound verses has deep roots in Indian literary history. The long courtly epics of classical times featured brief, well-polished verses that could be repeated out of context. In the vernacular literatures less energy was devoted to long epics as contexts, while the notion of unbound poetry was expanded to include short devotional lyrics. The *sant bānī,* then, generally come down to us as disconnected collections—of short lyrics, sometimes called *shabda*s; and of couplets, often called *sākhī*s, "witnesses."

Since the technical vocabulary that we will be studying appears in separate, unconnected *bānī,* "sayings," our attempts to understand it will take some cues from the techniques that scholars have used to understand the patterns of meaning informing the disconnected utterances of a language or the separate variants of a myth. The structuralist method that evolves may then help us realize something of the significance of *sant* technical convention for forming *sant* experience.

The Problem of Consistency

When the *sant*s attempted to express what they experienced in their religious practice, they drew upon a stock of Indic terms common to most postclassical North Indian traditions. Kabir, we recall, seems to have been particularly familiar with the idiom of the *nāth* yogis, and *nāth* expressions, through him, have remained central to *sant* technical vocabulary. Later *sant*s have, in addition, incorporated elements of the Perso-Arabic vocabulary of the Indian Sufis.

But while we can easily see common technical expressions recurring and recognize their similarity to those in other esoteric traditions, it is difficult to see any consistency in the patterns in which they are used. Not only does the usage of *sant*s from different sides of the tradition seem to diverge greatly, but a single *sant* may use the same set of terms in apparently different experiential contexts. These songs of Soamiji, however, illustrate the kind of consistency that *can* be found within the works of a single *sant.* All are taken from the section of *Sār Bachan* headed: "The Soul's Rising and Reaching the Heavens and the Play in the Places which the Soul Sees on Its Way." The first shows us in a somewhat devotional idiom visions of lotuses and lights reminiscent of more traditional yogic and tantric texts:

SOAMIJI'S SONG #1

Come, soul, look at the lanes of the sky
  Where the buds of the thousand-petaled lotus are spread. (1)
In each bud blossoms are seen;
  In the middle of each blossom sacrificial flames. (2)
The spotless flame Niranjan enjoys himself there;
  Variously colored flower gardens bloom. (3)

When it sees this form the mind spits out the world;
  Hearing the unstruck sound the soul rushes into the melody. (4)
What can I say of the unfathomable bliss that one finds
  Where pieces of karma are burned up every second (5)
Where lust, anger, and anticipation are crushed.
  Then the soul climbs further. (6)
The crooked tunnel *bank nāl,* three-pointed *trikuṭī,* and the *sushumna* open;
  It sees the sun, the moon, and flashing lightning (7)
It goes to be cared for on the summit of the void
  Where it sees white lotuses (8)
The great void and great time are met
  And the soul goes on to the whirling cave (9)
When it goes to the true name the secrets are opened
  And it meets the twin states of the invisible and unapproachable. (10)
Having touched the feet of Radhasoami, the dust is washed away.
  Now have I found great bliss.[3] (11)

The following song takes the form of an *āratī,* a very common convention with Soamiji. As the Upanishadic seer 'internalized' the Vedic sacrifice, so Soamiji often models his journey through the heavens on the popular Hindu practice of the *āratī,* the waving of lights in front of an image of the Lord: thus the reference in the third line below to the tray and the lamp. Note the relatively stronger attitude of devotion in this song, with the recollection of the *satguru* at the beginning and the humility at the end:

SOAMIJI'S SONG #2

I have seen the guru's unapproachable form;
  I have seen the true guru as the true name. (1)
The *satguru*'s strength has overpowered time;
  The stream from the *satguru*'s realm cut through the *karma*s. (2)
I fixed up the thousand-petaled lotus as a tray
  And lit the flame's lamp. (3)
The melody sounded the bell and the conch
  And set my gaze at the crooked tunnel. (4)
The gaze intent, the mind is happy
  And recognizes the thunder's melody within the heavens. (5)
I see the form of the sun's light;
  With darkness destroyed, I glimpse the sky. (6)
I find the self's massive station at the void
  Where I am intent on the melody of *rāraṃ*. (7)
I see the moon and silver crossing
  Where the white realm dispels the black. (8)

All at once the soul finds itself at that gate
  Where a great flock of loving swans are to be found. (9)
Joining Radhasoami's play, I perform *āratī;*
  The mind blooms full. (10)
I find *prasād* of blessings and of grace
  And annoint my head with the dust of his feet.[4] (11)

These songs differ in devotional tone, and in the specific experience they relate, but the general ordering of the technical vocabulary is the same. The terms the two songs have in common appear in similar *sequence.* First the thousand-petaled lotus associated with the flame (song #1, ll. 1–2; song #2, l. 3), later *bank nāl,* the crooked tunnel (#1, l. 7; #2, l. 4), followed by the sun (#1, l. 7; #2, l. 6); then the void (#1, l. 8; #2, l. 7), and finally the place of Radhasoami. In the first song, however, the soul seems to linger a while around the thousand-petaled lotus, so the crooked tunnel as next stage does not appear until the middle of the song. The following song, which in Soamiji's collection immediately follows our song #2, seems to offer a bare description of the general progression on the path seen in the first two. The journey here appears more conventionalized, less vivid than in the others. At the end of the next section, a verse of Tulsi Sahib reveals the ambiguous identity of the guru as both creator and experiencer of visions. In the following song, the frequent use of Hindi causative tenses makes it appear as though the speaker is indeed "causing" the experience to happen, and it remains finally ambiguous (to this writer, at least) just who is having what done to whom.

SOAMIJI'S SONG #3

Look, friend, I'll have you know the hidden;
  I sing now of the body's unapproachable secret. (1)
I take the soul to the thousand-petaled lotus
  And cause the eyes to see signs. (2)
I give you a glimpse of the flame;
  Abandoning the black I mix you with the white. (3)
Then climbing I come upon the crooked tunnel,
  And sound the *rāga* of three-pointed *trikuṭī.* (4)
As the soul proceeds I merge it in the void
  And make the holy lake reverberate. (5)
I intensify your love for the swans
  And have the lute played constantly. (6)
I have the name of Radhasoami uttered,
  And take the boat across.[5] (7)

All the technical terms here (except the lake) appear in song #1, and in the same order. Reference to the swans near the final goal is found in song #2.

Let us now turn to the *sākhīs* of Kabir and Vaudeville's interpretations of them. All of the following verses are from her ninth chapter, entitled "The Experience." The first shows the general similarity of aspects of Kabir's "experience" to the sound practice taught by Soamiji, indications of which we have seen in references in the songs to the unstruck sound, the melody, the bell and the conch.

Kabir, when the Śabda has entered the body,
  the lute resounds without strings . . .
Inside and outside, it pervades all
  and all wanderings are over![6]

Kabir's usage of the technical language, however, differs considerably from Soamiji's, particularly if we accept Vaudeville's interpretation of it. She sees Kabir as giving the same 'ultimate' significance to terms that Soamiji clearly distinguishes. Consider, for example, the following verses:

My mind entered the *unmani* stage,
  heaven (*gagana*) was scaled:
Where moonlight shines without a moon,
  there dwells Niranjan, the invisible King!

Crossing the boundary, I entered the Boundless,
  I took my dwelling in the Void*:
In that Palace which the Munis cannot reach,
  there I have my repose![7]

Thus Vaudeville sees both the void (*sunna*) and the heavens (*gagana*) as signifying the final "unconditioned" *sahaja* state (*sahajāvasthā*), which would imply that the Niranjan of which Kabir sings is an aspect of the Supreme Lord. For Soamiji, the void is clearly a stage on the way, and Niranjan is associated with the thousand-petaled lotus at the *initial* stages of the experience. The heavens that we see in Soamiji's song #2, line 5, do *not* appear as the final goal; moreover, the term "heavens" for him usually has a more literal force, representing as he does his experi-

[*Vaudeville's note: "*sunni* (Skt. *śunya*) refers to the *gagana maṇḍala* . . . ; the 'palace' to which even the Munis (great ascetics) cannot reach is the *sahaja* state."]

ence as taking place *outside* the body. His reference to the secrets of the "body" (or "head," lit. *ghaṭa,* "pot") in the first line of song #3, however, would indicate that his experience was tied to a form of bodily yoga.

Certainly, modern adherents of Radhasoami tradition can make sense of Kabir's sayings according to their own perceptions of the inner universe, but Vaudeville's stress upon the ambiguous continuity of Kabir with the *nāth* tradition makes good historical (and textual) sense. Seeing the yogic aspect of his experience as parallel to the realizations of the tantric and *nāth* masters of his day, she stresses his idiosyncratic and independent use of the tantric technical language:

> Whenever Kabir makes use of Tantric technical terms he does so with supreme detachment, as someone who is not impressed by such queer jargon. Often he gives these Yogic terms a new, non-Tantric meaning.

She notes the "great many uncertainties and discrepancies" in the glossaries various authors have compiled of Kabir's language, concluding that "often the context alone can give a clue as to the intended meaning."[8]

H. P. Dvivedi also demonstrates the futility of attempting to compile precise glossaries of Kabir's technical language, comparing the discrepancies in three such attempts.[9] In another work, he notes that just as Kabir's Ram was not the Ram with formal attributes of orthodox Vaishnava *bhakti,* so Kabir used "the definitional words of the yogis and *sahajīya*s in his own style."[10] Vaudeville writes about the problems of *sant* technical language in general:

> If some uncertainty and even confusion in the use of technical terms pertaining to Tantric Yoga is to be found in Nath-panthi popular literature . . . we shall not be surprised to find that the use of such terms by Kabir and the Sants is even more erratic—since the latter explicitly reject the value of [formal] Tantric *sādhanā* as a means of salvation, and they are also influenced by the concepts and practices of both Vaishnava Bhakti and Sufism.[11]

Barthwal, in an appendix to the *Nirgun School of Hindi Poetry,* does offer a technical glossary for the whole of *sant* tradition, which he calls "the Mystery Code." He gives many meanings for each entry and notes that "context" is the "deciding factor"[12] in choosing among them: as a precise "code," then, his "mystery code" becomes useless.

But in his text Barthwal also calls attention to different patterns of usage, in particular some of the differences we have pointed out between that of the earlier *sant*s and Soamiji.[13]

Understanding the basis of such patterns will depend on understanding the significance of the *sant*s' technical language as mystery "code" in two senses. The first is its synchronic, referential, and specifically linguistic sense (as in "Morse code"). Once we perceive this referential code we can see how the technical language also reflects a diachronic "genetic code" inherent in a lineage's spiritual substance. To understand better how *sant* technical language works as a referential code, we can turn to some other examples of esoteric language in India and their Western interpreters.

Code and Vision in Indian Esoteric Language

Tantric Paradox and Vedic Vision

Probably the most notorious form of esoteric expression found in Indian texts is the *sandhābhāṣā,* the "intentional language" of the Tantras.[14] Western perceptions of *sandhābhāṣā* have been formed in large part from the songs of the Buddhist *siddha*s Kanha and Saraha, translated into French by Shahidullah in 1928. This verse of Kanha, quoted by Eliade, illustrates the paradoxical and apparently nonsensical style of *sandhābhāṣā* expression:

> The Woman and the Tongue are immobilized on either side of the Sun and the Moon.[15]

Who is the woman and what is the tongue, and how did they stop beside the sun and moon? These paradoxes certainly need some explanation, which scholars have not hesitated to provide.

By all accounts[16] (including my own) Eliade's is the most cogent treatment of *sandhābhāṣā* in the religiohistorical literature. But Agehananda Bharati's chapter in *The Tantric Tradition* is the most comprehensive. Bharati reviews the different views Indian scholars have expressed as to the purpose of *sandhābhāṣā:* the relatively uncharitable—that it is to "camouflage instructions as may be resented by the orthodox" or to "entice people away from orthodox observance"; and the more sympathetic—that it is "to keep the non-initiate from dabbling with the implied practices." He also suggests a couple of possible purposes of his own: *sandhābhāṣā* as a mnemonic device, and as a form of teasing the orthodox. He admits finally, however, that Eliade has the "last word" on the subject:

> Eliade thinks that sandhabhasa has a double purpose: to camouflage the doctrine against the non-initiate, and "to project the yogi into the 'paradoxical' situation indispensable for his spiritual training."[17]

Shashibhusan Dasgupta in an appendix to *Obscure Religious Cults* stresses the continuity of the "paradoxical style" throughout the early Indian vernacular religious literature, giving extensive citations from Kabir.[18] But there are significant differences between the paradoxical aspects of *sandhābhāṣā* and the typical *sant* style of paradox known in Hindi as *ulaṭvāṃsī* (or *ultāvāṃsī*). Eliade takes the religious force of *sandhābhāṣā* paradox as the "semantic polyvalence of words" that replaces the "profane universe" by one "of convertible and integrable planes."[19] The force of the *sant*s' *ulaṭvāṃsī,* however, lies sooner in its shock value, as Barthwal states succinctly in a passage quoted by Vaudeville:

> The ultavansi is necessarily a paradox, while the sandhyabhasha is not . . . the ultavansi, the apparent meaning of which is usually an opposite representation of the actual behavior or order of things, is simply a means of startling the hearer and render[ing] him receptive to the real and hidden meaning hinted at.[20]

The different kinds of paradox natural to the two styles of esoteric language are related to the way in which the two styles worked as *referential* systems. As is well known, tantric practice sometimes (though not as frequently as generally imagined) involved a sexual ritual that was scandalous in the eyes of the orthodox, and potentially dangerous for the unqualified. It is especially this kind of "doctrine" that needed to be "concealed from non-initiates" and was a significant "key" to the ambiguous *sandhābhāṣā* "code." Eliade thus suggests three levels of meaning for Kanha's mysterious statement about the sun and moon, woman and tongue, and their immobilization. The first meaning is *haṭha*-yogic; the sun and the moon are subtle currents in the body. The second is philosophical: the woman is knowledge and the tongue is skillful means. The third is sexual, for gnosis comes with the immobilization of breath through the arrest of seminal fluid. And in addition to these three "keys" for understanding tantric texts, Eliade mentions the possibility of a fourth "liturgical" one, which would link the *sandhābhāṣā* as a referential system with concrete physical reality in another way besides the sexual.[21]

The *sant*s, however, had typically no liturgy and definitely no sexual *sādhanā*. More important, however, is the fact that they were not, for the most part, interested in intentionally concealing anything. As Alex Wayman writes:

> The esoteric is . . . of two kinds: natural and intentional . . . the first kind . . . eludes solution by its intrinsic difficulty . . . the second kind . . . is secret because it is not proper to be taught to all persons.[22]

Buddhist tantras, says Wayman, are intentionally esoteric. The experiential language of the *sant*s, I would argue, is naturally so. For understanding the referential value of the esoteric language of the *sant*s a more valuable comparison than the texts of the tantric yogis is, perhaps, the hymns of the Vedic seers.

What Soamiji was referring to in the songs above, we recall, were visions. He was on a journey, and he saw things. The *sant*'s perception of himself as recording what he spontaneously sees is, we shall soon find, explicit in the *sant bānī;* and the notion of the religious poet as visionary seer has deep roots in Indian tradition.

In the second decade of the present century Sri Aurobindo wrote about the Vedic *ṛiṣi*s as seers who gave their visions of transcendental reality substance in the concrete liturgical imagery of the hymns.[23] His specific interpretation of their symbolism, however, often seems to adhere too closely to the psychological perceptions realized in his own Integral Yoga, and rests, as well, on some rather occult presuppositions. Scholars who otherwise admire Aurobindo thus sometimes distance themselves from his interpretations of the Vedas.[24]

Only more recently has Western Indology begun to take the Rig Vedas seriously as inspired visionary poetry. In an important study of 1949, Renou writes about the Vedic *ṛiṣi*s' awareness of themselves as poets. Here he translates the Vedic term *dhīḥ* as "*inspiration (poetique)*" or simply "*parole, poème.*"[25] In *The Vision of the Vedic Poets,* Gonda takes specific issue with this translation, warning that it may lead one "to overlook the decidedly religious and psychological elements of the term . . ." For Gonda, *dhīḥ* means primarily "vision" or "intuition," and the Vedas should be seen in relation both to archaic religious poetry generally and to later Indian visionary poets: indeed, Gonda makes specific mention of *sant* Dadu.[26]

Of the many dimensions of the Vedic vision that Gonda describes in his lengthy treatment of *dhīḥ,* two appear particularly important for our discussion. First, visions sometimes seem to be the instruments of the gods, originating from them and executed by them. But at the same time the *dhīḥ* could also achieve an independent, substantial existence of its own. Indeed, "places are not wanting where Agni's favor is to be won by means of 'materialized visions'." Thus, Gonda sees the *ṛṣi*s as receiving divine "inspiration"—often from the gods—which they were able to craft into Vedic hymns. The hymns once formed could then manifest concrete spiritual power "pushing out into the sphere of the divine beings . . ."[27]

As visionary poetry, the *bānī* of Soamiji Maharaj are much like these hymns, but operate in a salvational and post-tantric framework. The vision, perceived as a substantial reality, is given by the guru, and can lead the disciple on a journey to the highest divine realm.

The following passage is from Tulsi Sahib, whom, we recall, many take to be Soamiji's guru. It introduces a long description of the inner worlds by offering homage to the *sant* who opens up inner vision:

Tulsi offers sacrifice at the feet of the *sant*
  Who has climbed the inaccessible and sheltered his soul.
He tells the secret as he sees it
  Singing *sākhī*s and *shabda*s in books.
Bowing again to the holy feet he sees and speaks
  Just as the grace of the *sant* has opened it.

We will now look more closely at the inner worlds Tulsi Sahib saw, the ways in which Soamiji treated the vision he apparently received from Tulsi Sahib, and the shape in which this vision has passed down in Soamiji's lineage.

Code and Continuity in the Radhasoami Line

Tulsi Sahib, they say, was born to the house of the Puna *peshwā*s, a Brahman dynasty that had achieved political dominance during the ascendancy of the Marathas in the eighteenth century. Whether or not he actually did, as tradition relates, abandon a throne to become a *sādhū,* he probably was a Brahman—or at least something of a scholar. His erudition is apparent in the *Ghaṭ Rāmāyaṇa,* one of the few extended treatises produced by a *sant.* Presented as arguments against adherents of a number of different religious persuasions, the *Ghaṭ*

Rāmāyaṇa appears in part as an attempt by Tulsi to come to terms with the various doctrines of the many traditions he found around him. At any rate, the cosmology that it reveals is most complex and bewildering: Tulsi Sahib tells of thirty-six kinds of waters, twenty-five kinds of airs, sixteen heavens, six whirling caves, six *trikuṭī*s, twenty-two voids, and more.

The passage below is from a description of the inner worlds, the introduction to which we have just seen. Tulsi's attitude now shifts from that of the grateful disciple who is granted a vision to that of the self-assured guru who presents one. The passage is found toward the end of the first chapter of the *Ghaṭ Rāmāyaṇa,* entitled "The Secret of the Body and the Universe." Here Tulsi refers to the secret states of the twenty-two voids, of which he describes six:

When the heart's eye opened the soul could see
  The states of the twenty-two voids
  . . . .
I'll tell again the six voids' secrets;
  Their separateness and differences I show.
Who lives in which void—
  I'll show that secret to the light.
In the first void is the nameless:
  The *sant*s perceive his reach and his intelligence.
The second void's state I tell,
  Where I saw the true name, *satnām.*
In the third void there's a certain sound.
  Any *sant* forgets himself if his soul should wander there.
I'll explain the fourth void,
  Where *pārbrahm* lives absorbed.
The *sant* who's seen it with his heart's eye
  Calls it *paramātman.*
I'll tell of the fifth void's secret:
  Total *brahm,* it's called the *jīva.*
The Vedas call it *ātman:*
  They know the *jīva*'s name as *ātman.*
The sixth void's in the mind and body,
  Clinging to the senses.
This is what the highest swans call *brahm,*
  Of which the Vedas say 'not this, not that.'
The mind calls this void *brahm,*
  But know its real name as Niranjan: "Spotless."
It's called the spotless flame—
  Brahm, Vishnu, and Shiva are its children.[28]

These verses seem to have described a descent from the "nameless" to the place of the "mind and senses." But when Tulsi finally concludes the chapter he recalls again the highest state, which is known to all the *sants*:

Now there is one separate, nameless Lord
  Beyond the void and great void.
That Lord is beloved of the *sants*.
  Sants make their court at his abode . . .[29]

Tulsi's usage of the void and great void here appears similar to Soamiji's: for both him and Soamiji the void and the great void are intermediate states. His description of the six voids above, however, seems somewhat confusing; though this description is parallel in certain respects to the progression we have seen Soamiji give, it is presented in descending order instead of in Soamiji's typical ascension: thus Niranjan Joti, "The Spotless Flame" is at the lowest level (vd. Soamiji's first song, l. 3); the place of the self, *ātman,* in the middle stages (Soamiji's second song, l. 7); the true name as near to the highest stage (Soamiji's first song, l. 10). The similarities between the world visions of Soamiji and Tulsi Sahib become more apparent from a broader examination of Soamiji's esoteric songs and their discussions in the secondary literature. In many of them, too, the trappings of Brahminical tradition are assigned to the different levels of the universe in much the same fashion as in Tulsi's.

At any rate, the point here is not a matter of exact correspondences, but of general perspective. What Soamiji seems to have done in his esoteric songs is to present systematically, and in precise language, aspects of a complex vision he probably received from Tulsi. This progression, once codified, remained reasonably stable throughout the lineage. Charan Singh of Beas presents a recent, fairly public explanation of it, which I present with a few additions gleaned from the secondary literature:

> In the first stage, we see the Lord and His 'Maya'—both 'Jyoti,' the Creative Force in the form of a Flame, and 'Niranjan,' the Lord of the three worlds. In Trikuti the Creative Force becomes dormant and only the Lord remains. In Daswan Dwar the Lord appears quite aloof and separated from the creation [this is the place of the void and great void]. In Bhanwar Gupha [the whirling cave] the soul realizes its 'sameness' with the Lord and cries out 'I am that.' Sat Nam means the Everlasting, Immortal Lord of all.[30]

We find this progression again in the next song we will see. It was composed by Shyam Lal, who traced his lineage through Soamiji's younger brother, Chachaji Pratap Singh.

Between Shyam Lal's group in Gwalior and the Radhasoami establishment at Agra tensions had developed, and these may have provided some of the earthly impetus for Shyam Lal's eventual revelation of a new name: he finally instructed his disciples to invoke the divine not as Radhasoami but as Dhara Sindhu Pratap. The new name gives a distinctive sectarian turn to the elements of the old one. Dhara consists of the syllables of Radha in reverse order and means "wave" or "current"; Sindhu contains the sibilant and nasal of Soami, and means "sea"; Pratap was the name of Shyam Lal's guru, and means "glory." In the following song, the new name is found in the last line, which conventionally indicates the author's signature. But Soamiji's codified progression, found in lines five through eight, persists through sectarian independence:

The guru had me drink the cup of love;
  Intoxicating bliss spread through my limbs. (1)
The guru made me understand about the Inapproachable;
  I learned then how to do the *āratī*. (2)
Beyond the stars and slanted moon
  The soul arrived within the earth-egg. (3)
The jewels of subtle principles and the three qualities
  The soul could wear on its own body. (4)
It climbed from there and got through the flame's door
  And then proceeded into *trikuṭī*. (5)
In the void I made *shabd-guru*'s *āratī*
  And took the full moon's colors. (6)
I saw the great void and the five cosmic eggs
  Then got through the cave to *sach khand*. (7)
I merged into the center of the sphere
  And found complete approach to the beloved. (8)
Dhara Sindhu Pratap, the utmost guru,
  Took his own disciple to the utmost realm.[31] (9)

As Shyam Lal's experience shows us, perhaps more deeply rooted in the devotee than any sectarian affiliation that he receives from his guru is the consistency of the guru's inner vision. This consistency is reflected in the selection and ordering of technical terms, which indicate discrete segments of inner experience that are *learned*. The variety in the esoteric songs of the Radhasoami masters reveals the different dimensions in which this segmented inner experience can spontaneously occur. What remains constant throughout the songs is the ordered progression of experience, which here appears as the lineage's visionary code.

The progressions of esoteric terms in other *sant* lineages, however, do not usually present the same degree of coded consistency as that seen among the Radhasoamis—and even when they do, they do not always seem to represent a transmission of learned experience. We will turn now to the factors involved in the transmission of esoteric vision from guru to disciple, and to the different dynamics between conventional technical language and spontaneous spiritual experience in the verses of the *sant*s.

Convention and Spontaneity in Lineage and Clan

The Radhasoami literature not only presents a well-codified technical vocabulary, but also gives us some insight into how its significance is passed on through the lineage. The published sources shed light on two important factors in the process: the disciple's expectations as to what he will see, and the guru's explanation to him of what he has seen.

Charan Singh's previously cited description of the progression of the inner worlds shows how the guru can provide his disciple with expectations. Some glimpses of how the guru shapes his disciple's vision by explanation can be gleaned from these excerpts from Charan Singh's letters to his disciples. We recall "the jewels of the subtle principles" referred to in line 4 of Shyam Lal's song above. Charan Singh writes to a disciple about these principles, called *tattva*s in Sanskrit and Hindi:

> The various, inconstant, different colored, bizarrely shaped lights that you see represent the lights of the tattwas. A little further concentration will make these look like beautiful flowers. Afterwards, only one Bright White Light will remain. But you need not bother about these things . . .[32]

Charan Singh speaks of the *tattva*s as beautiful flowers, which in their brightness, at least, seem similar to the jewels mentioned by Shyam Lal. But all jewels seen within may not be what they seem. We recall the frequent reference to the sun and moon in Soamiji's songs above; Charan Singh gives this advice:

> The shimmering round crystal diamond that you behold within you is not a diamond. It is the sun. Please give more time and attention to Simran [repetition], for then you will find its rays very soothing and enchanting. We have to pass through it in order to proceed further.[33]

Of course, the explanations the guru gives will make sense to the disciple only if there is some fit between the stages of the disciple's experience and the terms that the guru gives him to understand them. Radhasoamis commonly believe that this fit derives from the assimilation of the guru's spiritual power that is communicated to them at the time of initiation: in assimilating the guru's spiritual power through devotion and practice, the disciple grows to have a subtle nature like his, and can eventually move like him through the highest heavens. While the critical scholar will finally know little of the individual disciple's experience of merging and flight, he may see in principle how extended practice of the same meditational techniques can produce a fundamental similarity between the stages of inner experience realized by the guru and disciple. In the esoteric songs of the Radhasoami masters we see this similarity in the description of apparently spontaneous experiences occurring within a well-defined spiritual progression that is marked by set conventions.

Conventions Without Experience and With New Experience: Two Examples

While conventions of technical expression can mark similar experiences, they do not in themselves create them. Indeed, I spoke with two figures in different *sant* lineages writing verses today who seemed to use conventional terms without having realized the experiences to which the terms conventionally refer. One, in a lineage with well-set conventions, simply admitted that he had consciously used technical language without having experienced its corresponding state, though he gave a reason for so doing. The other, from an older lineage whose practice has changed over the years, adapted the language of the gurus of the past to describe experience that the early gurus may have spoken about in other ways.

Sant Vachan Das is a *sādhū* in the *panth* that continues from Tulsi Sahib, referred to variously as the Tulsi *panth* or the Sahib *panth*. Whether or not Tulsi Sahib was in fact Soamiji's guru remains a matter of sectarian dispute, but Tulsi Sahib did have a number of undisputed disciples, and these are the ones that have carried on the tradition that bears his name. Closer in time to the *sant* in whom they find their source than members of most other *panth*s, the Tulsipanthis generally seem to be more attentive than most to meditative practice. Yet even though Tulsipanthi *sādhū*s often boast that Soamiji and the Radhasoami establishment all ultimately "come from them," for their meditation they continue to use Tulsi's complex inner map instead of Soamiji's simpler one. They speak matter-of-factly about the sixteen heavens, six whirling caves, and twenty-two voids that Tulsi Sahib mentions, and a few continue to compose esoteric poetry in this tradition.

I first met Sant Vachan Das, one of these poets, at his natal village of Jogiya, just outside Hathras. This small city, situated between Agra and Aligarh, is the place where Tulsi Sahib finally settled, and continues to be the seat of the chief Tulsipanthi *mahant;* at Jogiya there is a small shrine to one of Tulsi Sahib's disciples, which I had gone to see. Like many of his village caste-fellows, Sant Vachan Das was from a Tulsipanthi family, but his guru was from eastern Uttar Pradesh, where the Tulsi *panth* has now come to have its largest following. At the time of our meeting in 1980, Sant Vachan Das said he was about forty-eight or forty-nine and had become a *sādhū* after living for some time as a householder. He had been staying at his guru's place in the east, I was told, but his family, involved in a land dispute, had asked him to spend some time in Jogiya. There he was well respected by many of the Tulsipanthi villagers, and often led them in communal worship and spiritual discussion.

When I started asking Sant Vachan Das about Tulsipanthi meditation practice he showed me a 131-page manuscript he had written about a year earlier. Illustrated with drawings showing the sights of different spiritual regions, it described an inner journey according to Tulsi Sahib's conventions. Interested in both Sant Vachan Das and his book, I made arrangements to return to spend some time in the village.

When I looked more closely at Sant Vachan Das' book on my second visit, I saw that it told of the highest regions of the universe described by Tulsi Sahib. Like most living *sant* poets, Sant Vachan Das affirmed that he wrote what he saw. During the time I spent with him I had certainly grown to respect Sant Vachan Das as a sincere *sādhū,* but I wondered whether he really thought that he had reached the high states revealed in his book. Just before I left Jogiya I asked him about it directly. Actually, he admitted, his own reach was only to here—he touched a point in the middle of his forehead, indicating an intermediate state. In fact, he said, he only wrote what he saw *as far as his spiritual reach would take him.* His description of the higher planes was added "for the sake of completeness."

Thus, in a lineage whose members use well-defined conventions, the conventions can sometimes gain an importance of their own. It becomes necessary to present them as doctrine, even if they no longer represent experience. In such situations we may then find the proliferation of experientially empty technical language. In lineages with looser conventions, however, we find a different problem. Here, as we see in our next example, the same technical term is used by different figures to describe what seem to be different experiences.

Shiv Prasad Das lives at Barauli, a small village in Barabanki district, west of Ayodhya. He is the sixth successor to the seat there of Hulas Das, a disciple of Paltu, and identifies with the larger Gulalpanthi tradition. Shiv Prasad Das has enough middle-class disciples to have been taken along by them on an all-India bus pilgrimage. Still, at about seventy, he retained both his humility and his vitality, working regularly in his vegetable garden, meditating, and composing verses in *sant* style.

I found Shiv Prasad Das the most radiant of the Gulalpanthi *sādhūs* I had met, and visited him twice in his village to ask about spiritual practice in his tradition. During my second stay at Barauli he said: "These things you are asking about are disappearing. Few people know them; they just read in books." Indeed, the spiritual succession within the Gulalpanthi tradition does not seem to have kept alive very well all of the secrets devolving from the great gurus in the lineage. The meditating *sādhūs* of the recent past are remembered as rigorous ascetics, and appear to have developed the yogic aspect of their tradition at the expense of the devotion found in the songs of Gulal, Bhikha, and Paltu.

Yet Shiv Prasad Das understands that he has verified the truths of past *sants* in meditation. "You read and read in the *bānī,*" he said, "meditate, and see that it's true." The experiences that the *sants* record in the *bānī* are objectively real, like the sun eternal, outlasting the embodied mortals who realize them: "The sun's reflection will shine in all the pots of water exposed to it; and even if one of the pots breaks, the sun is still there." At the same time, not everything in the available collections of *sant bānī* is to be trusted. The sayings of the *sants* can become corrupt as they are passed down. Shiv Prasad Das referred to printing errors; he may also have been thinking of the ways we have just seen in which experientially empty technical language can proliferate. He wrote verses, he said, because the old should be "swept away" (he gestured as if sweeping with a hand broom); new songs needed to be put in their place. Shiv Prasad Das, too, emphasizes that he records what he sees: "You wouldn't want to write lies, would you?" *Sant*s, Shiv Prasad Das affirms, compose verse to inform people of spiritual truths.

Shiv Prasad Das said that he had not yet produced very many songs, though he added that he planned to write some more during the rainy season, when he would have the time. He was able, however, to show me a neatly written notebook filled with his verses that he said the *mahant* at the Paltu Akhara in Ayodhya had talked about publishing. Most of the songs in it are in styles popular in his lineage; the following one is a *kuṇḍaliyā,* the form for which Paltu is most famous:

Through the *satguru*'s magnificence
  Turn 'round and climb the sky. [Refrain]

Turn 'round and climb the sky:
  Take up the path of *sohaṃ.*
Once you know that pleasing place
  You find new bliss each day. (1)
Near the whirling cave
  The unstruck sound is heard;
Its beginning, middle, end—
  All three give happiness (2)
He's sleeping there with legs outstretched
  And no one else around:
His faithful wife alone
  Remains with her beloved, (3)
And every moment Shiv Prasad
  Remains with him close by.
Through the *satguru*'s magnificence
  Turn 'round and climb the sky. (4)

Certainly, earlier gurus in the lineage had written of experiences that sound similar to those presented here by Shiv Prasad Das. In the following song Bulla tells of the greatness of his guru Yari, which is known at the whirling cave:

Gopal has given me his *darshan.*
  I was enraptured, and I saw Niranjan's beauty. (1)
At the whirling cave's gate
  All the spheres burn with light. (2)
And the Brahmas and the Vishnus and the Shivas can't be counted—
  The beginning and the middle and the end in all. (3)

There rules the royal Lord
  And the state of Yari Das is reached, supreme and inapproachable. (4)
To tell of it is his affair;
  The creature Bulla grasps his feet, (5)
A light merged into light.[34] (6)

In this song of Bulla, as in that of Shiv Prasad Das, we find the beginning, middle, and end of the spheres at the whirling cave, and a traditional association of the spheres and the cave in the lineage may have served as a basis of their common usage. The association of *sohaṃ* with a region near the caves in Shiv Prasad Das' song may have an even broader basis in *sant* experience, for it is a definite convention of the Radhasoamis. But Shiv Prasad Das' whirling cave is definitely not the whirling cave of the Radhasoamis—for them a high sphere whose bodily counterpart is close to the very top of the head. When I asked Shiv Prasad Das just where the whirling cave was located he pointed to a region in his spine—an explanation which at the time, however, did not seem too surprising. Other Gulalpanthi *sādhūs* had previously explained their old gurus' esoteric songs to me in terms of the *haṭha*-yogic centers in the trunk of the body. The question arises, then, as to whether Shiv Prasad Das' usage represents an adaptation of an old term to new *haṭha*-yogic conventions; whether it derives from his own spontaneous meditation on the old texts; or whether it might indeed represent at least one aspect of the meaning given to the term by the old gurus themselves.

In any event, the *haṭha*-yogic references Shiv Prasad Das may give to his terms probably did not *exhaust* the meanings that the old gurus attributed to them. For the songs of the great early *sants* in the lineage—Yari, Bulla, Gulal, Paltu—suggest that they knew much of the experience of which the Radhasoami gurus sing, though they do not appear to have been limited by it, and were certainly free with their use of yogic language. The following song of Yari Sahib, for example, which combines the images of the yogi sitting in postures with the bird flying away, does seem to refer to a yoga of ascension similar to that which the Radhasoami gurus teach: the yogi should leave his monastery,[35] probably a reference to the body, to experience light coming forth and the sound of *sohaṃ:*

Yogi, store up yogic knowledge [Refrain]

Sitting in your posture on *suṣumna*
  Turn attention to the unconditioned. (1)

Explore the void that you've made visible;
  Suppress the self, destroy it! (2)
Experience light's form coming forth
  And the sound of *soham̩* sung. (3)
Move, leave your monastery, yogi,
  Fly away without wings! (4)
Yari says: this intelligence-bird
  Climbs the Inapproachable and eats its fruit.[36] (5)

Just how far the experience reflected in this song of Yari actually approaches that sung of by the Radhasoami masters is perhaps best left for adepts to judge for themselves. Yet whatever the similarity of experience between the Radhasoami masters and the *sant*s within Yari's *paramparā,* the patterns of technical usage within the two lineages clearly present different dynamics of vision and code.

Consistent Scenes for Inner Experience in the Bauri *Paramparā*

The most easily available texts of the *sant*s in the Bauri *paramparā* are those in the *Sant Bānī Pustakmālā* series of the Belvedere Press, Allahabad. But as a basis for comparing the esoteric usage within the Bauri *paramparā* to that within the Radhasoami line, these texts prove problematic. The *Sant Bānī Pustakmālā* was assembled by a remarkable individual named Baleshwar Prashad, who succeeded in both holding high office in the Uttar Pradesh government and loyally following a line of Radhasoami gurus. His devoted capability was recognized within his Soami Bagh circles, and he was appointed secretary of their Central Administrative Council when it was established in 1902. Baleshwar Prashad certainly made sincere efforts to save old texts from oblivion: we hear of his traveling about to old monasteries and shrines. At the same time, we also hear of his "correcting" manuscripts and "revising" them.[37] Yet Baleshwar Prashad seems not to have corrected his texts any more than many editors. In fact, the other editions of Paltu and Charandas that we have cited more often show standardized Hindi spellings, while the Belvedere Press editions retain the dialectical forms. On a few occasions Baleshwar Prashad seems to have found a small collection of a particular fairly obscure *sant* and published it whole.[38] But for *sant*s with more voluminous available works—like many of those in the Bauri *paramparā*—he published selections, and his selections naturally reflect Radhasoami sensibilities. Out of Charandas' large corpus, which in many places elaborates on themes from Hindu tradition, the *Sant Bānī Pustakmālā* presents us with only two slim volumes of verses in the *nirguṇ* style.

Baleshwar Prashad was a professor at Queen's College, Banaras, before he went into government service, and his editions, sometimes giving variant readings, show more critical awareness than most popularly available editions of the *sant*s. For the verses of many *sant*s, moreover, they are the only editions in print. We have thus readily cited verses from the Belvedere Press editions, when relevant, in our general discussions of *sant* piety above. But for an examination of the specific patterns of technical language in the Bauri *paramparā,* Baleshwar Prashad's Radhasoami-oriented selections and possible "revisions" might lead us astray. We will thus restrict our examples to those found in a large collection published in 1933 at Bhurkura, the main center of the *sādhū*s who look to the gurus of the Bauri *paramparā,* usually called Gulalpanthis. This text could conceivably contain as many spuriously attributed songs as those in the Belvedere Press editions, but the songs it does offer, in any event, are those that have been preserved in the lineage.

The collection, entitled *Mahātmāom kī Bānī,* was printed from a manuscript called *Rām Jahāz,* "The Ship of Ram," which I have seen kept respectfully high on a shelf in the *mahant*'s receiving room in Bhurkura, and have had a chance to inspect. According to a scholarly Gulalpanthi *sādhū* who has diligently compared the book with the manuscript, the two differ principally in that the manuscript contains a number of songs signed by Sur, Tulsi Das, and Kabir that the authorities at Bhurkura saw no need to publish. Certainly, the lack of order with which the songs in the book follow one another distinctly suggests an unedited version of a traditionally preserved text.[39]

The most extended connected passage in *Mahātmāoṃ kī Banī* is a series of questions and answers between guru and disciple on matters of esoteric experience. The passage is headed "*Shrī Gulāl Sāheb Kṛit Jñān Guṣṭi*": "The Knowledge-Meeting Made by Gulal Sahib." Yet the name we find repeated within the text is not Gulal's, but that of his disciple Bhikha, a presumably literate Brahman, who thus seems a more likely author of the text than his guru. Of course, even if the text were written by neither, its inclusion in a revered manuscript indicates its importance for the lineage. At any rate, to preserve the coherence of the dialogue between Bhikha and Gulal, I have translated Bhikha's name as a term of address in the answers and as the traditional signature in the questions. The name Bhikha, moreover, derives from a root that means "beg" (*bhikṣ,* whence the Buddhist *bhikṣu*), and the poet frequently refers to the disciple as a beggar.

In the *Jñān Guṣṭi* the guru gives detailed answers to his disciple's questions, often describing internal scenes that make aspects of the meaning of certain technical terms very vivid. Indeed, one of the first questions the disciple asks is about the esoteric significance of the everyday words for the moon and the sun:

PASSAGE #1

The disciple's petition:

Give me the teachings of the moon and the sun,
  In which abodes do you invoke them? (1)
Explain to me the logic behind
  What are called the moon and sun: (2)
They're not the moon and sun that rise with
  All these nights and days that come and go? (3)
O guru, I know absolutely nothing;
  And hearing of so difficult a yoga,
    This beggar is afraid. (4)

. . . .

The guru's grace:

Listen to the secret of the moon and sun:
  Do their service sitting in the city of the nose. (5)
The moon and sun inhabit the *brahmāṇḍ*
  Making light there night and day. (6)
Two areas are found within the city of the nose:
  At the left is the moon's seat;
    At the right is the sun's. (7)
Put the moon aside and climb the sun—
  The *iḍā* and the *pingalā* go into the *suṣumna;* (8)
At that one place then make your effort.
  When the void occurs, the soul becomes confused; (9)
But the void will disappear, becoming brilliance:
  The day takes incarnation as the sun. (10)
Light comes, giving the soul happiness,
  And making all its fear of darkness flow away. (11)
Bhikha, I don't think
  The sun moves slowly through the day (12)
And the moon comes out at night.
  Know the sun to shine throughout the night (13)
And the moon throughout the day.
  There's no yogic knowledge more than this.[40] (14)

Some of the yogic referents in the passage above seem clear: the *iḍā, pingalā,* and *suṣumna* (l. 8) are three yogic veins that meet at the place between the eyebrows, the probable referent of "the city of the nose" (ll. 5, 7). The *iḍā,* at the left, is commonly associated with the moon; the *pingalā,* to the right, with the sun. But the moon and the sun of the passage above appear to have a larger mystical meaning than the veins of yogic physiology. As bearers of light, they give the soul happiness after an experience of fear (l. 11). Their roles reversed, the moon giving light during the day and the sun at night—they provide the essence of yogic knowledge (ll. 13–14).

The passage below similarly begins with a description of principles associated with methods of *haṭha* yoga, and then presents a more profound wisdom that transcends them: the airs, or vital forces (*pavan*), which the guru first mentions, have no access to the transcendent "guru-knowledge" (*guru-jñān*). The places of access to the guru-knowledge seem to be the top of *merudaṇḍ, bank nāl* ("the crooked tunnel"), and "three-pointed" *trikuṭī*—about all of which the disciple asks at once:

PASSAGE #2

The disciple's petition:

Tell the path of *merudaṇḍ*
  And how to climb bank nāl; (1)
How the western way is open,
  How the soul impels its vital forces on. (2)
How does one see *trikuṭī*
  And the self as Ram? (3)

The satguru's grace:

Bhikha, here is what to contemplate;
  Listen, ponder, grasp it deep within your mind: (4)
The forces of the sky go down into the netherworlds
  Then back they come half way. (5)
Contemplate *bank nāl;*
  Climb *merudaṇḍ* and ponder. (6)
Be steadfast, call to mind the knowledge of your guru—
  The vital forces have no access there. (7)
They get confused to death by thinking about guru-knowledge
  Only when the guru gives his grace is it unveiled. (8)
Bhikha, there the ego's conquered
  And the door will open right away. (9)

Beggar, gaze at *trikuṭī*,
  Which offers light and holds the highest self (10)
And understand you're contemplating Ram . . .[41] (11)

In both of the passages above, transcendent principles are realized together with a vision of light: here, light comes with a knowledge of the highest self; in the earlier passage, light emerges out of the void. Below, the guru elaborates on the fullness of the void and its identity with light. Now light as fire consumes all into itself, and the void seems at once to hold everything and nothing. The vital forces that had no access to the transcendent in passage #2 above are here contained in it with everything else:

PASSAGE #3

The guru's grace:

In the sky-void, Bhikha,
  All things have a place: (1)
Anhad nād, shabd, vital forces
  Consciousness, I tell you. (2)
That void lives in the body—
  Manifest in all, in all unmanifest. (3)
When someone comes in touch with it
  He finds the guru's *shabda.* (4)
The body doesn't merge with it.
  The soul does, though, and leaves the body (5)
Going off in *shabda.*
  The air then takes the body's place. (6)
Where *shabd* is, air is also—
  Know this to be true. (7)
Who comes to the void goes into the void;
  Coming and going take place in the void. (8)
The lamp that's in the void's just like
  The flaming light within the body: (9)
In every body a blazing flame of knowledge—
  The form of *brahma* great and bright. (10)
A flame burns at all stations of the body:
  One void goes in four directions. (11)
The lamp of knowledge stays with him
  To whom the guru's grace gives eyes to see. (12)
The lamp has come from nowhere:
  It occupies the same space as the void. (13)
When they see the blazing lamp of knowledge
  Mind and *māyā* right away are burned up in the fire. (14)

The soul, a flame, becomes a moth:
  It merges in the void, its form destroyed. (15)
Bhikha, know the flame's in every body.
  The lamp of knowledge—
    That's what's called the void. (16)
Grasp your lamp, make brilliance!
  Then you'll understand how far the void extends. (17)
Bhikha, fire lives in the void:
  The lamp's home's where the void is.[42] (18)

In the *Mahātmāoṃ kī Bānī* collection, a number of other songs recall one or another of these three scenes from the *Jñān Guṣṭi:* (1) the sun and the moon; (2) the lights at *trikuṭī* and *bank nāl;* and (3) the void, which contains everything and nothing. The following song, attributed to Bulla, recalls the scene of passage #1. Here, too, the sun and moon are joined to eliminate the distinction between day and night, allowing the devotee to dwell in pure whiteness:

SONG #1

Once you make the sun and moon one planet,
  Destroying day and night (1)
You'll settle right away into a pure white island. (2)
Make the triad of the qualities your mother
  And comprehend the five essentials. (3)
Waves arise there, great and endless,
  To which the creature Bulla makes his offering.[43] (4)

The word translated here as island (*dīp,* from Sanskrit *dvīpa*) is homophonous with one meaning light or lamp (Sanskrit *dīpa*). The "settling in" (*basāvanaṃ,* l. 2) and "waves" (*laharī,* l. 4) suggest rendering the word as "island," though we have seen the images of the flame and lamp recurring in the passages above and they may be deliberately evoked here as well. In the following song, "sparkling flame" occurs with the victory of the guru's words at *tribenī* and *bank nāl*—a scene recalling one observed before in passage #2:

SONG #2

If someone turns inward to gaze at the self . . . [Refrain]

Look, look! Take your longing within:
  Repeat the holy names without a rosary. (1)

Adopt the guru's words' true nature—
  Make the journey to the Inapproachable. (2)
The blossoming lotus grows, its face unspoiled,
  And the devotee-bee remains in longing. (3)
The ornament of victory lies at *tribenī,*
  Ascend *bank nāl:* (4)
In ten directions sparkling flame
  Without a mother or a father— (5)
The fearless, indestructible, unearthly subtle idol,
  The Lord giving life to the *sant*s. (6)
Flitting about there in ardor—the creature Gulal,
  And no one else around.[44] (7)

The word translated as "unspoiled" in line 3 is *sahaj,* which often means "natural" in colloquial usage, but as a metaphysical term in esoteric verse is probably best translated as "unconditioned."[45] Several songs in the *Mahātmāoṃ kī Bānī* collection attempt to evoke the *sahaj sunya,* the unconditioned void of passage #3 that contains everything and nothing. The following is one of the best:

SONG #3

Climb, mind, to dwell at the unconditioned void. [Refrain]

No shape there, no outline; no caste there, no rank:
  There dwells the indestructible, the formless. (1)
A drum resounds with no one beating it;
  A song is sung without a tongue. (2)
A sound is heard with no one playing music;
  A dance is danced without a foot. (3)
No moon, no sun, no night, no day,
  Nor three *dev*s nor four *veda*s. (4)
Gulal says: win the game there;
  Come home, mind, win the unconditioned.[46] (5)

Perhaps the greatest difference between these esoteric songs from *Mahātm̃aoṃ kī Bānī* and the *āratī*s of the Radhasoami gurus seen earlier is the means of approach to the transcendent that they offer. The Radhasoami *āratī*s present definite progressions from one well-marked sign to the next, leading finally to a vision of the "Inapproachable" (*agam*) Lord. In the songs we have just examined, however, we see instead consistent clusters of signs constituting recurring scenes, with breakthroughs to the transcendent apparently occurring in each of them. The scenes we have observed include not only those represented in the three passages and three songs just cited but also the whirling cave told of by Shiv Prasad Das and seen as well in the song of Bulla, also from *Mahātmāoṃ kī Bānī.*

Whatever the oral instructions that may have been transmitted through the gurus in the lineage, in their poetry, at least, the different scenes in which visions of the transcendent are available are not clearly hierarchized. Thus, the consistency of technical language in these songs is found in the clustering of esoteric terms, not in their order. Recurring among the different *sant* poets of the Bauri *paramparā,* it is this clustering of terms that appears as the specific "code" informing the esoteric experience of the lineage. But both code and experience are less highly structured than they are among the Radhasoamis. Instead of ordered progressions of terms and experience, we find clusters interconnecting with one another. Thus, both the sun and moon of passage #1 of the *Jñān Guṣṭi* and the *bank nāl* and *trikuṭī* of passage #2 lead to a vision of the light in the void described in passage #3. The first two passages themselves, moreover, seem to present different experiences of much the same yogic territory. In its threefoldness, *trikuṭī,* "the three prominences," of passage #2, certainly resembles *trivenī,* even if it is not identical with it. *Trivenī,* the yogic "triple-braid," normally refers to the place where the moon as *iḍā* and the sun as *pingalā* come together with *suṣumna,* a situation described at length in passage #1. The consistent scenes that occur in *Mahātmāoṃ kī Bānī,* then, often appear as different visions of a similar ground.

Occasionally, however, we do find in *Mahātmāoṃ kī Bānī* progressions from stage to stage that in fact recall those in Soamiji's *āratī*s. But since the songs in this collection are usually shorter than Soamiji's *āratī*s, the progressions we see are more compact:

The moon and sun become one planet;
  Pure water on *tribenī*'s shore.
When airs reverse you climb the sky:
  The lamp's light and the unconditioned void.[47]

This verse recalls elements from all three of the passages we have examined in the *Jñān Guṣṭi,* and in the same order that they are presented there: the sun and the moon of passage #1; the reversal of the vital airs of passage #2 as well as *trivenī* (as *trikuṭī*'s reflex?); and the lamp's light and unconditioned void of passage #3. In the following song, attributed to Bulla, we find a progression that includes the whirling cave we have seen mentioned earlier; the poet begins with the image of the dutiful wife going out in the morning to fetch water:

In the morning the enthusiastic bride
  Glimpsed *trivenī*'s confluence. (1)
The guru gave a water-jug that morning:
  Back and forth she swayed and drank of love. (2)
Once she cleaned root *mantra*'s home
  She climbed to realize *bank nāl*'s home. (3)
When the whirling cave resounded
  She prayed at the tenth door's home. (4)
So says the creature Bulla:
  The mad one makes his home there
    And burns up in white flame.[48] (5)

Both the clustering of terms into scenes in the *Mahātmāoṃ kī Bānī* collection and the progression of scenes as far as it is evident bear some striking resemblances to the Radhasoami conventions, particularly to those that the Radhasoamis use to describe the lower regions of the universe. The sun and moon as yogic veins belong to the lowest stage of the Radhasoami cosmos, *bank nāl* and *trikuṭī* to the second stage, and the void to the third. The order of this hierarchy is the same one in which we have seen the technical terms taken up in the *Jñān Guṣṭi* and presented in the first progression just cited. The second progression, attributed to Bulla, also presents *trivenī* and *bank nāl* at lower levels, but the order in which it shows the whirling cave and the tenth door reverse Radhasoami conventions: the Radhasoamis usually associate the tenth door with the void, the third stage, and see the whirling cave as the entrance to the highest heavens.

Thus, while there is certainly divergence in the use of technical language between the gurus in Soamiji's line and those of the Bauri *paramparā,* there are also some similarities. The similarities suggest that by the end of the seventeenth century, norms of esoteric language may well have congealed among the *sant*s of the North Indian plain. But for *sant*s of different lineages to share elements of a common esoteric usage means that the inner referents of the terms they used also had something in common. Certainly, Radhasoami gurus today make inner sense of the verses of the gurus of the Bauri *paramparā*. Their intuitions, perhaps, should not be discounted: it may well be that by the eighteenth century *sant*s from Delhi to Banaras were using similar terms to refer to similar experiences within an esoteric *sant* tradition that had taken on large and common dimensions.[49]

In our study of *sant* technical usage from Kabir to the Radhasoamis we have seen four increasingly specific degrees of consistency. These different degrees of consistency appear to be linked to the increasingly specific patterns of coherence we find within *sant* tradition itself: the two most general patterns of coherence in *sant* technical language derive from principles of clan; the two most specific, from principles of lineage.

The most general level is that in which *sant* usage coincides fairly well with technical usage among the majority of Indian yogis. Here we have terms such as *iḍā, pingalā,* and *suṣumna,* which, as we have seen in the *Jñān Guṣṭi,* can be used by *sant*s in much the same way as they are by other yogis. Next we have a set of terms that seem particularly characteristic of *sant* texts. Some of these terms are also used by yogis generally, but they are used by many *sant*s in certain specific ways (*trikuṭī,* for example); others appear less commonly in the yogic literature (for example, the whirling cave). Most of this technical vocabulary is found in profusion in the extended Kabirian corpus and helps to define the *sant*s as a unique clan among more distantly related yogic brethren. The commonality of technical terms certainly might indicate some commonality of esoteric experiences, especially among certain later *sant*s. But particular technical expressions can, as we have seen in the case of Shiv Prasad Das, be used idiosyncratically by individuals who are exposed to them more through texts than through teachers.

Coming to the more specific patterns of coherence, we find first the somewhat loose consistency among *sant*s in a lineage as seen among the gurus of the Bauri *paramparā* and in the correspondences between the texts of Soamiji and Tulsi Sahib. Here we notice definite, if inexact, similarities among spiritually related *sant* poets. These similarities are, moreover, understood within traditions to derive from factors of lineage: the guru gives his disciple a vision (as declared by Tulsi Sahib)[50] or instruction (as found in the format of the *Jñān Guṣṭi*). The most exact usage occurs among gurus within lineages such as the Radhasoami or Tulsi *panth,* where most people knowledgeable in tradition are aware that the technical terms are being used in certain highly specific ways. Here, as we have seen in the case of Sant Vachan Das, an emphasis upon full and exact usage can lead to the creation of some experientially empty esoteric verse.

The patterns of esoteric usage based on a presumption of a clan of *sant*s reflect an attitude of faith in the *sant* tradition as a heritage: what the *sant*s said is true, and the forms in which they expressed themselves are both eternal and adequate for us now. It is in such patterns of usage that the esoteric language appears most perplexing as a referential code that must be figured out, or "broken." The patterns of esoteric usage within a lineage, however, in transmitting specific experiences of subtle reality through time, can appear as a lineage's "genetic" code. They reflect an attitude of faith in the *sant* as a holy man ("I should try to understand what my guru told me"). In a well-structured pattern of usage like that found among the Radhasoamis, this attitude can be combined with the perception of the lineage originator as a singular personality ("Soamiji revealed the true path"). We shall now turn to the various theological expressions of these attitudes in different developments within the Radhasoami line.

6

Doctrine and Succession in the Radhasoami Line

The knowledge passed down in *sant paramparās* comes through living gurus, whose eventual death leads to regularly recurring problems of succession. For some disciples, these problems require a theoretical as well as a practical resolution. We have already seen some of the practical problems of succession among *sants*: succession to the guru's wealth and authority leading to protracted legal battles; succession to the guru's experience through an assimilation of his esoteric vocabulary that may not be complete. Theoretical questions about the meaning of succession have been sharply articulated by thinkers in the Radhasoami line. For, more like the early *sants* than were many intervening figures, the leaders of the important Radhasoami lineages have usually pointed to the guru alone as immanent focus, giving little spiritual legitimacy to the forms of the Hindu heritage. At the same time, unlike the mostly illiterate early *sants* and their followers, the Radhasoamis are able to draw on both Hindu and Islamic lettered traditions to come to terms with just who the guru is: In what ways are successive gurus spiritually the same? How do the gurus in their line compare with other *sants*?

Answers to these questions are clearly shaped by the contrasting socioreligious situations at the two major regional centers of Radhasoami tradition, which foster the different attitudes toward the problem of Soamiji's guru discussed near the end of chapter 4. At Beas, in Sikh country, Soamiji is thought to have had a guru and to have been a *sant* of the order of Guru Nanak, whom the Sikhs revere. At Agra, Soamiji's own birthplace, he is thought to have been a singular, guruless personality, who for the first time revealed the highest truth. These two contrasting ideas about the place of Soamiji in the general dispensation of salvation lead to different theological problems among the lineages at Agra and those coming down through Beas. At Agra, the problems entail understanding the way in which the spiritual force that came with Soamiji continues to manifest in a guru, and the proper form of the religion that finds a focus in him. Devotees of gurus in the Beas sublineages face these problems in a somewhat different form, together with a problem of their own: how can the idea of the existence of realized holy men within different traditions be reconciled with a very definite teaching about the progression of experience to the supreme?

The gurus in the minor Radhasoami lineages often present teachings about the nature of the guru and spiritual reality that are substantially different from those at both Agra and Beas, teachings that evolve from their own development as holy men outside an established Radhasoami institutional framework. This chapter will treat the interplay between succession and theology within the established lineages at Agra and Beas, and the ways in which two unorthodox masters with Radhasoami roots have consciously modified the teachings and experience they pass on. Figures 3 through 5 in the Appendix outline the relationships among some noteworthy gurus in the lineage, indicating their significance in the development of tradition. The reader may wish to refer to these diagrams during the narration of the complex dynastic history that follows.

Agra: The Singular Personality as Divine Current

Soamiji's relics remain at Soami Bagh, his former retreat on the outskirts of Agra, about three miles from the center of the city. Devotees with allegiance to the line of gurus who have had control of Soami Bagh pride themselves on being of the "parent stock." They recognize a succession of five and only five gurus including Soamiji, the last of whom, unfortunately, died in 1949. Nevertheless, some of the last guru's important disciples have continued to give initiation in his name, teaching doctrines that justify this practice.

The parent lineage split with the passing of the third guru, Maharaj Sahib. At his death, many of his disciples were attracted to the head of the branch *satsang* at Gazipur, Uttar Pradesh, a successful lawyer who would eventually be revered as Sarkar Sahib. Sarkar Sahib, however, was not recognized by the Central Administrative Council that his guru had set up, and his Gazipur group eventually broke away from it. His disciple, a very dynamic Punjabi Hindu called Sahibji Maharaj, settled in Agra across the street from Soami Bagh. Within the colony he founded, Dayalbagh, a number of colleges and factories flourished, and through them the colony became known to many Indians not involved in Radhasoami tradition.

At the same time that these lineages were developing around Soamiji's retreat outside Agra, another has been continuing in the heart of the city, at the seat of Soamiji's principal successor, Huzur Sahib (who is also counted within the lineages of both Soami Bagh and Dayalbagh). After Huzur Sahib's death his son was generally acknowledged as an inportant *satsangī,* qualified to grant initiation. Many of those whom he initiated, however, revered him as a guru in his own right, and a succession of gurus developed among his physical descendants. Today, relics of Huzur Sahib's son and grandson are offered devotion daily at the family residence, called Huzuri Bhavan, where they are unstintingly maintained by the last guru's grandson, who himself commands the allegiance of many devotees.

In Agra today, then, Radhasoami lineages continue at three seats: Soami Bagh, Dayalbagh, and Huzuri Bhavan. People in all these groups understand the earlier *sant* tradition to have provided the groundwork for Soamiji's arrival on earth. But in Soamiji the Lord incarnated to reveal a unique name, "Radhasoami," which comes from the highest region of the universe, attained by no previous *sant.* The salvific force bearing the Radhasoami name and embodied in Soamiji is sometimes spoken of as the *dhār,* "current," which will remain accessible to man until its work is complete at the dissolution of the universe. The different groups, however, have their own ideas as to just how the *dhār* remains on earth. These ideas appear to depend in part on the actual events of succession that have occurred in the Agra sublineages.

In his discourses, Maharaj Sahib spoke about the divine's "own current" years before the major split in the lineage that occurred with his passing. For whatever the import it would gain in sectarian politics, the concept of the *dhār* emerges easily from the common religious idiom of fluid substance familiar from the devotional poetry of chapter 1. The sectarian translation of these extracts from a discourse by Maharaj Sahib tell of channels, rivers, reservoirs, and currents (*dhār*s):

> When Sat Guru departs, the Current is still there; it does not recede but remains 'withdrawn,' as it were. . . . 'Withdrawal' signifies that the Current does not flow with as great a force as it does at the time of flow tide in a river, like the river Hooghly. . . . Formerly it used to come into the

> river Hooghly, and now it comes into another river, the sea being the same. So also is the case with the Reservoir and Current, the only difference being that of the channel or the body.[1]

The "withdrawal" spoken of by Maharaj Sahib refers to the period after the passing of a recognized guru, when the succession remains unclear. It takes time, some say, for the *dhār* to manifest. The perfect disciple, having cultivated humility, will have to overcome his shyness and grow into his new identity as guru. Only gradually does the new guru begin to act like a guru. Indeed, after Huzur Sahib's passing it seems to have taken three years for the succession to become firmly established in Maharaj Sahib himself. Huzur Sahib, moreover, had already given Maharaj Sahib a good deal of visible spiritual responsibility, sometimes having him preside over communal worship and deal with devotees' correspondence.[2] But, as Maharaj Sahib assures us in the passage above, during the interval between manifestations of the *satguru*—normally referred to even in Hindi by the English term "interregnum"—we need have no anxiety: the *dhār* has not totally receded, just withdrawn somewhat like the tide; the work of redemption still goes on. And when the *dhār* does finally manifest in another "channel or body" the new personality is to be understood as the same cosmic being as the departed master.

The major difference between the Soami Bagh and Dayalbagh theories of the *dhār* is in their ideas about the normal interval between its manifestations, in other words, about the length of interregnums. The succession within the lineage now at Soami Bagh has gone through some trying times, and remains without a guru today. People there have learned to see a long interregnum as part of the natural course of things, and to realize the particular virtues it can offer.

According to the people at Soami Bagh, after the departure of Maharaj Sahib, the *dhār* manifested again in his sister, called Buaji Sahiba, "Madam Father's Sister." About a month before his death, they say, Maharaj Sahib had dropped hints regarding the role she was to play. He was talking about the *nij aṃsh,* the Highest Lord's "own part":

> The Nij Ansh is in the female form and as such she cannot be expected to function fully. If it be the Mauj, she can function more or less in the same way as did Mira Bai and Sahjo Bai. This Nij Ansh shall in the future function fully as an Acharya in the male form.[3]

Not only was Buaji Sahiba older than Maharaj Sahib and well on in years when she succeeded him, but she also remained in *purdā,* "seclusion," as ladies from respectable traditional families often still do. Access to Buaji Sahiba was difficult to come by, and in her the *dhār* still remained for practical purposes somewhat withdrawn. Yet this withdrawal, they say, had the effect of purifying the community: those dependent on enjoying the outer play of the guru and unable to be content with inner discipline fell away.[4] The seclusion of Buaji Sahiba also gave valuable experience to her chosen disciple, called Babuji Maharaj, who was to succeed her and "function fully as [the] Acharya in . . . male form" alluded to by Maharaj Sahib.

Babuji Maharaj was the grandson of Soamiji's sister, and as a child had enjoyed early contact with his illustrious granduncle. A friend and associate of Maharaj Sahib when both were young men, and the visible representative of Buaji Sahiba, Babuji Maharaj had long been respected in the Radhasoami community. His reign as guru was also the most enduring. He took over from Buaji Sahiba in 1913 at Allahabad and died thirty-six years later at Soami Bagh, where he had settled with many of his disciples in 1937.

Babuji Maharaj had been very weak for the last years of his life, but his end was sudden, and he had not clearly designated anyone to succeed him. Nor has anyone emerged who could or would command the spiritual allegiance of the majority of Babuji Maharaj's disciples. One of the leaders of the Soami Bagh colony, an allopath known as Doctor Sahib, tells of a time when some devotees tried to make him the guru, but, he says, he would have none of it: he was no *sant.* Sant Das Maheshwari, formerly the personal assistant to Babuji Maharaj, had written and translated dozens of books on Radhasoami teachings, but was respected by most as a senior devotee, not revered as guru. One disciple of Babuji Maharaj, however, a Boston-trained homeopath named J. N. Hazra who kept an office at Soami Bagh, did manage to command the allegiance of a sizable minority of his guru's devotees. Before he died in 1966, he formally appointed a successor: his guru's daughter, called Bibi Rani. She too, they say, appointed a successor before she passed on, but in 1981 he was far away from his devotees at Soami Bagh. For he was employed as an official in the Indian Railroads, and his service had taken him to Calcutta.

While a small following still assembles nightly at Dr. Hazra's house in Soami Bagh, and a few people speak in excited whispers about a new guru they won't identify, soon to manifest himself publicly, most people at Soami Bagh continue to try to understand the significance of interregnum. Maheshwari writes of the distinct spiritual benefits that interregnum can offer: love for the guru now becomes intense love-in-separation; detachment arises; the spiritual level of both the individual and the community consolidates.[5] Yet for many these benefits are not enough, and a number of Soami Bagh *satsangīs* I met admitted sadly that no one ever really expected the current interregnum to last for so long.

Across the street at Dayalbagh, people do not put much stock in the idea of a long interregnum. The gurus they acknowledge have in fact for the most part been dynamic individuals who have managed to establish themselves in fairly short order. Accordingly, Dayalbagh literature shows us how the *dhār* is able to manifest itself right away: "Immediately after the departure of Maharaj Sahab, Satsangis began to be blessed with internal experiences." We are told that they had spontaneously seen the image of Sarkar Sahib, the successor recognized by Dayalbagh people, or that Maharaj Sahib came in a dream proclaiming Sarkar Sahib to be the new guru.[6]

The day after Sarkar Sahib's funeral, his successor, Sahibji Maharaj, showed distinct signs of being possessed by the *dhār* in his turn. Sitting with a group of disconsolate devotees, he told one of them "to look at Him and have the *darsana* of Soamiji Maharaj who had arrived and everyone was astonished to find that instead of Sahabji Maharaj, Soamiji Maharaj was there." All the gurus in the lineage would come, announced Sahibji Maharaj, and he appeared to his devotees as each of the gurus in turn. Then, very distinctly, Sahibji Maharaj began to act in the authoritative manner that a guru can adopt. Since the spiritual current was flowing through him, he said, those assembled should pay obeisance. Accusing two people present of petty theft, he commanded them to apologize. His young son should address him not by the respectful "Babuji," but by the much more respectful "Soamiji."[7]

Under the guidance of Sahibji Maharaj, the Dayalbagh colony grew into a vital community. Factories of all sorts were established—for leather goods and soap, scissors and textiles; colleges were built. During the 1920s and 30s the colony gained fame in British India as a model community, and Sahibji Maharaj was honored with a knighthood: his name in law was now Sir Anand Sarup, Kt.

Sahibji Maharaj was not one to disdain the material goods the Lord had put in his path; he lived well. Indeed, four days before his passing in 1937 Sahibji Maharaj said:

> If He makes me a king, I will sit on the throne in a way that no king ever sat before, and if He makes me roll in the dust, I will roll and roll in such a way that no beggar ever rolled before.

Many devotees understand Sahibji Maharaj to have actually lived in certain ways like a king and to have been able to forsee his passing; so his reference to a possible future as a beggar is said to allude to the next manifestation of the divine current in his successor, Mehtaji Sahib:

> Everyone has observed during all the period since 1937 how Mehtaji Sahab has lived a life of stark simplicity and his work in the dust and dirt of the fields reminds one of Sahabji Maharaj fulfilling His promise, in His New Form, to roll and roll in the dust as 'no beggar ever rolled before.'[8]

Sahibji Maharaj had apparently given another, more concrete indication that Mehtaji Sahib was to be his successor. He had found himself approaching death once before, they say, and before the divine will had changed to restore his life forces, he had announced that Mehtaji should take charge.[9] Mehtaji in his turn, however, had decreed that after his own passing his successor should be agreed upon by acclamation of the *satsang*. Many of those present in the assembly that chose Mehtaji's successor were very moved by their experience. The names of a number of candidates were proposed, and those assembled were instructed to say Radhasoami three times to indicate the one they felt to be the new guru. The crowd was completely silent, we are told, until the name of the present successor was called, but then the room reverberated with the sound of Radhasoami, Radhasoami, Radhasoami.

For decades, the administrators of Dayalbagh ("The Garden of the Merciful") have been involved in legal proceedings with those of Soami Bagh ("The Garden of the Master"). Of the different types of *sant* succession disputes so far examined, the issue between them seems closest to that over which the successors to Charandas quarrelled: the rights of the true successor to the relics of his master. If the Soami Bagh successors were in fact real gurus then there is no question that they could do with the relics what they liked; but if they were mere human administrators, then they should be made to open the relics to the Dayalbagh people, who also have a religious interest in the relics.[10]

Given the open animosity between the two groups, it is no surprise that the Soami Bagh people find the enthusiastic exercise in spiritual consensus of the people at Dayalbagh merely a sign of how low they have fallen. How absurd to think, say the Soami Bagh people, that a guru could possibly be "elected." Of course, on hearing of this accusation by his neighbor across the street, someone from Dayalbagh will commonly counter with something like: "Well there's no guru at all in Soami Bagh."

Yet Soami Bagh may not need a quick succession of competent spiritual authority as much as Dayalbagh does. As people of both groups recognize, the patterns of routinization within the two communities have taken different courses. Soami Bagh people, making light of Dayalbagh industries, are proud that their establishment is devoted solely to spiritual practice; the Dayalbagh people, on the other hand, see their industry, agriculture, and educational institutions as a mark of the "better worldliness" that Sahibji Maharaj took as one of his main ideals. And with increased value given to fruitful activity in this world at Dayalbagh comes an increase in the practical importance of *sevā,* "spiritual service." Not only Soami Bagh people, but some internal dissenters as well have thought the attention paid to external work as *sevā* at Dayalbagh excessive; but Mehtaji had an answer to critics who suggested that devotees spend more time listening to spiritual discourse: "Let such people feel happy and blessed by keeping away from His *sevā* (service) and let us enjoy the happiness and bliss of engaging in His *sevā.*"[11]

To give increased opportunity to the population at Dayalbagh to engage in fruitful work as service to the guru, Mehtaji instituted a morning program of work in the fields. In the dawn hours, before their regular salaried jobs, many of the residents of Dayalbagh, both old and young, assemble at one of the fields under seasonal cultivation. There they work at whatever simple task is required: perhaps they weed, or transplant rice. While engaged in work, however, they are also able to enjoy the guru's *darshan.* For he comes to the fields too, often receiving people with personal problems and consulting with the administrators of the diverse Dayalbagh concerns:

> . . . though some individuals may have stayed behind, Mehtaji Sahab has always gone there to cheer, encourage and guide people in their manual work in the fields.[12]

Thus, the presence of a capable spiritual authority at Dayalbagh serves both to evoke enthusiastic outward service and to keep complex institutional affairs running in order.

The spiritual practice stressed at Soami Bagh, on the other hand, is internal, and seems to be carried on well enough without the presence of a living master. True, contemplation on the form of the master is a crucial element in Radhasoami meditation practice; but until the new guru is manifest, we are told at Soami Bagh, his past bodily form remains a spiritually effective object of contemplation.[13] The characteristic mode in which devotees offer outward service at Soami Bagh is cash offerings for the building of an impressive temple to Soamiji Maharaj. The temple has been decades in construction and people at Soami Bagh say that it will be decades more before the temple is finished, pointing out that they take donations for this work only from their own *satsangīs*.

Soami Bagh *satsangīs* are scattered throughout North India but often assemble at Soami Bagh at yearly feasts in honor of each of the gurus in the sublineage. Thus, Soami Bagh begins to serve as a spiritual and pilgrimage center for a far-flung religious constituency. Indeed, with its imposing temple and yearly cycle of feast days it begins to recall Nathdwara, the site of the chief *puṣṭimārgīya* shrine, described in chapter 2. As at Nathdwara, the *prasād* taken at the special feasts is said to have special ritual power, though the authority of no living guru is needed to sanctify it—much less a hereditary successor like the Nathdwara *tilkāyit.*

A small, if elaborately kept, Radhasoami shrine is already complete in downtown Agra at Huzuri Bhavan, the seat of Soamiji's successor, Huzur Sahib; it, too, sometimes serves as a pilgrimage center for a limited, though widespread group of devotees. Here, however, a guru in a hereditary succession does in fact preside over the shrine, though the idea of hereditary lineage is not a well-developed doctrine, as it is among the *puṣṭimārgīs*. According to the present guru's bright and personable younger son—who certainly has a stake in the issue—"it just happened" that gurus have occurred within his family; he couldn't say that it would always be so. His father, called Dadaji Maharaj, tells of Huzur Sahib's doctrine that *sant*s should openly nominate their own successors;[14] and in practice the gurus at Huzuri Bhavan do seem to have designated some spiritual authority to one of their sons or grandsons.

Dadaji Maharaj is revered as a perfect master and is able to be less doctrinaire than the guardians of Soamiji's relics at Soami Bagh, who of all the Radhasoami groups in both Agra and Beas present the best-developed theology. Dadaji Sahib offers *satsang,* has written verses, and has seen his discourses published. Thus, even though the Huzuri Bhavan group does recognize *de facto* a *bindu paramparā,* it bears less resemblance to a *panth* than does the Soami Bagh group. A history professor at Agra college, Dadaji Maharaj has written a book on the Radhasoamis in academic style that is remarkably generous toward the minor sublineages. Yet he, like the other gurus at Agra, teaches that the Radhasoami Faith is "a separate religion,"[15] finding a focus in a unique singular personality, the one *sant satguru* of the age.

Beas: The Perfect Master in *Sant* Tradition

At Beas, too, the idea of the single *satguru* of the age eventually emerges, but in a somewhat different form. At Agra, as we have seen, the same current that first came down from the highest heavens with Soamiji Maharaj is understood to continue its manifestation on earth through a succession of spiritually prepared beings. Devotees at Beas, on the other hand, speak little of the unique current, the *dhār,* and sometimes mock the idea; instead, they understand succession to take place between distinct perfected individuals. The different understandings of the cosmic identity of the guru at Agra and at Beas is reflected in two important aspects of Radhasoami practice: contemplation of the guru's form, and repetition of the divine names.

After Sarkar Sahib's passing, we recall, Sahibji Maharaj was seen by many to appear in the images of all the gurus in the lineage: they are all manifestations of one *dhār.* In the same spirit, Agra devotees are enjoined to contemplate in their daily practice the image of the new guru once he becomes manifest, not that of the old. Some devotees to gurus in the Beas sublineages, like the new devotees of Sahibji Maharaj described above, have reported seeing the images of past gurus merge with that of the latest successor, and, like the disciples of Sahibji Maharaj, they take their vision as an internal proof of the new guru's legitimacy.

Yet not all Beas people are so enthusiastic about spiritually embracing a new successor. Since they usually see their gurus as individual persons with powers of their own, many of them will talk about loving a new guru and respecting his teachings, but will still continue to contemplate the form of the guru who initiated them. This attitude is consonant with the official Beas version of Soamiji's prose discourses, *Sār Bachan,* which differs from the Agra version precisely on the matter of whose form to contemplate when the old guru passes on. The Agra version presents a long passage explaining why the disciple should seek out the successor and contemplate his form, recommending contemplation of the old guru only for those not keen on further progress and ready to take another birth.[16] The Beas version presents a much shorter rendering of the passage. Using the same phrases, it is apparently adapted from the Agra text, but its import is radically different.

> If anyone is accepted by a perfect *Sat Guru,* has love and faith in Him, serves him devotedly, but before he has advanced far the *Guru* departs, he should continue just the same with his love and faith, and go on contemplating His form and performing the exercises prescribed by the late *Guru.* In the end, that *Sat Guru* in that very form will do this work to the extent that he deserves.[17]

Thus, should his guru pass on, the devotee at Agra is enjoined to contemplate the form of his guru's successor; at Beas he is told to contemplate the form of the deceased guru who initiated him.

Kirpal Singh, an important guru whose lineage comes through Beas, argues that the prose discourses of *Sār Bachan* were "not written by Swami Ji himself, but [were] based on dictations and notes taken by disciples, and published several years after his death."[18] Jaimal Singh, he continues, the disciple of Soamiji who founded the seat at Beas, simply did not believe that the Agra version of the passage represented the teachings of Soamiji that he remembered, and so made the substitution.

Jaimal Singh also remembered different teachings about the divine names to be repeated in meditation practice. According to devotees at Agra, we recall, the singular divine current that came with Soamiji manifests as uttered sound through the name Radhasoami, which is understood to have a unique spiritual power. As among the *puṣṭimārgī*s, the form of the divine words bestowed at initiation, if not their power, is given out publicly, becoming in fact a revealed basis for religious community. People at Beas, on the other hand, will frequently say that the exact form of the utterance imparted by the guru is not of such great consequence. What is important, rather, is the power the individual guru imparts to the words, and for this to be effective, their exact form should not become common public knowledge.

In practice, Beas gurus initiate devotees into *pāñch nām,* "the five names" said to be invoked in Sikh scripture. Soamiji's family were traditionally followers of Guru Nanak, and all admit that at least at the beginning of his career as guru, Soamiji initiated devotees into the five names of the Lord. For Jaimal Singh, a Sikh, these names were enough, as they were for his successors in the predominantly Sikh

Punjab. Indeed, there the gurus in his lineage appear to devotees less as propagators of a new religion than as masters in an extended *sant* tradition of which Guru Nanak and the early Sikh gurus were a part.

Yet while the *sant* tradition as understood by disciples of Beas masters usually posits a plurality of holy men scattered over space and time, it does not always include a plurality of perfect holy men at *one* time. This point in fact remains ambiguous in Beas tradition. Indeed, less routinized in a number of ways than the large Agra groups, Beas tradition presents less neatly codified doctrine on many issues. The ambiguities of Beas teachings on the single *satguru* of the age reflect tensions understandable in a devotional tradition when the disciple's awareness of his guru's finiteness confronts his loving adoration of him. Thus, most informants will usually admit that there can be more than one perfect guru on earth at a given time, sometimes citing Kabir and Nanak as contemporaries. But simultaneously, most really seem to believe that normally there is only one, and now it is theirs.

Thus, at Beas, the idea of the guru of the age appears not as the continuing manifestation of a unique entity, but as an eternal office, always filled by a living person. This concept of the guru of the age bears some resemblance to the Sufis' *qutb,* the "pole" of the universe, the axis of the spiritual hierarchy. Carrying with it a whole set of lower spiritual offices, the Sufis' *qutb* is a more complex concept than the Radhasoamis' guru of the age. But it is also a well-known concept among Sufis, and given the Urdu-Persian overlay to Radhasoami tradition, one with which the Beas gurus were no doubt familiar. In any event, both the Sufis' *qutb* and the Radhasoamis' guru of the age serve to give some kind of unique cosmic status to certain living holy men.

For someone to become the uniquely qualified holy man of the age, according to Beas tradition, he himself must be initiated into the supreme truth. Thus, every perfect master has needed a guru, including, of course, Soamiji, whose guru is usually said to be Tulsi Sahib. The relationship between a perfect master and his guru is sometimes described through the metaphor of the guru as lamp that we have already seen mentioned by Sahajo Bai: even though one lamp may be perfectly adjusted and brimming with oil, it still needs contact with another one already lit to shed light by itself.

A doctrine that all true *sant*s must themselves have living gurus leads to the theological problem of the "first guru"—which is not, however, much of an issue. The abundant literature from Beas usually deals with more vital problems of spiritual life, leaving this theoretical question unanswered. According to one devotee, in fact, no teaching exists on the question. The gurus, though, when asked, provided some answers. One successor to Kirpal Singh said that a perfect master came along with the creation, and that there normally remained only one perfect master at a time. Another of Kirpal Singh's successors affirmed the second half of that statement, adding that otherwise there would be no more souls left for the world—a remark that recalls the theme of the overcrowded heaven that frequently recurs in classical Hindu mythology.[19]

Taken more seriously than theoretical worries about a primal perfect guru are the immediate practical criteria used for determining succeeding *satgurus* of the age. An examination of the important split in the Beas lineage that occurred after the passing in 1948 of Sawan Singh, Jaimal Singh's illustrious successor, can help in identifying these criteria.

Of Sawan Singh's tens of thousands of disciples, two gained substantial followings: Kirpal Singh and Charan Singh, who holds the seat at Beas. Disciples of Charan Singh affirm that Sawan Singh not only definitely selected his successor before his passing, but also specifically designated him in a formal will. This successor, they say, was Jagat Singh, who before his death left a will nominating Charan Singh. Among the eighteenth-century disciples of Charandas, we have seen an earlier precedent for claims of formal written designation to succession, but written testaments do not in fact seem to have been customary among *sants*. So disciples of Charan Singh sometimes say that Sawan Singh provided for a will because he foresaw the problems that would follow upon Kirpal Singh's claim. But the will's lack of precedent can at the same time give Kirpal Singh's disciples some justification for questioning the circumstances surrounding its composition and signing; and Kirpal Singh understands that Sawan Singh, during the days of his final illness, gave him clear verbal directions to carry on his work.[20] His disciples also make reference to events of a more public nature: remarks made by Sawan Singh in front of witnesses that suggested Kirpal Singh's successorship; jealousies aroused on his giving initiation through Kirpal Singh; Sawan's bestowing upon Kirpal a mantle, a symbol of succession among Indian Sufis.[21]

In addition to such external criteria of legitimacy, both Charan Singh and Kirpal Singh speak of certain internal signs. In answer to a disciple's question about Kirpal Singh, Charan Singh mentions, in addition to Sawan Singh's will, an internal "key," "given at the time of initiation":

> As regards S. Kirpal Singh, let him say or do anything he likes. Sooner or later he will have to render account for his actions. You have been

given the key at the time of Initiation and can satisfy yourself as to whether or not he is a true Master. It would not be in good taste for me to go into detail, but I will say this much, that the Great Master Sawan Singh Ji never gave him permission to initiate anyone, and duly appointed Sardar Bahadur Jagat Singh Ji as His Successor by a legally executed will, in writing and duly witnessed, so as to leave no doubt about the matter . . .[22]

While Charan Singh's disciples can look to a public "legally executed" will to resolve any doubts as to the legitimacy of their guru, those of Kirpal Singh stress the importance of internal criteria. Kirpal Singh is emphatic that a true master should be able to give his disciples some spiritual experience at the time of initiation—and this, he gives reason to believe, does not usually occur at Beas. When a disciple questions him about initiation at Beas he replies matter-of-factly:

> The other day I gave initiation to six hundred and fifty-three people. All saw Light—about two hundred saw the Master's Form. The teachings at Beas are the same, but the words given at initiation now *are not charged.* That is the difference. . . . They're afraid of asking for any experience . . .[23]

Thus, while the basic grounds for legitimacy in succession is designation by the previous guru, the criteria used for recognizing that designation are both internal and external and can be stated in terms of formal evidence (the wills, the mantle, the "inner key"), or as the successor's evident spiritual power. The disciples of Charan Singh, who actually holds the Beas seat, seem to look sooner for criteria involving trustworthy forms; those attracted by the spiritual personality of Kirpal Singh—for whom formal public evidence is undeniably more tenuous—cite instead the guru's demonstrated power.

In the passages from Charan Singh and Kirpal Singh just cited, each guru manages to keep a diplomatic reserve; yet neither really tries to hide his attitude toward the fact that the other is giving initiation. The open antagonism that can develop between strong personalities—if not between groups of their less-gifted followers—would also seem to give emotional support to the idea of the one perfect master: not only are there definite criteria for determining just who is a true *sant,* but those who do not meet them are patent imposters.

Still, among those attached to the Beas sublineages, the one perfect master of the age nevertheless remains within an open-ended *sant* tradition in which holy men from the different world religions are respected. This tradition is almost always extended to include those Persian Sufi masters mentioned by Soamiji.[24] Thus, L. R. Puri, writing from a Beas perspective, notes that not only did "Guru Nanak, Kabir Sahib, Swami Ji, Tulsi Sahib, Dadu Dayal, Paltu Sahib . . . all [reach] the final stage of 'Sat-Purush Radha Swami'," but so did "Mansur Hallaj, Shamas-i-Tabriz, Maulana Rumi and Hafiz Sahib."[25]

In the modern world it is easy for the idea of a great fellowship of *sant*s to become that of a brotherhood that encompasses the globe. "All true saints are equal," declares Puri. Admittedly, the qualifications he gives for being a true saint are stringent indeed, but he does admit that people within the different world religions can achieve the highest goal. Explaining "how religions come into existence," Puri writes:

> When true Saints disappear from a Spiritual mystic school, then it degenerates into a common Religion and loses its deep spirituality and the method of inner realization of Reality and Truth. The so-called followers of the original Saints . . . forget the universal principles and methods that were taught by the original Saints, Gurus or Masters.[26]

Kirpal Singh, in a similar unifying spirit, was the moving force behind three well-attended international conferences of religion in Delhi. Darshan Singh, his natural son and one of his successors, has, moreover, made plans to establish an institute for the study of comparative religion at his ashram. Thus, in certain circumstances the Radhasoami master can appear as one holy man among many, presenting a teaching that represents the essence of the religions of the world.

Yet a grandly syncretic and unifying vision of religious truth does not in itself usually offer a firm basis for a functioning religious tradition; leaders of active religious movements usually have to narrow their teachings to present a less relative truth concentrated in a more definite immanent focus. In the larger Radhasoami centers, as we have seen, the guru himself is often perceived in the role of a singular—or at least very special—personality: the unique perfect master of the age. However, in one small group around a successor to Kirpal Singh I saw less attention paid to the singular cosmic status of the guru himself than to the defining role of the Hindi *sant* tradition as heritage.

More than most other devotees I spoke with, those of Ajaib Singh, known as Santji, seem to take seriously ideas about multiple succession and a legitimate plurality of gurus. Santji himself, in answering a disciple's query, mentions two individuals whom he believes Sawan Singh commissioned to give *nām,* and suggests that there may be others. At the same time, Santji seems to pay more attention than do most Radhasoami gurus to the figure of Kabir. He has, in fact, commissioned an English translation of *Anurāg Sāgar,* one of the most important books of the Chhatisgarhi Kabirpanthis. This book not only uses *sant* vocabulary to reveal an extensive cosmology, but also presents Kabir as having incarnated in the four previous Hindu ages. The doctrine of Kabir's previous incarnations can then provide an answer to the theoretical problem of the primal guru: Santji for his part has publicly declared "that Kabir was the *very first* Master of this world."[27] Instead of an emphasis on the one true living *sant* who presents the essence of the world's religions, we are here offered the possibility that a number of *sant*s manifest within a specific Indian heritage.

While the guru in Beas tradition, then, is seen to have access to the highest truth, his position as a being in the cosmos depends in part on just how *sant* tradition itself is perceived. To what extent is it a global tradition focusing on a singular personality? To what extent is it a specific, if pluralistic, Indian one? Certainly almost all people connected with the Beas sublineages who are versed in sectarian matters will identify their tradition as *sant mat,* in contrast to the Radhasoami "religion" of Agra. But in understanding their tradition as the somewhat open-ended "teachings of the *sant*s," Beas people are faced with two problems. One is the fact of spiritual diversity on earth: all holy men everywhere in fact do not seem to practice the exercises Soamiji distilled from the Hindi tradition. If the *sant* tradition is extended to include all great masters, in what way are "all true saints equal"? The second involves the dynamics of personal devotion and spiritual rivalry: how does the devotee manage to worship his guru as god and not think less of other, perhaps competing, holy men? A more characteristic Hindu context offers some specific avenues of approach to these problems, and in studying our next two figures we will see alternative varieties of unifying truth and different modes of devotion.

The Reassertion of the Holy Man and the Hindu Resources

The spiritual careers of Pandit Faqir Chand of Hoshiarpur, Punjab, and of Thakur Mansingh—called Malik Sahib—of Gwalior, Madhya Pradesh, are similar in a number of ways. Both trace a lineage to Soamiji, but through relatively minor sub-branches: Faqir Chand through Maharishi Shivbrat Lal and Huzur Sahib; Malik Sahib through Shyam Lal and Chachaji Maharaj. Both feel that they have completed the Radhasoami *sādhanā,* and both have acted as gurus in that tradition. But both have subsequently had other experiences that convinced them that there is more to spiritual reality than Radhasoami devotion alone. Both are thus consciously aware of giving their disciples something other than just what they received from their Radhasoami gurus. For both, moreover, the Hindu heritage serves as the source of the new gifts they offer. Neither is a narrowly sectarian Hindu, each finding in his Hinduism a greater unifying truth; but the unifying truths presented by each are different indeed.[28]

The Holy Man Who Would Not Be a Guru

Pandit Faqir Chand in 1979 was an agile ninety-three, getting up to close windows and open doors himself at his ashram in Hoshiarpur. His following is larger and more diverse than that of Malik Sahib, and the more plebeian elements in it sometimes put him into the role of a popular holy man—a role he will play, though he complains about it. "These people don't come to see me for spiritual benefit," he says, "but for material gain." Nevertheless, during the few days I spent with him he regularly acceded to devotees' requests for material blessings: several times he accepted someone's proffered rupee-note, signed it, and handed it back; and once, receiving a request by mail, he thought a moment and then provided a new store with a rather prosaic, Hindi-English name: "Amar Cloth House."

He stated then, and it is affirmed in his recorded discourses, that his major realization came through his disciples: *they* served as his guru. "They say they see my form inside, and they think it's me," he said. "But I'm not aware of being there. It's all in their mind." Hearing so many reports of his false form appearing to his devotees made Faqir Chand look for his real form, his true self. He says to his disciples:

> My True FORM is a STATE within me, where nothing manifests, and if at all something manifests I do not accept it. He who dwells in such a state is known as a Saint or a recluse. A Faqir (recluse) dwells in his own FORM. I feel indebted to you, who helped me to realize my "SELF".

Earlier, he says, he used to see wonderful scenes in Radhasoami meditation, but his disciples' inner visions of him made him understand just what these were:

> Your experiences proved [to] me, that whatever forms, visions or scenes I used to enjoy within, they were all the creations of my mind. It helped

> me to go beyond the realms of mind, while living in mind. I have understood the mind and its working. Now I do not allow my 'Self' to get involved in mind and its creations.[29]

Faqir Chand's teachings thus take a decidedly Vedantic turn: the guru's image is a product of the disciple's mind, *māyā* like everything else; one should attempt to live in the self beyond mind.

But since the guru's image is merely a product of the disciple's mind, the living, outer guru insisted upon in most Radhasoami tradition becomes all the more important: if the disciple's mind is not pure, the inner guru will guide him falsely. For most people, then, Faqir Chand stresses the role of the guru as counselor for everyday living. He no longer gives the traditional Radhasoami initiation; instead, he says, his words are the initiatory *nām.* His followers should meditate on what he says and act accordingly. Still, for those of his devotees who might profit from Radhasoami practice, he has a number of disciples authorized to give the traditional initiation in his name.[30]

Faqir Chand's radical revision of the teaching on the guru is, not surprisingly, rejected by some of his most devoted disciples. One close disciple, who was living at the Hoshiarpur ashram when I was there, tells of seeing Faqir Chand's image in his heart before he ever met him. He was trying to meditate on Shiva, he said, and was upset at seeing a strange *sādhū* there instead. He still doesn't believe that this image wasn't somehow connected with Faqir Chand's person, and says he disagrees with his guru's interpretation. Two other Radhasoami gurus questioned later affirmed that, yes, the image of the guru the disciple sees within was somehow emanating from them, and that they were aware of a connection between the image and themselves. So Faqir Chand has some grounds when he proclaims that he was the first to reveal that the image of the guru is not really the guru. He understands this proclamation as part of a commission from his guru, Maharishi, to "change the (Radhasoami) teachings." The teachings need to become simpler, says Faqir Chand, so that they might be more accessible to the common people who approach him.

The *Sant* Who Is Also a Yogi

Malik Sahib also emphasizes how difficult it is to advance far on the Radhasoami path. But the easier path he provides is of a very different nature. It is a yogic path, but one which places great weight on the actions of the guru's grace. The power of the guru's grace is known in this tradition as *guru-shakti,* and it comes to the disciple through *shaktipāt* initiation.

This *shaktipāt* initiation has a lineage of its own, a lineage with which Malik Sahib came in contact in the later part of his life, after having served for many years as a guru in the Radhasoami tradition. Radhasoami gurus have traditionally been self-supporting—often, like Malik Sahib, through careers in government service. The story goes that one day while posted in another town, Malik Sahib became acquainted with a major Swami in this *shaktipāt* lineage, and between the two a close spiritual friendship developed. This Swami's guru, still alive, eventually met Malik Sahib and invited him to his ashram in Rishikesh. The two meditated together for six days, after which time Malik Sahib was authorized to give the *shaktipāt* initiation.[31]

Malik Sahib's disciples, however, are still said to have access to the Radhasoami devotion, now interpreted in a Hindu context as the essence of Vaishnava experience. This interpretation is reflected in the verbal form of a *nām* that Malik Sahib very frequently gives, which is based on the names of important Vaishnava deities. *Shaktipāt* experience, however, derives from Shaiva tantra, and entails a *guru-bhakti* less sweet and adoring than the Radhasoamis'.

This different attitude of devotion can be seen in different practices of succession. Less emphasis on the virtues of humility allows qualified disciples to give initiation in their own name during their guru's lifetime, not a normal practice among Radhasoamis. A lesser degree of personal attachment to the guru makes it easier for disciples to accept the fact of multiple succession—particularly when, as is not unusual, qualified successors have been clearly functioning as gurus during their common guru's lifetime. This was, in fact, the case with Malik Sahib and his *shaktipāt* guru. So while there was a heated succession dispute after the passing of Malik Sahib's Radhasoami guru, Malik Sahib is accepted by most people concerned, if perhaps somewhat grudgingly by some, as one of his second guru's five or six qualified disciples. (Two were not giving initiation during their guru's lifetime and are not recognized by all.) The principle of multiple succession is indeed the norm in Hindu tantric traditions, within most of which, as we shall see in the next chapter, the appearance of a plurality of gurus is taken as a matter of course.

Malik Sahib's dual role as the source of both Radhasoami *nām* and Hindu *shaktipāt* initiation has led to some temporary minor predicaments regarding Hindu traditions of caste and life-stage. One of these recalls the story told above, where Govind sought initiation from

Gulal,[32] though it has a happier resolution. While the followers of Radhasoami gurus in fact come largely from clean castes, Radhasoami tradition does not sanction the spiritual legitimacy of caste distinctions. Thus Malik Sahib, like Gulal a *kṣatriya* householder, would give initiation to all he deemed qualified; but unlike Gulal in the case of Govind, he had no qualms about initiating Brahmans, of higher traditional rank than he.

After Malik Sahib began giving *shaktipāt,* his old Brahman disciples naturally received that too. But when a Brahman *sannyāsī*—senior to him even in years—approached him specifically for the *shaktipāt* initiation, Malik Sahib began to have some of the same doubts that Gulal apparently did. *His* reaction, however, was to write to the senior guru-brother who had led him to his *shaktipāt* guru. His guru-brother confirmed his doubts: in fact, he wrote, it was better not to give the initiation; however, the *sannyāsī* could be sent to him, the guru-brother, who was himself both a *sannyāsī* and a Brahman. But, the story goes, the *sannyāsī* insisted that he wanted initiation from Malik Sahib alone, so Malik Sahib wrote to his own guru in the *shaktipāt* tradition, a Brahman householder. The householder-guru's decision differed from that of his *sannyāsī* disciple. In a long letter citing precedents from Sanskritic tradition, he replied that it would indeed be proper for Malik Sahib to give the initiation, which he did.

In bringing *sant* tradition into a full synthesis with elements of Hinduism, Malik Sahib shows less resemblance to Gulal than to Charandas, the liberal Hindu of Mughal Delhi. As a matter of fact, Charandas seems to be one of Malik Sahib's favorite *sant*s, his *bānī* being read frequently at Malik Sahib's ashram. Both Malik Sahib and Charandas offer a type of synthetic, unifying truth that differs markedly from the unity seen by Faqir Chand. The Vedantic perspective taken by Faqir Chand looks to the one truth underlying all forms of knowledge. Malik Sahib, on the other hand, describes both Radhasoami and yogic experience as total, though in different ways. Faqir Chand's is a reductive truth: the many are finally one. Malik Sahib's is more integral: the one has many aspects.

Certainly, no unifying synthesis is completely integral. Regardless of the religious tradition in which it is based, each has at least some one unifying principle. But traditions within a Hindu context, with its subtle fluid substance, are probably the most comfortable among those within the world religions about incorporating pieces of other traditions *whole.* Thus, alongside the severe reductions of a Shankara, India has always known more integrative approaches to unifying truth: in classical times, the Gita; today, the exemplary experience of Ramakrishna and the all-encompassing spiritual intellect of Sri Aurobindo.

Faqir Chand and Malik Sahib, in presenting their inherited Radhasoami traditions within the greater unifying truths they came to know, tend to lose their identity as Radhasoami masters. At the same time, the unifying Hindu context on which they draw gives them new identities as holy men. What changes in their images occur as they move between the Radhasoami and more traditional Hindu contexts? And in what guises does the holy man appear within the other great religious contexts of India, which highlight distinct immanent foci of their own?

III

THE HOLY MAN IN INDIA AND THE PLACE OF THE *SANTS*

7

The Indian Master in Greater Religious Contexts

The *sants* do not stand alone as holy men against the postclassical Indian landscape. The same religiocultural soil out of which they emerged also nurtured figures from Buddhism and Indian Islam, as well as from Hinduism. These greater religious contexts necessarily add their own dimensions to the image of the holy man, seen so far among the *sants* in a bare and unadorned form. We shall now consider the ways in which the different universes of meaning central to the world religions flourishing in India inform the figure of the holy man as focus of the divine. How does the image of the holy man vary in traditions where iconic worship is the norm—or where there are normative strictures *against* iconic worship? How is the holy man at hand seen in relation to a sanctified heritage or a cosmically unique founder of tradition? The distinctive identities revealed by Hinduism, Buddhism, and Islam in India will eventually suggest some conclusions about the particular religious synthesis presented by the *sants*.

The specific Hindu, Buddhist, and Islamic traditions to be discussed here, though in many ways highly diverse, have a number of characteristics in common. Most fundamental from our analytic perspective, they all present the holy man as the dominant immanent focus. Moreover, the spiritual power of the holy man is seen to be linked in some vital way with his practice, a practice which can be typified as "yogic" in a middle-range sense of the term (somewhere between Sri Aurobindo's "All Life Is Yoga"[1] and the classical yoga sutras of Patanjali). In this chapter "yoga" will refer to those practices of Indian asceticism (which we can stretch to include those of some Indian Sufis) that entail a perception of the subtle dynamics of the physical body. When these practices are grounded in the developed philosophy and ritual of the

Hindu and Buddhist tantras, they are sometimes called tantric—a term that to the ears of the Hindi speaker most often connotes magical practice, not the sexual ritual that excites many Westerners.

The guru, with his yogic power, can serve as an esoteric master for serious disciples and can, according to his specific tradition, lead them to apparently different kinds of realizations. But the image of the powerful guru, tantric or otherwise, can also serve as a figure in more popular mythologies. The *sant*s have shown us the importance of the image of the guru for both yogic vision and popular imagination. They have also revealed the crucial role of concepts of lineage in sectarian developments featuring holy men. These two perceptions of the master—his image in space and his lineage in time—will be the bases for our comparisons here.

Both the esoteric and the more popular traditions of holy men are found in Hinduism, Buddhism, and Indian Islam. While we will be concerned primarily with the Indian variants of these world religions, we will not be overly rigorous in limiting ourselves to strictly Indian materials. Though an examination of Indian Sufism can be grounded fairly well in Indo-Persian texts and the continuing tradition on the subcontinent, literate Indian Sufis were conversant with their greater Islamic heritage, and themselves made use of Persian and Arabic sources. It is, moreover, the Tibetan Buddhists who have preserved most of what we know of Indian Vajrayana, the "Diamond Vehicle" of the Buddhist tantras. Thus, an intelligent treatment of tantric Buddhism usually demands substantial consideration of Tibetan developments, many of which stand in close continuity with their Indian sources.

Guru-Bhakti and Enlightenment in the Indic Traditions

The idiom of fluid substance familiar to *sant*s and Vaishnavas also lies behind the phenomenal world known to *tantrika*s, both Hindu and Buddhist. Yet the Buddhist *tantrika* differs from the Hindu in his perspective on both the roots of phenomenal reality and the means to achieve ultimate knowledge. While the Hindu knows the real as rooted in a constant ground of being, finally continuous with his person, the Buddhist is more aware of constructing the reality he knows. And while the Hindu seeks to recapture the visions revealed to ancient seers, the Buddhist seeks to understand a definite teaching. As conduits of sacred knowledge, then, holy men in Hinduism and Buddhism are likely to present contrasting images.

The differences between Hindu and Buddhist tantric gurus are evident in both popular story and esoteric tantric practice. Where the Hindu guru, existing in a world of continuous substance, gives the disciple a chance to merge with him through offerings of "body, mind, and wealth," the Buddhist master constructs situations that illustrate the value of a teaching. Where the Hindu yogi knows the guru within as an eternal divine being who may appear to him when recollected, the Buddhist is, again, more careful about constructing divine forms according to learned conventions. Finally, as a basis of faith, the Hindu guru is for his disciples a channel of ancient wisdom more accessible and trustworthy even than the gods—who are many, and sometimes capricious; in Vajrayana, on the other hand, the guru vividly embodies the immortal teachings once revealed by the Buddha.

Trials and Their Rewards in the Hagiographical Literature

As among *sant*s, popular stories of guru devotion among Hindus and Buddhists often play upon the tension between the disciple's ardent desire to serve and the guru's mysterious wisdom and unfathomable will. One common resolution to this tension comes through the guru's deliberate trial of his disciple, which may then lead to the disciple's enlightenment. In the Hindu and Buddhist religious contexts, however, both the trial and enlightenment take different forms.

Within postclassical Hindu popular tradition, the image of the powerful yogi is well represented in the stories of the early *nāth*s. Buddhists find comparable figures in the lore of the illustrious *siddha*s. The legendary figures of both traditions are said to have lived in the earlier part of the postclassical period, from about the eighth century onward. Many of the legends, particularly of the *siddha*s, probably do revolve around historical persons who lived during an era when both lettered tantric traditions and spiritually independent yogis flourished widely. But the most important of these yogis have been delimited in later lettered tradition to manageable—and auspicious—numbers: the *nāth*s are nine; the *siddha*s eighty-four. Today, certain *nāth*s and *siddha*s are particularly revered in specific religious communities. Householder *nāth*s continue to look to their illustrious ascetic predecessors, as well as to the early *sant*s who carried on the *nāth* tradition of iconoclastic holy men. Important *siddha*s figure prominently in some Vajrayana lineages. Beyond these limited communities, stories of illustrious *siddha*s and *nāth*s are current in popular regional lore, presenting common people with both images of powerful yogis and models for guru-devotion.

To understand the way in which a characteristically Hindu idiom presents the disciple's trials, we shall examine two stories. The first is about the devotion of Gorakh, the most illustrious of the *nāth* yogis, to his guru Matsyendra; the second is the famous legend of Guru Gobind Singh's creation of the Sikh *khālsā* out of a *sant* lineage. The story of Gorakh is well known, and has been depicted in Hindi cinema. The version to be presented here, however, follows that heard from a professional Vaishnava story-teller at Malik Sahib's ashram.

Gorakh Nath, we are told, had gone to beg food for himself and his ailing guru. Unsuccessful and desperate, he met an old woman who offered to trade cooked food for one of Gorakh's eyes. Gorakh Nath accepted the terms without hesitation ("his fingernails were very long," the storyteller noted). When Gorakh returned in the evening he tried to hide his wound from his guru, who acted as though he did not know of Gorakh's sacrifice. Gorakh was again unsuccessful on his begging rounds the next night, but he met the same woman and again accepted her terms. Now completely blind, Gorakh managed to stumble home and offer his guru a meal. At this point, the latter revealed that he had known what had happened, and Gorakh "saw something he had never seen before."

Many of the same devotional elements in the tale of Gorakh and Matsyendra are found in the story of Guru Gobind Singh's founding of the *khālsā,* the "pure" Sikh order. While in fact telling of the origins of the Sikh sectarian community, the story has become part of common North Indian lore. Max Macauliffe, staying close to his Sikh sources, gives us a spirited rendition of the tale. Guru Gobind Singh had summoned his followers outside his tent, and when they had all assembled he asked if " 'any one of his beloved Sikhs [were] ready to lay down his life for him?' . . . All grew pale. . . . A third time he spoke in a louder voice, 'If there be any true Sikh of mine, let him give me his head as an offering and proof of his faith.' " One disciple finally accepted the challenge and entered into the tent with the guru. Outside, the assembled followers heard the sharp thud of steel cutting through flesh, and the guru emerged alone, his sword dripping with blood. One by one, four more volunteers came forward. Four more times the thud of the sword was heard, and the guru displayed it soaked in blood.

Finally, the guru revealed that his demands for a disciple's life had only been a test: the disciples were still alive and goat's blood was on the sword. Guru Gobind Singh addressed the five who had offered themselves to him: "My brethren, you are in my form and I am in yours. He who thinketh there is any difference between us erreth exceedingly." The devoted disciples were to be known as the *pānj piāre,* "the five beloved," and to be the foundation of the *khālsā;* they are given *amrit,* "immortal" nectar, a special *prasād.*[2]

Both *nāth* and Sikh stories extoll selfless devotion to the guru's person. Conscious surrender of self in the guru results in a divine reward that comes directly through the guru's grace. The reward as well as the offering is presented in substantial terms: Gorakh gives his eyes and receives a materially transformed vision; the *pānj piāre* are ready to give their heads and receive a special *prasād.* The pānj piāre, in fact, have realized a substantial merging with their guru: "You are in my form and I am in yours."

The stories of the famous *siddha*s' devotion to their gurus are probably more familiar in popular Tibetan lore than are any comparable examples in Hindu lore. But the more monastic orientation of Vajrayana in both India and Tibet has given some hagiographies classical literary forms that have made them much more than recensions of popular narrative. The way the tales are told reveals characteristic aspects of Vajrayana religious experience, an experience less of union with the substantial divine than of insight into the real nature of phenomena—which in fact entails a leap out of the substantial universe.

To find a test of faith comparable to those seen above, we can examine the life of Naropa as found in a Tibetan text that stands fairly close to the Indian tradition.[3] Both Naropa and his guru Tilopa, lest we forget, were Indian, and, according to Guenther, "it is likely that this text [belonging to the late twelfth century] is the first authoritative Tibetan account of Naropa's life that has been written."[4] After a number of minor visionary experiences in which his guru appears to him in various guises, Naropa finally meets Tilopa in person. In twelve years Tilopa instructs Naropa twelve times, usually within the context of a rather amusing situation of guru devotion. One year, when Naropa is sucked cold by leeches through Tilopa's design, he receives from him an instruction on mystic heat. The next year, Tilopa burns Naropa with heated reeds and then gives him instruction on the "apparition," which is free from pleasure and pain.[5]

Like the trials of Gorakh and the *pānj piāre,* these situations are presented as tests of faith: Naropa, at the suggestion of his guru, unhesitatingly gets himself into obviously foolhardy and painful predicaments. But they prove to be more than simple tests rewarded directly by the guru's grace. Tilopa constructs each painful situation to give Naropa insight into an aspect of the suffering inherent in the phenomenal world. The lesson for Naropa to learn is less that he should surrender himself to the guru (which is taken for granted) than that he misunderstands the true nature of phenomena. So Tilopa usually asks him to "look into the mirror of his mind," and proceeds to give him a *teaching*.

These characteristics of the disciple's test in Vajrayana hagiography do not seem to be dependent on the sophisticated form of the biography of Naropa that we have referred to here. Abhayadatta's short narrations of the lives of the eighty-four *siddha*s also show us gurus constructing situations that help reveal mystical teachings. Here, the future *siddha* Bhadrapa, a Brahman, receives instruction only after his guru breaks his pride by forcing him to sweep and plaster a house. But through this humbling situation, the guru—an enigmatic yogi—is able to present a cryptic teaching:

> The color of the plaster is the symbol of meditation. The conjunction of the three—the wall, the plaster, and the act of applying it—is the symbol of the result.[6]

While the gurus in both the stories above construct situations to illustrate teachings, the content of the teachings revealed in the stories depends in part on the literary genre of each: Tilopa's instructions consist of complex tantric doctrines embedded in a hagiography of his disciple; the yogi's instruction to Bhadrapa about the wall and the plaster appears as an enigmatic insight in a brief didactic sketch. Moralistic narratives in a more popular genre, moreover, often conclude with a statement that the protagonist received enlightenment through hearing the Buddha's teachings, but present nothing at all of the content of these teachings. As a symbol, then, the Buddha's teachings can represent the source of all spiritual accomplishment.

For Buddha as a singular personality revealed a basis of personal salvation in his discourses, and the different traditions of Buddhism give a crucial place to specific received teachings understood to derive from these discourses. Specific received teachings, as we shall see, certainly seem to be more crucial for the Buddhist *tantrika* than for the Hindu in constructing his visualizations. The different patterns of Hindu and Buddhist meditation that emerge, moreover, seem related to the differing attitudes of the Hindu and Buddhist *tantrika* toward the guru, whose image for both is routinely contemplated within, like that of a god.

Gurus and Gods in Tantric Practice

For the Radhasoamis, too, the image of the guru within is a reflection of the deity. Most Radhasoamis, moreover, see this image as a manifestation of the living guru's psychic presence, which can lead to passionate argument over just whose image to contemplate at the time of succession. Since the guru's image within is really the projection of a living spiritual being, an attempt to visualize it consciously from an icon outside is of little spiritual benefit. A disciple asks Babuji Maharaj, the last Radhasoami guru at Soami Bagh:

> So long as Guru's form does not become manifest within, can one contemplate His photograph, or not?
>
> Answer: If you fix your gaze on the photograph, you will see nothing but the photograph in *Dhyān* [contemplation], too. Only this much help can be taken from the photograph that, by looking at it, one can refresh one's remembrance of the form.[7]

The insistence of Babuji Maharaj that the internal image must precede its outer representation appears consonant with central tenets of Hindu iconographic tradition. In a brilliant essay on art in Indian life, Coomaraswamy stresses the importance of the maxim *dhyātvā kuryāt:* the Indian image-maker should "contemplate, then make." The image-maker must certainly be aware of the traditional descriptions of the deities learned from teachers and found in texts. But before he creates he should know the god inwardly, visualizing and identifying with him. The way is then open for the image-maker to "have direct realizations of his own, for he may gain 'direct access to the highest source of knowledge—Vac Saraswati, or the Lord . . . of image-bearing light.' "[8]

The creators of the Hindu calendar art that flourishes today, while following well-known conventions, seem to function adequately without first hand knowledge of the classical texts—which in any case were more concerned with temple architecture and sculpture than with painting. In adhering to traditional models without being tightly bound to them, the more inspired of these artists might sympathize with the following comment on the reality of divine forms by Shri Aurobindo, himself long concerned with problems of both art and yoga:

> . . . the supraphysical planes are not bound to . . . forms like the physical. The forms there are expressive, not determinative . . .
>
> As to the gods, man can build forms which they will accept but these forms too are inspired into man's mind from the planes to which the god belongs.[9]

Even though the artist may create divine images, they remain genuine, inspired from the heavenly worlds. Thus, more refined works of Hindu calendar art often find their way into the meditation room of the practicing yogi, where they may be used, like the photograph of the guru, to "refresh the remembrance of the form."

Present-day practitioners of Buddhist tantra in Tibetan tradition, on the other hand, are more likely to build up detailed visualizations from icons *outside.* Indeed, one Tibetan monk I met in India insisted that at his monastery most were instructed to visualize the guru himself from a photograph, instructions that clearly run counter to those of Babuji Maharaj above. Similarly, while early Buddhism seems to have given a significant role to the artist's inspiration in the creation of images,[10] modern Tibetan *tanka* painters are concerned about the exact reproduction of the image prescribed in their manuals. One artist I talked to, stressing the importance of his work, said that if he made a mistake the monks would meditate incorrectly. In exceptional cases, he continued, a high lama may see a form in a slightly different posture and tell an artist to prepare a new image, which might eventually find its way into the manuals. The manuals themselves are very precise and systematic. Students are taught to sketch out the meditational deities against lined grids so that the limbs are placed in just the right attitudes.[11]

The contrast between the Hindu's realization of traditionally inspired forms and the Buddhist's constructing them according to the correct teachings is certainly not absolute, but rather a matter of emphasis. Hindu *yantra*s are indeed exactly reproduced and handed down. But these are line drawings oriented around a point, not normally featuring images to be visualized, as in the Buddhist *maṇḍala*s, though commentaries sometimes assign deities to a *yantra*'s various directions. Hindu *tantrika*s, too, commonly make an effort to visualize the deity systematically, "from the sole of His foot to His face, or from His face to the sole of his foot"; but in Buddhist tradition attention is also systematically given to degrees of visual plasticity.[12] From a Buddhist perspective, moreover, the deities can seem at least as real as anything else in the phenomenal universe. Thus, despite broad similarities among yogic techniques throughout India, the different epistemological perspectives of Hinduism and Buddhism inform the practice of contemplation in the two traditions, and in so doing, give characteristic tones to devotees' attitudes toward gods and gurus.

The difference between the attitudes of the Hindu and Buddhist *tantrika* toward the reality of divine images is revealed through the way in which each typically visualizes his deities. The Hindu devotee usually contemplates his deities one at a time, with only their conventional mounts or spouses as appendages. He may, moreover, subtly offer to his object of worship the parts of his inner being, as the devotee is enjoined to do in the *āratī*s of the Radhasoami gurus. The Buddhist *tantrika*'s contemplation of a deity is usually more detailed, and is very often preceded by a meditation on the ten directions of space, filled with countless compassionate Buddhas and bodhisattvas. The Buddhist *tantrika* may, moreover, move the deity about, controlling it as he worships it. The Hindu's offering of the various aspects of his inner self to the deity recalls the substantial offerings of disciples in the stories of Gorakh and Gobind Singh. The adept Buddhist meditator consciously building up and manipulating divine images within recalls Tilopa (and Bhadrapa's yogi-guru) constructing revelatory situations outside.[13]

The Buddhist *tantrika*'s conscious manipulation of images is perhaps better seen in his practice of magically absorbing the deity's power, usually more frequent with him than with the Hindu. At the same time, these meditations demonstrate more profoundly the Buddhist turn that can be given to the Indic world view seen earlier in Hindu devotion. Stephan Beyer translates a meditation on Tara as Chintachakra that clearly reveals a world of flowing substance and the yogi's definite identification with the deity's person.

When the Vajrayana master instructs his disciples to "visualize the guru as the Holy Lady," they should see Chintachakra over their heads, "surrounded by the Conquerors and their sons." By the power of the guru's prayers, "a measureless stream of the nectar of deathless life" then enters the disciples from "all the parts of the bodies of the gurus of the lineage and of the Holy Lady." The stream enters the disciples through the tops of their heads and fills their bodies. With this their sins "emerge black and thick" through their pores and sense organs "in the form of smoke and soot." At the master's word, the gurus visualized above and the innumerable surrounding deities "dissolve into the Holy Lady." The conclusion of the meditation has the goddess separating another body from her own. This second body, "melting" into the the essential "nectar of deathless life . . . dissolves" into the disciples through the tops of their heads. The "body, speech, and mind" of the disciples are then "inseparably of a single taste" with the goddess.[14]

The disciples' identification with Chintachakra here is clearly one of fluid and personal substance: the stuff of the goddess' "body, speech, and mind" "dissolves" into the disciples'. Nevertheless, it differs from the patterns of uniting with the deity that are likely to occur in Hindu contexts. The Vaishnava of the songs in chapter 1 has to endure the involuntary pull of the Lord's divine vision. And in order to realize the eternal substantial unity of his own true nature with the godhead's, the Hindu yogi—like the Radhasoami performing inner *āratī*—can offer the subtle parts of his being to the deity in a more controlled way. By contrast, the Buddhist yogi's identification with the deity in the passage above takes place in one deliberate movement preceded by an extended process of directed attention, a definite act in an elaborate world of constructed images. The meditational deities of Hinduism and Buddhism, then, reveal a typical contrast: the Hindu god is adored alone as a single, attractive, and essentially real divine source, while the Buddhist is not only an attractive focus of all the beings existent in the ultimate emptiness, but is also sometimes subject to conscious manipulation within it.

These different perceptions of the divine image in space correspond to different attitudes of devotion to the deity in Hindu and Buddhist tantra. The important Hindu deities, representing a development of unity, usually have complex personalities that contain contradictions kept in balance. The powerful mythologies that present these contradictions are suggested by the mounts and consorts sometimes included in their *dhyānas*: Ganesha, the elephant god, rides a mouse; the beautiful Adya Kalika stands supreme as her consort Maha-Kala dances humbled before her.[15] Essentially real, the Hindu deities often act spontaneously of their own accord, giving their devotees unsought *darshan.* For the yogi, Shiva and Devi can, indeed, become intense and concentrated objects of devotion.

The divine love of the Buddhist, however, is more spread out. Together with a focus on a particular deity comes compassion for the myriads of beings. A number of the myriad beings that can be visualized by the Buddhist *tantrika,* moreover, are mere abstractions, with little subconscious mythological support. Tucci writes of the deification even of different instruments of worship: the incense, the drum, the mantric formula. Indeed, the Lord of one of the central Buddhist tantric cycles,

Hevajra (literally: Hey, Vajra!), seems to be a deification of the formula for invoking the symbol of both thunderbolt and diamond that has given its name to the Buddhist tantric path.[16] In Vajrayana, the Buddhas proliferate as well, one for each of the infinite worlds. And even the most important Buddhas appear less as complex and involving beings than as perfected ones, masters of the diamond vehicle.

The guru, too, is seen as one of these perfected beings, though more compassionate than any other:

> The scripture *Five Stages* states,
>
> The self-born Buddha
> Is a being gone to perfection;
> But kinder than Buddha is one's own teacher,
> For he personally gives one the oral teachings.
>
> Contemplate how your Guru is kinder than all the Buddhas of the past, present, and future.[17]

While the disciple may normally see the guru as kind, this may not always be easy: he is enjoined to meditate on the guru's kindness. To see the guru as perfect is no doubt even more difficult, and texts and commentaries emphasize how important it is for the disciple to overlook any apparently base qualities he may see in his guru, or at least to understand them as deriving from his guru's compassion. If the guru seemed completely perfect, he would be inaccessible to the disciple, beyond human relationship. The guru's apparent weaknesses stem from his desire to help; using skilful means, he mirrors the disciple's own flaws.[18]

The guru, then, unlike the flawless Buddhas, necessarily manifests contradiction and ambiguity. The disciple, moreover, clearly does not have the direct control over the guru that he has over the perfect beings he constructs within. As the only divine being that can offer the disciple intense personal involvement, the guru as an object of devotion surely occupies a special place for the Buddhist *tantrika.*

For the Hindu *tantrika* as well as the Buddhist, the guru as focus of the divine can be given explicit priority over the singular personality highlighted in tradition. Knowledgeable Hindus sometimes recite a *shloka* recalling the famous couplet of Kabir that exhorts the disciple to choose his guru over Lord Govind:

> When Shiva gets angry, the guru can save;
> Should the guru get angry, there's no one at all.[19]

The guru, then, may be the ultimate spiritual support of the yogi, but Shiva too appears as a living personality (an irascible one here!) and may share some of the disciple's personal devotion. And unlike Shiva, who when upset with a disciple at least knows that the guru will take care of him, the guru can get angry and leave his disciple with no spiritual recourse anywhere. Indeed, the ideal of compassion for all living beings cultivated among the Buddhists is not presented in the Hindu tantric texts as a primary motive for the guru to take on the burden of disciples. The Hindu guru is seen rather to be fulfilling dutifully the lot prescribed for him by nature. A *jīvanmukta,* "freed while alive," he has come to his situation as guru through his *prārabdha,* that share of *karma* predestined to be lived out in this life.

While the compassion of the guru's nature is not particularly emphasized in Hindu tantra, it is sometimes extolled in the Hinduized *sant* tradition—where, as we have seen, the cosmic dimensions of the guru's person become magnified within a sweet devotional context. *Dayāl,* "merciful," is a common epithet of Dadu, and *Dātā Dayāl,* "the Merciful Giver," was the honorific name for two different Radhasoami gurus.[20] But the bestowing of grace implied by this epithet nevertheless lends itself to traditional Hindu notions of duty and obligation. Malik Sahib, with links to both tantric and Radhasoami traditions (the latter, in fact, through a master called Data Dayal), once said that his work as guru was the fulfillment of a debt: he had taken spiritual gifts from the culture (*sanskriti,* the "sanskritic" heritage), and now he had to give them back.

While the living guru may be relatively more important as a focus for the disciple's personal devotion in Buddhist tantra than in Hindu, in both traditions he is readily identified with the supreme deity. Both Hindu and Buddhist *tantrika*s are frequently enjoined to contemplate the guru in the heart, or, more characteristically, at the top of the head, which Hindu yogis generally understand to be the seat of the ultimate experience. The Radhasoamis too, we recall, see the image of the guru finally appearing "in his physical form" at the very top of the head.[21] But Hindu and Buddhist tantric *sādhaka*s also often contemplate the guru in the form of a singular personality featured in their tradition. Above, we saw the Vajrayana guru visualized as the goddess, though he is perhaps more routinely visualized as a Buddha. In the following passage a modern commentator cites a scriptural source to assert the identity of the guru with the *iṣṭadevatā,* the disciple's patron deity:

. . . it has been said in the Yamala:

Siva alone is Guru, and I am that Śiva. O great Devi, Thou too art Guru, and Mantra alone is Guru. For this reason as regards Mantra there is no difference between Gurudeva and Iṣṭadevatā. That Gurudeva must sometimes be contemplated in the thousand-petalled lotus (in the head), sometimes in the lotus of the heart (as Iṣṭadevatā), and sometimes in His visible worldly form.[22]

The ultimate state to which the Hindu guru as *iṣṭadevatā* leads his disciple, however, is different from the ultimate realization that the guru as Buddha grants to his, as are the identities between guru and perfected disciple understood by Hindu and Buddhist yogis. A modern Hindu yogi begins the chapter of his book that deals with "Guru-Tattva and God" by invoking Dakshinamurti, the being who gives initiation:

I bow to Dakshinamurti
  Pervading the body like ether,
One image in three parts:
  The Lord, the Guru, and the Self.[23]

Thus, the Hindu *sādhaka* who merges into the Lord as Shiva or any other deity, realizes the unity of his true self with that of his guru. Similarly, in Vajrayana, the perfected guru is understood to be a Buddha, and if the disciple achieves perfection he in turn becomes a Buddha. Yet unlike the Hindu disciple, united with his guru through the one divine essence, the guru and his perfected disciple in Vajrayana remain distinct beings. Both are Buddhas, but different ones. Thus, if the guru and disciple in Hindu tradition are finally one through their essential substance, in Buddhist tradition they each seem to achieve an essentially perfect Buddha-*form*.

The different kinds of identification between guru and disciple in the two traditions reflect resolutions of different philosophical problems of personal individuality. The Hindu realizes the identity of the individual self (*jīvātmā*) with the universal self (*paramātma*) through his guru, who has already realized the two as one. From its beginnings, however, the central Buddhist problem of the self has taken a turn fundamentally different from the Vedantic realization of the unity of *jīvātmā* and *paramātmā*. The early Buddhists were faced with the problem of *anātmā:* no self at all in a world of momentary disparate entities. Buddhist yogis by Vajrayana times may have begun to resolve this problem through the subtle bodies that we have seen them build up in the world of inner phenomena. Though the stuff of these bodies resembles the fluid consciousness-substance by means of which the Hindu yogi ultimately merges into the supreme self, it becomes for the Buddhist the basis of an ultimate *individual* selfhood: the Vajrayana master is transformed into *a* Buddha, with an indestructible "diamond-body."

The Tantric Guru as a Basis of Faith

The indestructible diamond-body of the Vajrayana master surely appears as a firm foundation for the disciple's religious faith, thus fulfilling the primary role that we have given to our notion of an immanent focus of the divine. But himself a Buddha, the Vajrayana master is a holy man assimilated to the image of a singular personality—as is the guru in Hindu tantra, though not in just the same way. We will now look more closely at the configurations of immanent foci offered by Hindu and Buddhist tantra and the place of the guru within them. As we shall see, the meaning of the guru as basis of faith in these traditions depends in good measure on the relationships posited between the holy man and the other immanent foci that the traditions encompass.

While the great host of Buddhas and bodhisattvas that struck us in the evocation of Chintachakra is characteristic of Mahayana, and the ideal of successfully becoming a Buddha is characteristic of Vajrayana—the idea of a Buddha per se is rooted in the historical appearance of Shakyamuni Buddha as a singular personality sometime in the centuries before Ashoka. As a singular personality, Shakyamuni Buddha left something for the world. In the Buddha's case especially, what was left is in part conceived as a teaching, which is supposed to be understood. So—as we see best illustrated, perhaps, in Theravada tradition—scripture, ideally, has referential meaning.

But as the teachings of the Buddha began to penetrate diverse lands beyond his original home, they grew liable to divergent interpretations. In what ways could the doctrines held by all those who looked to Buddha as founder of their tradition be conceived as Buddhist? Becoming increasingly visible across space, the Buddha presented a problem characteristically posed by singular personalities: how does the singular personality fulfill the needs of devotees from varied cultural and sociological backgrounds, while still presenting a single distinctive divine truth? For the most part, members of different traditions appear first to develop their characteristic doctrines, and then to find for them an authoritative Buddhist source. Thus, in Theravada, which offers the publicly revealed teachings of Shakyamuni as a basis of salvation, an extensive scriptural collection is represented as Shakyamuni's historically uttered discourse.

In traditions where the more hidden esoteric teachings of the holy man come to dominate, we often find principles of lineage used to link the person of the holy man at hand with that of a great Buddha of the past, if not with Shakyamuni himself. The early Zen schools present traditions of holy men whose lineages were seen to extend clearly all the way back to Shakyamuni. With the Vajrayana ideal that all realized masters were Buddhas, it was enough for practical purposes to trace genealogies to great gurus of the past. If their lineages from Shakyamuni were not always so clear, as Buddhas of wide experience they themselves were dependable sources of doctrine. The guru in a respectable lineage can be taken as a basis of faith by his disciple because he too has become a Buddha, having realized a trustworthy teaching.

Instead of teachings from a singular personality, the Hindu heritage presents us with certain assumptions about the way the universe works and has always worked. As a heritage potentially encompassing all the members of a single culture, moreover, Hinduism as it develops faces problems of religious distinctions that differ from those presented by the teachings of the Buddha as they spread to diverse Asian populations. For Hindus what is crucial is an understanding of the ways in which each element in their own sanctified society plays its distinct religious part. Hinduism thus tells us that natural cosmic order is reflected in the religiocultural forms that the forefathers knew, the most central of which are rooted in ideas about caste and Veda. New groups then come into the culture by finding a distinct place within the caste hierarchy. A multiplicity of different religious developments attempt to relate themselves to the ancient heritage of the Vedas: sectarian authors write commentaries on established scripture; new scripture is attributed to ancient *ṛṣi*s. And since the eternal includes the present, there is even room for frankly new revelation from an eternal source such as Shiva—revelation apparently more *frankly* new than corresponding Buddhist strategies that attribute new teachings to different stages of Shakyamuni's ministry.[24] The *referential* meaning of the Vedas themselves has become for the most part irrelevant: they are very specially sanctified *mantra*s that contain power. Tantric gurus hold powerful *mantra*s and can be taken as bases of faith because they have access to the ancient eternal truth.

Certainly, Buddhist *tantrika*s too wield powerful *mantra*s, and share with Hindus many basic Indic ritual forms—though they give these forms different shape, and often radically different meanings. Indeed, the ritual heritage of Buddhist tantra today usually seems at least as rich as that of the Hindu. But the fact that the tradition is preserved within lineages that devolve from very special personalities gives it somewhat more codified forms. Since authoritative tradition is constituted by specific teachings coming down through lineages of great gurus, the patterns of practice established by those gurus are best preserved intact. A monk might accept teachings from someone from another school, but he is clear as to the spiritual pedigree he has inherited from his principal guru and the central teachings associated with his lineage.

Hindu tantra, on the other hand, appears in the larger, much less codified regional traditions of Kashmir, Bengal, and Kerala. Instead of skillful means to realize the essence of the Buddha's teachings, as basis of faith the Hindu tantric guru offers the power to realize the truth preserved in a vast and ancient heritage. Certainly, masters of both Hindu and Buddhist tantra—independent holy men—make their own syntheses of tradition. But it is easier for the Hindu guru to pass down his own syntheses to his disciple as a version of the eternal truth than it is for the Buddhist to pass down his as the transmitted teaching.[25]

Even freer than Hindu *tantrika*s in making their own syntheses and passing them on, have been the Hindi *sant*s. Several, like Kabir and Paltu, were not only independent of tradition but also disdained it. The lack of value given to the Hindu mythic heritage by most solitary *sant*s and their followers has, we recall, often made the living guru, divine guru, and *shabda* appear collapsed in *sant* tradition into an extended guru-*tattva*. Hindu tantra can also reduce its corresponding categories of guru, *devatā,* and *mantra* into the principle of the guru. Yet within the context of a developed Hindu heritage, even when collapsed together each of these terms retains an independent existence. A modern commentator gives the following precise analogy from the *Muṇḍamālā Tantra:*

> Mantra is born of Guru, and Devata is born of Mantra, so that, O Beauteous One, Guru stands in the place of a grandfather to the Istadevata. Just as service done to the father or grandfather pleases the son or grandson, service done to Guru pleases Mantra; service done to Mantra pleases Devata; and service done to both Guru and Mantra also pleases Devata.[26]

Characterizing the guru as the father of *mantra* and the grandfather of *iṣṭadevatā,* this passage surely reveals the holy man as dominant focus within the context of the Hindu heritage. But a passage from another tantra soon quoted by the same commentator radically equates the three categories. Here the holy men loses his dominance, which seems to be reclaimed by a heritage that includes the guru and *mantra* as well as the *devatā:*

> Just as the words Ghata, Kalasa, and Kumbha designate the same thing [a pot], so the words Devata, Mantra and Guru designate the same subject. Devata in its ground is the same as Mantra, and Mantra in its ground is the same as Guru. Thus the effect of worshipping Devata, Mantra, and Guru is the same.[27]

These two passages taken together (as they are by our Bengali commentator) show us again how the Hindu heritage presents a reality that appears one "in its ground" but is clearly hierarchized in its manifestation, an all-pervasive substrate that is realized after a careful ascension through the realms of matter. These perceptions of ultimate ends and soteriological means differ from those offered within the Vajrayana heritage, which, however developed, still looks to a source in the Buddha as singular personality. Instead of attempting to merge into the most subtle aspect of a continuum of flowing substance, the Buddhist looks for insight into the reality *beyond* the world of substantial phenomena. The Hindu perception is commonsensical in its own terms; once the premises are accepted, the end is continuous with the beginning. By contrast, much of the point of the Buddhist insight is just that it is *not* commonsensical in this way: it demands seeing things in a radically new set of terms (or no "terms" at all), a break, a leap. To make such a leap, the religious individual needs a stable basis of faith, provided in this case by the Buddha as singular personality. The Hindu, on the other hand, sees the common sense he accepts working in all the aspects of his culture and the many different religious paths it offers. The stability of his faith is less a concentrated point than something all-pervasive, a perspective on the way *everything* works.

The fluid all-pervasiveness of this commonsensical Hindu logic in Indian culture has provided problems for other religions in postclassical, predominantly Hindu India. For both Hindu and Buddhist yogis, the phenomena of inner reality appear as continuous and substantial. And as Buddhist yogis worked within this Indian common sense it apparently became difficult for them not to be led to some important conclusions similar to those of the Hindu. Like their Hindu counterparts, the Buddhist yogis posit a continuity between the guru and the deity. The ultimate "store-consciousness" of Indian Buddhist *yogāchara,* moreover, seems suspiciously substantial and Brahman-like. The Sufis of Islam, too, faced similar problems in adapting the common-sense reality of India, though as we shall see, with tensions more acute and vociferous.

Islam as "Submission" and the Master-Disciple Relationship

The Indian *guruvāda* is not unique in asserting the necessity of a spiritual master for progress on a mystic path. Ideals of the relationship between the Sufi *pīr* and his disciple had been formulated within the Persian orders well before they began to develop in India. In Sufism these ideals developed within the idiom of Islam as submission, the literal meaning of the word Islam. This idiom permitted, as in India (and the Christian West) the Master's being spoken of as "father" to his disciple, and the perception of his *baraka,* "blessing," as a substantial divine power.[28] But Islam is grounded in a Semitic world view that takes personal identity to be considerably less fluid than it is in the Hindu. So while *baraka* could be seen as inhering in the sheikh's person as substance (and thus potentially transmittable to his descendants) it was not identified with his person in the same way that the Hindu's *guru-shakti* is with the guru. Instead of attempting to merge into some substantial emanation of the master, as a Hindu devotee might, the disciple of the *pīr* is to approach his master in a spirit of utter submission. A new disciple, "the sheikhs have said, . . . is like a dead man in the hands of a washer—he turns whichever way he is turned!"[29] The sheikh's discipline involved a conscious humbling of the disciple, illustrated in the following story about Nizamuddin Auliya, no doubt the most illustrious of all the Indian Sufis.

Nizamuddin had been a bright and rising theologian before he met his master, Baba Farid. One day while Nizamuddin was still fairly new at Baba Farid's hostel, an old school friend inquired about him outside. Baba Farid ordered Nizamuddin to carry a tray of food on his head to his friend on the road, a humiliating act, and to tell him that their ways had parted:

You are not my fellow traveller;
Follow your own path, get along!

May prosperity be your share in life
And misfortune mine.[30]

As a test of faith in the spiritual master, this incident differs from the stories of *siddha*s and *nāth*s we have seen earlier not only because it is more plausible and may well record events that actually took place, but also because the terms of the test are different. In the Hindu tradition disciples are ready to offer their limbs to the guru, and in the Buddhist they are ready to undergo obvious suffering at the guru's behest. Here, however, submission to the master's will leads the disciple to sacrifice his self-esteem and spiritual pride.

Conscious humility is particularly characteristic of devotional mysticism—which is on the whole a much more dominant element in Sufism than in *nāth* or *siddha* piety. Indeed, the story of Nizamuddin recalls forms of discipline within Christian monasteries in both the Roman and Eastern Orthodox traditions. The story is not, however, particularly reminiscent of anything from Vaishnava *bhakti.* Vaishnava devotees were certainly ready to add Das, "servant," after their names, but as Hari Das or Ram Das they were servants of Hari or Ram, the Lord whose bliss they sought. A great guru like Chaitanya is characteristically portrayed as lost in ecstasy much of the time. He baffles his disciples through his enigmatically divine behavior, rather than humbling them through conscious exertion of his authority, as Baba Farid did.[31]

The dynamic of humility and authority evident in Islamic mysticism has roots, perhaps, in the figure of the Prophet himself, at once the "slave of God" and the leader of his community. Muhammad as a singular personality providing a focus for tradition was certainly to inform the development of Islamic mysticism in India, though in a very different fashion from that in which the figure of the Buddha informed Vajrayana. In Vajrayana Buddhism we have seen a developed Indic heritage of myth and ritual produce a plethora of godheads, among whom Shakyamuni Buddha appears as an important focus of the divine, but hardly a unique one. In Islam, however, a developed semitic legal heritage reinforces the status of Muhammad as a singular personality within the community he founded.

Thus, before the flowering of Indo-Islamic culture under the Mughals, most Sufis kept within the bounds of their own, Islamic, community; only a few were to find a place for themselves in the general popular yogic and devotional melee, though more did later. In the earlier centuries we hear of Sufis from the *qalandariyya* tradition, famous for their rough, ascetic style, who sometimes seem to have mixed with *nāth* yogis.[32] Later they were joined by ecstatic devotees, often called "enraptured ones"—*majzūb*s. This term, in addition to being used by common people to refer to the religiously unbalanced, could also be employed with definite derogatory connotations by sober Sufis to refer to the ecstatics they condemned.[33] The Mughal era saw a flowering of both ecstatics and sober sufis: at the same time that the number of convention-mocking *majzūb*s increased, the more aristocratic Naqshbandi order took firm root in India. Naqshbandi tradition, of whom the first great Indian exponent was Sheikh Ahmed Sirhindi, would then have a lasting influence on the later cultural and intellectual history of the Indian Muslims.[34]

With the emphasis Islam gives to the religious community as a political entity, problems of authority and submission among Indian Sufis often showed up in debates about the correct attitude to take toward the royal court and its patronage, and the place of Hindus in a Muslim state. Naqshbandis (and others) generally believed it was the duty of the Sufi to attempt to influence those in authority. Nizamuddin, along with many other (but not all) Chishtis, scrupulously avoided the court, preserving an attitude of humility. A similar difference is found between the ideas of Chishtis and Naqshbandis in their attitudes toward Hindus. Of course, both Chishtis and Naqshbandis usually believed that the one really true path was to be found in Islam. But conversations of Nizamuddin's show him as seeing some virtue in the Hindus' error and dealing honorably with Hindus as individuals.[35] He is reported to have been impressed with some of the yogis who occasionally visited Baba Farid's hostel and to have conversed with them on matters of spiritual practice.[36] Sirhindi, on the other hand, waxed vitriolic at seeing Hindus in any position of authority at all, and advocated sumptuary laws of a politically most unrealistic kind.[37]

In both orders the iconoclastic strictures of Islam provided for spiritual practices less visually elaborate than those we have seen in the Indic traditions. The emphasis was auditory, on *zikr,* "repetition" of Islamic formulas. Visual contemplation, when it occurred at all, was generally aniconic. Thus, lights could appear to Sufis as they practiced *zikr:* white, green, red, and black; and the significance of the lights' colors and place of appearance in the body were discussed. Although sometimes these lights were discounted as potentially distracting allurements, they could also provide images for sublime experience in meditation:

This meditation should be like the lotus seeing the sun,
Or the Greek partridge seeing the moonlight . . .[38]

In addition to looking at inner lights, Sufis sometimes contemplated the Arabic letters.[39] The only lifelike image that was regularly contemplated by Indian Sufis was that of the spiritual master, called *pīr* in Persian and *murshid* in Arabic. Nawab Gudri Shah Baba, a twentieth-century Sufi, tells us the benefits of such contemplation for the *murīd*, "disciple":

> The contemplation on the Murshid is the first step towards mysticism. By constant contemplation on the Murshid, the face of the Murshid will appear in the eyes of the mureed. His light will radiate from the eyes of the mureed and his whole outlook will change. At times the radiance in his eyes is clearly visible and then it influences those he looks upon.
>
> When the image of the Murshid manifests in the mind of the mureed, he will develop the power to transmit his thoughts to the minds of others and gradually he will be able to read the thoughts of others.
>
> When the image of the Murshid takes its abode in the heart of the mureed, his heart will be filled with light and under the influence of the Murshid the mind will find enlightenment.[40]

The murshid, moreover, was sometimes known to reciprocate by directing his attention to the disciple's image to strengthen the bonds between them—bonds seen to be substantial, as among Hindus.[41] Certainly, we hear of Chishtis contemplating the *pīr*'s image, but even more remarkable was the importance of directed attention (*tawajjoh*) between sheikh and disciple among the Naqshbandis. Indeed, the Indian Naqshbandis seem to have known complex esoteric practices, which, like the Radhasoamis, they might refer to in terms of an inner journey: *safar dar watan,* "travel in the homeland." Since Sirhindi's day these practices had been integrated into a context of orthodox Islam, but Sirhindi himself, in one of his less-restrained statements, tells of rising to states proper to Usman, Umar, and Abu-Bakr, the first three caliphs of Islam. Like them, however, Sirhindi returned to the holy community on earth, giving it a new mystical basis.[42]

Sirhindi, with his experience of ascension and stations, finds a place on Soamiji's list of accomplished holy men.[43] His conscious sobriety, however, was no particular advantage: he is listed along with his near contemporary Sarmad, a naked *majzūb* intoxicated by divine love directed toward a Hindu boy. Sarmad "followed the tradition of Hallaj, longing for execution as the final goal of his life."[44] His longing was fulfilled by Aurangzeb, who had him put to the sword for heresy. Eaton tells us of a more interesting emulation of another aspect of Hallaj's piety in the Indian environment. Here, a flourishing *majzūb* of Bijapur unpopular with the orthodox invoked a phrase recalling Hallaj's famous *an-al-haq,* "I am the Truth." In the Indian case, the sheikh's invocation of this statement led soon enough to accusations of *pīr* worship. The issue was resolved, according to the sheikh's followers, when a legalistic distinction was made based on types of prostration (*sijda*), a problem long discussed among Indian Sufis. The type of prostration the sheikh's disciples made to him was one of respect (*sijda-yi ta'zim*), not the prostration of servitude (*sijda-yi bandagī*) reserved only for God.[45]

Not all Sufis, however, were fortunate enough to escape the consequences of appearing to be worshiped. We hear, for example, of Sheikh Ahmad Bihari, executed by the fourteenth-century Sultan Firoz Shah; the Sultan claimed that "Ahmad's disciples preached that God had appeared in Delhi in the form of Ahmad."[46] So Indian Sufis have had reason to hesitate in making an Indic identification of the spiritual master with the Lord. But they can extend themselves fairly far if they are so inclined, and those obviously influenced by Hindu ideas sometimes seem to have been.

'Abd Al-Quddus Gangohi is presented by Simon Digby as a sheikh of unextraordinary spiritual gifts who demonstrates the profound ambivalence toward Hindu tradition often found among Indian Sufis. This sheikh's political views can appear comparable to those of the most zealous Muslim: no Hindu should hold any responsible position in a proper Islamic government, he writes to Babur; non-Muslims should be subordinated and taxed. But 'Abd Al-Quddus was familiar with the vocabulary, at least, of hatha yoga, and liked Hindi verses, collecting many in the *nirgun* style and some that invoked Gorakh and Niranjan. And while the sheikh's ideas about the spiritual master were expressed in traditional Islamic terms, they reflect a Sufism most comfortable with indigenous Indian attitudes. The *pīr* is God's mirror, he tells us; when reflecting God's glory, the *pīr* can himself be destroyed, leaving only God. In such a case, he adds, prostration before the *pīr* is not only permissible, but legally obligatory.[47]

In the more popular syncretistic Sufism of medieval Bengal described by Asim Roy, the spiritual master is often known simply as the guru. Striking parallels appear between the roles of Hindu and Muslim spiritual masters, but also an important conceptual difference: though the disciple should merge his self-consciousness into that of the *pīr*, who is to be "served after the manner of the Lord himself," the *pīr* is not, like the Hindu guru, taken to be an incarnation of the Lord.[48] Nawab Gudri Shah, writing in a twentieth-century secular Indian state, is not afraid to blur the distinction between human and divine masters publicly; he tells us plainly that "the Murshid is not different from God or from the saints . . ."[49] For almost all Muslims, however, the spiritual master did remain distinct from the Prophet.

The Holy Man in a Singular-Personality Context: The Buddha, the Prophet, and the Person of Shiva

Sufis, like tantric Buddhists, use a strategy of lineage to link a spiritual master at hand with the singular personality of the past. But Muhammad as a singular personality is conceived in more definite historical terms than is Shakyamuni among the Buddhas, and Sufis seem more insistent than Buddhist yogis on tracing a lineage back to the source of their greater religious context. The chains of succession, called *silsilahs*, usually go from the present *pīr* to the founder of the order, then through illustrious classical Sufis to Ali and the Prophet. A new disciple may be presented with a certificate listing the members of the *silsilah* in succession (together, perhaps, with a space for the disciple's name at the bottom).[50] This general strategy of lineage (without the written particulars) is similar to what we have seen in Vaishnava *sampradāyas* and *sant panths*, where historical founders are seen as very special personages. It differs, however, from what we normally see among Hindu *tantrikas*, who often lose sight of lineage after several generations.

While Brahmans and Rajputs may value lengthy biological genealogies going back to legendary figures, there is less urgency in Hindu tantric traditions concerning spiritual lineages. When it describes how oblations should be offered "to the line of gurus," the *Mahānirvāṇa Tantra* includes only four generations. Oblations should be offered

> in the first place to the Sadhaka's own Guru seated together with his wife on the lotus of a thousand petals, and then in the same way to the other three Gurus who are the Parama Guru, the Parapara Guru, the Paramesti Guru successively.[51]

The gurus of the last three generations, then, sometimes given specific names (*parama-guru, parāpara-guru, parameṣṭi-guru*), can appear as definite relations within a spiritual family sanctified by the Hindu heritage. But the family's lineage itself is as eternal as the heritage that gives it sanctity; neither has a fixed point of beginning. Shiva is sometimes spoken of as *ādi-guru,* "the primal guru," but this is less for legitimating specific lineages than as a divine basis for the principle of guruhood: "Paramaśiva Himself in human body secretly wanders on the earth in order to favour Śiśyas."[52] It is enough to know that there are gurus in the world, who make new gurus, and better not to worry too much about where lineages historically begin.

Thus, the extent to which lineage is traced in a North Indian esoteric tradition seems to depend in part on the relative values of heritage and personality in that tradition's greater religious context. The Indian Sufi, revering the person of the historical Muhammad, usually tries to trace a direct spiritual lineage all the way back to him. Within the Vajrayana heritage the Buddha becomes less a unique personality than a cosmic principle manifesting through different individuals; so while Buddhist yogis take their lineages very seriously, they are often content to trace them back not to Shakyamuni, but to some eminent Buddhist personage of the more recent past. Hindu *tantrika*s, finally, looking to no historical personage as source, are likely soon to lose the history of their lineages in the eternity of their heritage.

But the guru's relative lack of lineage in Hindu tantra can help give him comparatively more exclusive claims on his disciples. Since the Hindu is supposed to see the very Lord himself embodied in a specific individual, he is often expected to have a stronger loyalty to a single guru than is found in traditions where many lineages are seen to lead to one historically manifested person. Like the chaste wife, the disciple is normally supposed to take initiations—seen as something of the guru's substantial power—from one master alone. Only in exceptional cases (Abhinavagupta, Ramakrishna, Malik Sahib on his own scale) are gurus portrayed as having more than one spiritual master, who then initiate them into fundamentally different "paths" (*yoga, bhakti, jñāna,* etc.) within the heritage.[53]

In Vajrayana, too, the disciple maintains an attitude toward one individual as "root guru"— who plays a special role in his practice. But, living in a monastic environment, he may routinely take initiations from other qualified masters. Among the most important of these initiations are evocations of specific deities, rites that usually entail complex visualizations like that of Tara Chintachakra above. Certainly, an accomplished lama may be understood to lend his personal power to the disciple's initial meditation. But "the primary signification of 'initiation' in Tibet is as a guarantor of lineage—of authenticity of doctrinal transmission—and as a preliminary and proper authorization of practice."[54] A Vajrayana initiation, then, is first of all perceived as a trustworthy teaching, not, as among Hindus, means of assimilating the guru's personal spiritual emanation.

The different Sufi orders, like the Vajrayana lineages, represent authoritative lines of teaching, often seen as ultimately deriving from the same source. And despite the importance that Sufi tradition gives to the role of the master, its later Indian developments saw individual Sufis freely seeking affiliation with more than one order. But the effects on tradition of an individual's having multiple lineages showed different emphases in Vajrayana and Sufism. In Vajrayana the convergence of multiple lineages helped give some obvious coherence to the larger community; in Indian Sufism it more often gave weight to the individual holy man.

We frequently hear of accomplished Tibetan monks who have received initiations from a number of sources. The variety of these sources, however, does not seem to be crucial to their spiritual authority; it is taken for granted that a master from one school might want access to the teachings of others, for they were all finally of the same divine origin.[55] Indeed, many of these schools owed their existence to the work of Atisha, popularly known as the master "who brought Buddhism to Tibet." Said to have had access to all the lineages devolving from Shakyamuni, and the evident source of more than one significant Tibetan school, Atisha through his own integration of Buddhist sources provides a means for Vajrayana as a whole to be seen as complete and integral Buddhism. He thus serves as a special personage who provides a focus of consolidation for a large part of Tibetan tradition.

The plural lineages sometimes traced by founders of minor Sufi orders can serve a similar function in a more limited tradition. But the multiple lines of authority that converge on the special personage who founds an order can also give weight to the independent power of the living holy man who does not. For in practice, *pīr*s finding multiple lines of authority seemed to claim less the ability to transmit several coherent lines of traditional teachings in their integrity than a sanction for fashioning their own individual syntheses out of them all.

Among Indian Sufis, succession was normally certified through a document called a *khilāfat nāma,* which might also designate certain books the sheikh gave his disciple permission to teach. Granting a disciple a *khilāfat nāma* certainly meant that a sheikh vouched for a disciple's spiritual worthiness. But *khalīfa*s, appointed by a sheikh during his own lifetime, often appeared simply as deputies of their master. Only the closest disciples of Indian Sufis seem to have been personally identified with their masters in ways reminiscent of Indic traditions. Indeed, Baba Farid, Nizamuddin's *pīr,* distinguished different classes of successors: those whom God spontaneously inspired him to nominate; those he himself chose on consideration of their merits; and those appointed on the recommendation of others.[56]

Baba Farid describes the degree of his successors' spiritual closeness to him in terms of the extent to which he was influenced in their selection by spiritual forces alone. Indeed, one suspects that the "recommendation of others" may in fact imply factors of sectarian politics. During the later stages of Indian Islam such factors seem to have gotten out of hand. We find an apparent inflation in the value of *khilāfat nāma*s, which were sometimes even traded by Sufis among themselves, each one initiating the other into his own order. Certificates of succession began to look less like indications of practical spiritual training than like honorary degrees. And while the multiple lineages of Buddhist yogis often involved the empowerments of various independent deities that could come through different gurus, the multiple lineages of the Sufis (who recognized no such deities) were those of the teachers' own authority. Thus Baba Farid's *khilāfat nāma* for Nizamuddin tells its reader that "obedience to him is obedience to me."[57] The eventual effects of the gross collecting of *khilāfat nāma*s, as Eaton points out, was to obliterate the role of the specific order as a defined traditional path, thus enhancing the significance of the *pīr* himself as holy man.[58]

While the Sufi *pīr* as holy man could have at least as much practical importance as his Indic counterparts, even a moderately orthodox Islamic context would tolerate no easy Indic identification of the holy man with the singular personality and the ultimate divine goal. The *valī* ("friend") of God, the "saint," was clearly distinguished from the *nabī,* "prophet." The kinds of miracles that could be attributed to them were different and had different names. There were frequent discussions as to which of the two occupied the higher station, with only a few of the most radical Sufis opting for the saint. Sheikh Sharafuddin Maneri, a moderate thirteenth-century Sufi from Bihar, gives us both sides of the issue, but he makes his position clear:

> . . . great saintliness is merely the starting point of prophecy . . . . Heretics . . . reason that saints are always engrossed in God, whereas the prophets are mostly concerned with the affairs of men. They presuppose

> that anyone who is continuously absorbed with God is holier than anyone who is only sometimes caught up in this fashion. . . . [But] just as the rank of saints is concealed from the understanding of ordinary people, so, too, that of the prophets is hidden from the grasp of the saints![59]

Despite his negative polemics in the passage above, Maneri reveals a conception of the saint as analogous to the prophet, though on a smaller scale and with a clear demarcation between the two. Sufis can also use parallelism of expression comparable to Maneri's to describe the *similarity* of the saint and prophet in their own spheres. They frequently recall this tradition attributed to Muhammad: "As the prophet is to the nation so the sheikh is to his people."[60] *Fanā-f'il-sheikh,* "annihilation in the sheikh"—the closest the Sufi normally comes to an Indic-style identification with the divine through the spiritual master—is traditionally followed by "annihilation in the prophet." The thirteenth-century Chishti poet Mas'ud-i Bak compared the saint to the prophet as brilliance to light.[61] Contemporary Indian Sufis, when asked about the relationship between *pīr* and prophet, consistently reply to the effect that the *pīr* "carries on the prophet's work."

In the following meditation instruction attributed to Nizamuddin, the distinction maintained between the *pīr* and the prophet in Sufism stands in sharp contrast to the identity often posited between the holy man and singular personality in Indic tantra. In tantric meditation, we recall, the disciple is regularly instructed to contemplate his guru as Buddha or Shiva (or Shiva or Buddha as his guru), but the disciples of Nizamuddin were not told to identify the *pīr* with the Prophet Muhammad so readily. Nizamuddin, they say, was once asked whether one should contemplate God alone or God, the Prophet, and the *pīr.* He replied that both meditations were possible, but that if someone wanted to contemplate the *pīr* and the prophet together with God, he should meditate on God in front of him, the prophet on his right side, and the *pīr* on his left.[62] Even when the three are contemplated at once, then, they remain separate.

8

Hindi *Sants* in North Indian Tradition

Against this complex Indian religious landscape of Sufis, yogis, and devotees, how, finally, are we to comprehend the *sants*? Certainly, the *sants* were more Indic in their outlook than even the most liberal Sufis, but they were often much more iconoclastic than traditional Hindu holy men. Perhaps, then, we should look for the sants' roots in an older form of Indic heterodoxy: the Buddhist *siddha* tradition. There do seem to be parallels in usage and style between the songs of *sants* and of *siddhas*, who aptly exemplify the image of the erratic, occasionally contradictory individual sometimes presented by *sants*.[1] But the similarities between *sants* and *siddhas* will probably have to remain morphological only, suggesting comparable socioreligious roles for like pieties, but no direct historical links. For the gap between the final collapse of North Indian Buddhism with the twelfth-century Muslim onslaught and the fifteenth-century appearance of Kabir appears too great for unbroken continuities between the two traditions. Any Buddhist roots of the *sants* probably must have come through the *nāths*, who shared a common yogic culture with the *siddhas*, but have endured through the centuries in increasingly Hinduized forms.

The image of the *sant* as a figure apparently Hindu, in some ways Sufi, but not quite either, thus remains. The problem is to understand the significance of this image—what it meant for early *sants* to have forged a style of piety that in its different dimensions resembled sometimes Hindu, sometimes Islamic mysticism. I will approach this problem in two ways. The first is morphological—by comparing the forms of piety found among *sants* to those of the holy men in the other yogic traditions just examined; the second is historical—by suggesting some routes through which Sufis may have influenced formative *sants*, and more important, pointing to the parallel socioreligious roles *sant*s and Sufis seem to have played at a critical epoch in pre-Mughal India.

Sufi Style; Indic Interpretation

To distinguish the Islamic from the Hindu aspects of *sant* piety, it will help to distinguish two broad categories of phenomena: those derived from experience, vision, and practice; and those of speculation, interpretation, and understanding. Tables 1 and 2 present some of the forms in which the Indian holy man as basis of faith elicits these two aspects of religious life. Comparing the forms of *sant* tradition seen in part II to those of the yogic traditions studied in the last chapter, we find that *sant* vision and practice (table 1) is strikingly similar to that of the Sufis, but the speculative, interpretive forms of the *sant*s (table 2) are clearly Indic—in a Hindu devotional idiom surveyed in chapter 1.

The parallels between the *sant*s' understandings of the holy man and those found in Hindu tradition should come as no surprise. More unexpected is the closeness of the parallels between the *sant*s' experience and that of Indian Sufis. Despite the *sant*s' Hindu appearance,

TABLE 1. Experience of the Divine Through the Holy Man in the Yogic Traditions.

BUDDHIST	HINDU	SANT	SUFI
1. Complex visualization that includes the Buddha-field	1. Often complex meditation on deity	1. Frequent meditation on lights and guru's unadorned image	1. Frequent meditation on lights and *pīr*'s unadorned image
2. Both visualization and *mantra*	2. Both visualization and *mantra*	2. Basic practice auditory (*shabda*)	2. Basic practice auditory (*zikr*)
3. Yogic concentration and compassion	3. Yogic concentration with some devotion	3. Attachment to the Lord leads to world-scorning concentration on Him	3. Attachment to the Lord can lead to ascetic concentration on Him
4. Attention paid to physical body	4. Attention paid to physical body	4. Very little cultivation of the physical body	4. Little cultivation of the physical body

TABLE 2. Understanding of the Holy Man in the Yogic Traditions.

BUDDHIST	HINDU	SANT	SUFI
1. Lineage very important; relates holy men at hand to authoritative teacher of the past	1. Idea of lineage important, but not source of lineage	1. Lineage sometimes very important but no one historical source	1. Lineage very important; relates holy man to singular personality at source of tradition
2. Guru as compassionate bodhisattva and all-knowing Buddha	2. Guru dutifully acts out his mysterious divine nature	2. Guru compassionately acts out his mysterious divine nature	2. *Pīr* as "friend" of God; analogous to prophet but distinct from him and on a smaller scale
3. Disciple can become Buddha like his guru	3. Ultimate identity of Guru and disciple in Brahma	3. Disciple's ultimate identity with guru and *shabda*	3. Disciple can become "friend" of God like his *pīr;* but both distinct from each other, Prophet and God
4. Flowing consciousness-substance leads to radical insight	4. Merging into divine substance	4. Merging into divine substance	4. Humility and love lead to "nearness" to the Lord

there really do seem to be some aspects to their devotion that resemble Sufi piety, and it is time now to identify these more closely. We can begin by distinguishing the Hindi *sants* from the Marathi ones, their nearest Indic predecessors. In studying the formative beginnings of the Hindi tradition, we have already seen that the Hindi *sant* Kabir diverges clearly from Namdev, rooted in the Marathi tradition. We will now examine some of the ways in which this divergence represents a turn toward Sufi style.

First of all, the Marathi *sants* were, on the whole, more seriously Vaishnava than the Hindi *sants*. Most Marathi *sants* participated to some extent in the burgeoning cult of Vitobha at Pandarpur and practiced *saguṇ* worship in addition to *nirguṇ*. The Hindi *sant*s, on the other hand, were famous primarily as *nirguṇ* devotees. In Hindi popular tradition, *nirguṇ* devotion does not denote a piety in which the Lord is conceived as absolutely "without qualities"—the literal meaning of *nirguṇ*. It does imply, however, that the devotee does not wax ecstatic over a vivid description of the image of the deity—as Sur was famous for doing, and the Marathi *sant*s sometimes did. The Hindi *nirguṇ* poets normally did write of the divine as a being, often addressed by a Vaishnava name, and frequently used suggestive, personifying analogies. But the iconic terms they used did not normally recall any sustained image of a Vaishnava deity, whose names sometimes in fact do *not* appear in their songs.[2] The Lord might, for example, be called Sahib, the very common Indian honorific of Perso-Arabic derivation. The *sant*s could thus, like Sufis, talk about the Lord in the loving but aniconic ways frequent in Islam, where Allah is regularly invoked as merciful and compassionate.

Second, we saw that *sant*s in the Kabirian tradition were closer to the *nāth*s than were the late Marathi *sant*s. They are thus, like Sufis, linked to a developed tradition of esoteric practice. But as Vaudeville has pointed out,[3] Kabir used the *nāth* jargon in his own way. And just as important, he used only pieces of it, pieces that reflect a clear difference in his (and general *sant*) values from those of the *nāth*s. The *nāth*s were famous for being "spiritual alchemists" in search of immortality conceived in physical terms, and it is clear that *nāth*s were concerned about the state of their bodies, practicing complex forms of *haṭha* yoga. Kabir, on the other hand, is concerned about death and a more spiritualized immortality. As Vaudeville notes,

> Death, its inescapable, frightful, tragic character, appears to be at the core of Kabir's thought . . . No other poet in India—perhaps no other poet in the world—has spoken about Death as Kabir does, with such striking, tragic intensity . . .[4]

While later *sant*s have indeed incorporated descriptions of the six *chakra*s in the body, the well-attested Kabir hardly mentions them. The terms he adopts from the *nāth*s refer primarily to regions in the head—the place from which yogis want to be able to make their final exit: Kabir speaks of *sunna,* "the Void," and of *gagan,* "the heavens." Soamiji, too, while offering descriptions of the *chakra*s in the body, disdains them, saying that meditation in the higher realms is necessary and sufficient for salvation. The attempt to transcend the bodily world through devotion, together with a basically aniconic form of spiritual practice grounded in the repetition of holy words, is just what we find in the early Chishti Sufis.

In fact, many of the images, issues, and attitudes in certain Sufi texts seem reminiscent of those we have seen in our discussion of *sant* literature. A long passage from the *Jñān Guṣṭi,* where the sun and moon were more than yogic referents, is brought to mind by the Sufi's meditation on the heavenly spheres:

This meditation should be like the lotus seeing the sun,
Or the Greek partridge seeing the moonlight . . .

Nawab Gudri Shah tells us of the identity of the master's inner image with his person:

> When . . . the impurity of the lower self has been removed, the heart becomes clean like a mirror and in it the image of the Murshid becomes clearly visible. The reflection of the Murshid is not different from the person. The blessings of the image of the Murshid are manifold and manifest themselves in various ways as supernatural powers. The manifestation of these supernatural powers is a proof of the Truth and shows to the world the special quality of those who seek God.[5]

The identification of the master's image with his person is essentially the common Radhasoami position with which Pandit Faqir Chand takes issue. Nawab Gudri Shah's mention of the blessings of the image of the master as proof, moreover, brings to mind the assertion of Babu Shyam Lal's song from chapter 2:

The satguru gives proofs within the body
  And a little faith begins to grow.

And as it has for Radhasoamis and other *sant*s in *paramparā*s, Nawab Gudri Shah's love for the Lord beyond form leads him to take the living guru himself as the primary object of devotion:

> Thinking of God depends on the love in the heart and the real centre of this love is the Guru or the Murshid (Spiritual Guide). A perfect Murshid manifests the qualities of God. The Murshid is the only link between the seeker and the attainment of that which he seeks . . . Real love means loving this centre of love—the Murshid—more than anything else in the world.[6]

The power of the devotee's love for his master is a motif in the hagiography of the *sant paramparā*s, as are the virtues of humility and submission characteristic of Sufism. We have seen Bulla, in the lineage of Bauri, content with his station as a humble laborer; Gulal, moreover, in submitting himself to Bulla—his servant—is understood by devotees to have demonstrated an extreme form of humility. The Radhasoamis have even shown us how the guru is in fact expected to humiliate his disciple when they describe Sahibji Maharaj's marking his succession by exercising his authority dramatically. The Radhasoamis also tell us about the conscious authority of the guru and the humble love of his successor in a story about Soamiji and his disciple Huzur Sahib a story that moreover reveals the necessity of the disciple's readiness "to consider every difficulty a comfort" as Nawab Gudri Shah advises.

Oral accounts tell us that Huzur Sahib had confessed an apparently trivial spiritual fault to Soamiji, who recognized it as a great evil and told him to fetch water daily as penance. The example of Huzur Sahib's water-carrying service to his guru is striking for devotees, and is described in almost all narrations of his life as a disciple.[7] The well from which Soamiji wanted his water was two miles away, and we are shown Huzur Sahib, a high government official at the time, with a jug of water on his shoulder, unmindful of what people thought.

This story bears some striking resemblances to that told of Baba Farid and Nizamuddin above. Not only was Soamiji, like Baba Farid, trying to humble his disciple, but he did so by prescribing similar actions: carrying water/food, on the shoulder/head, in public, by a person of some rank. Such actions are symbolic of humbling service in India, and are commonplace enough to derive spontaneously from immediate situations. But the story of Nizamuddin was a well-known one, recounted in important Indian Sufi literature with which the early Radhasoami literati, given their Urdu-Persian orientation, could easily have been familiar. Thus, as an example of a type of story about submission to the master's authority, that of Baba Farid and Nizamuddin may itself have served as a model for the biographers of Huzur Sahib, if not for Soamiji himself.[8]

On examining the forms of religious life in *sant* tradition, then, what we find are Indic elements coming together in a way particularly characteristic of mystical Islam. Clearly, the Indic elements of *sant* piety were in existence long before the emergence of the first Hindi *sant*s, so there is little question of the *sant*s taking over their devotion wholesale from the Sufis. We ask instead just why and through what means did *sant* piety take its distinctive shape when it did, at a time when Sufis also flourished. To answer this question we must turn to some specific dynamics of interaction between the Hindu and Muslim communities in pre-Mughal times.

On the Margins of Community

The first *sants* emerge in North India toward the end of the age of the Delhi Sultanate, after the Muslims had established a lasting political foothold in India, but before the flowering of the Indo-Muslim culture under the Mughals. The Delhi Sultans sometimes commanded large territories, yet political union was never very stable for very long. The decentralized postclassical feudal political structure developed within Rajput culture was thus still visible, but now found parallels in diffuse traditions of holy men among Muslims as well as Hindus. Militarily victorious, the Muslims tended to rule as aloof outsiders, making few consistent attempts at cultural synthesis with the infidels. Nevertheless, the power of Muslim rulers and the visibility of Islamic religion represented a conspicuous new factor in the religious perception of large numbers of Indians, most of whom did not proceed to embrace the religion of the conquerors. The Hindi *sant* tradition appeared during this period as a response to the new religious universe that presented itself.

The Impact of Islam on the Rise of the *Sants*

Though illustrious Hindi *sants* do not appear until the beginning of the fifteenth century, they stand in continuity with a type of convention-mocking holy man that had developed in a particular yogic way in earlier postclassical times. From a socioreligious perspective, however, the first known Hindi *sants* differ from the *nāths* and *siddhas* who preceded them in one important respect. The yogis of *nāth* and *siddha* tradition, while becoming figures of popular legend, do not appear to have taken much interest in the religion of the people at large: they were engaged in their own internal practice and did not entertain large numbers of lay disciples. The *sants*, on the other hand, were usually themselves lay people, householders with trades. And while most *sants* certainly did seem to have forms of esoteric devotional experience, most also wanted to communicate something of this experience to the public at large. This dual role of the early *sant* is reflected today in the socioreligious dynamic of close and distant disciples among the Radhasoamis, discussed in chapter 2. But during the Sultanate period, a similar role was characteristically played by Chishti Sufis. Several Chishtis are known to have attracted at least two circles of disciples: an inner group who were instructed in spiritual practice, and a much larger circle of more casual devotees, whose attitude called for less individualized attention.[9]

Within the outermost circles of many Chishtis, Hindus as well as Muslims could no doubt be found; and yogis, it seems, came to their *khānqā*s. But the early Chishtis were not particularly concerned with the propagation of Islam among common Hindus—their energies were devoted to the spiritual welfare of Muslims. In an oft-cited story from *Fawa'id-ul-Fu'ad,* Nizamuddin stresses to one devotee (probably himself a convert) the value of the pious Muslim's example for converting Hindus, and admits the inefficacy of preaching. Even the Sufi's moral example, however, was a highly questionable factor in most cases of conversion. More clearly significant was the example of his lifestyle and forms of piety among those who had, for whatever reasons, already accepted Islam. In the understanding of what it meant to be a Muslim for a population more conversant with *guru-bhakti* than with books or high culture, the Sufi as a religio-cultural model played a crucial role. A number of *khānqā*s were situated in the outskirts of cities, where many of the newly converted low-caste artisan groups lived.[10] And it is out of such castes that several important *sant*s arose—including Kabir and Dadu, and two most influential for later tradition.

Orr, in fact, argues with some credibility[11] that Dadu's spiritual preceptor came from Sufi tradition, though the influence of mystical Islam on the Hindi *sant*s was probably not primarily through Sufis as masters demanding loyal submission. Preceding the great early Hindi *sant*s remembered today there were presumably forgotten figures who thought of themselves as *sant*s in a tradition continuous with the Marathi. And if the early Hindi *sant*s did in fact recognize single living gurus, these were more likely to have been from this tradition, the one with which the earliest *sant*s seem most to have identified.

The Islamic turn we have seen in the piety of the Hindi *sant*s is probably better explained through the role of the early Sufis in providing religiocultural models among newly converted Indian castes. As mystically inclined members of these castes, figures such as Kabir and Dadu, at early stages of their development, may very conceivably have frequented the Chishti *khānqā*s, where they might have found *nāth* yogis. From the liberal Sufis these figures certainly did not assimilate much orthodox Islam. But they probably did learn some practice, and may have been impressed by a style of piety both devotional and aniconic, one which recognized the virtue of humility, but was more outspoken and virile than that of the Vaishnavas who were beginning to appear in abundance. While the early *sant*s finally sang in their own Indic idiom, the image of the Sufi may have determined to a large extent their pereption of what it meant to be a holy man—thus, perhaps, helping them find the dual, popular-esoteric role of the *sant* congenial.

But what of the extreme iconoclasm of some *sant*s, which was characteristic of neither Marathi *sant*s nor moderate Sufis? And what of the wide spread of *sant* tradition in the North? To understand these facets of *sant* tradition we can examine aspects of Hindu-Muslim interaction in the pre-Mughal period, particularly the large-scale adoption of Islam by groups of Indians. The factors leading to conversion were complex, and neither the stereotype of "Islam by the sword" nor of "Islamic egalitarianism" seems to have carried much weight in India: the Hindus were too many and their traditions too deep for the sword to penetrate—though it seems prisoners of war were sometimes presented with "an offer they could not refuse"; and those low castes that did convert remained just as low in the eyes of well-born Muslims, who had pedigrees of their own.[12]

Nevertheless, city-dwellers in service to the Muslim ruling classes often did become Muslim themselves. Lack of enthusiasm with their place in the Hindu order, solidarity with their new masters, and the economic benefits conversion might bring were all factors that led some urban artisan castes to opt for Islam en masse. In many cases identification with a leader acting from personal motives, either worldly or religious, seems to have been a significant factor in group conversions, and Muslim officials sometimes did make efforts at proselytizing individuals of some rank. These included, most notably, Hindu chiefs and tribal leaders; claimants in land disputes, who during some regimes might automatically win their case through conversion; and those of the gentry seriously attracted by Islamic religiocultural tradition—or just as likely, by the spiritual charisma of a particular Sufi or the worldly benefits he (or his tomb) might bestow. A high-ranking individual who converted would often take most of his retainers and dependents with him.

But what did it mean for members of such groups to accept Islam? For most it certainly did not mean a thorough grounding in Islamic theology, but rather a slow adoption of Islamic religiocultural ways, together with some ideas about the Prophet, the *pīr,* and the Quran that could easily be assimilated into Indian patterns. It also meant a different attitude toward the members of Hindu society, who, once having identified an individual as Muslim, could no longer deal with him on the same terms—and would not easily take him back.

While the new Muslims certainly had a revalued perception of the sanctity of orthodox Hindu norms, those who remained Hindus might be led to reconsider the value of their own tradition by the presence of large numbers of converts in their midst, and at least as important, of Muslim rulers. Perhaps the elaborate legal and ritual forms of Hinduism were not so eternally valid after all, especially since they diverged so greatly from those of Islam. In fact, perhaps the external paraphernalia of both traditions was just a bunch of hokum. At any rate, this is what many Hindi *sant*s declared in no uncertain terms.

But while the *sant*s reject the sanctity of the Hindu heritage, with its social and mythological forms, they retain a general Indic world view, which, as we have seen, may give license to the most extreme ontological inclinations of the *guru-bhakta.* So the Lord of whom the *sant*s sing, while inapproachable through the sanctified traditions of both Hinduism and Islam, still remains accessible through the guru, who can take on radical dimensions. Since the *nirguṇ sādhanā* depends on no traditional icons, the *sant* is able to serve as a focus that rises above apparently conflicting heritages. He can, moreover, become the basis of a community toward which personally unconvinced members of converted groups—now outside the pale of Hindu society—might turn. Thus both the strongly iconoclastic direction that *sant* tradition sometimes takes and its widespread popularity can be traced to the *sant* as holy man offering an alternative to the heritages of Hinduism and Islam.

The Continuing Place of *Sant* Piety

The moment of impact between conflicting heritages that gave rise to the *sant*s was eventually followed by a moment of reaction. Among Hindus as well as Muslims, the staunchly devout grew suspicious of the syncretic Indo-Muslim culture encouraged by Akbar, the great Mughal whose reign began a century after Kabir's era. Opening his secular bureaucracy to Hindus from the old ruling classes, Akbar undermined the sanctified bases of Hindu political authority: hereditary princes could wield power under the new system, but their authority no longer derived from Hindu law. At the same time, with a laissez-faire religious policy and eccentric beliefs of his own, Akbar was seen as a heretic by conservative Muslims upholding a narrow construction of Islamic rule. In reconsolidating their communities, both Hindus and Muslims found new foci in powerful traditional personalities. Hindu poets and devotees began to see eternally present deities transforming their everyday realities into heavenly worlds. Muslim Naqshbandi leaders, identifying themselves as special, recurring Islamic personages, gave communal law renewed sanctity. These mythic figures and their living representatives then served as foci for the reintegration into orthodox society of the devotional and esoteric traditions that had previously been the preserve of sometimes unorthodox holy men.

Hindus became increasingly devoted to the incarnations of Vishnu. Many prayed ecstatically to Krishna, and treated gurus in the lineage of Vallabha and others with royal dignity. But perhaps more important for communal ideals was the revival of the cult of Ram, the upright king, embodiment of pristine Hindu virtues.[13] The courtly imagery of Tulsi Das' Ramayana hearkens to an earlier royal reality, ignoring the accoutrements of the contemporary Mughal empire.

Meanwhile, at about the same time, special personages were appearing in Indian Islam. In the years just prior to Mughal rule, Saiyid Muhammad of Jaunpur spoke out against corrupt Indian Sufi practice and declared himself the Mahdi, the one who would usher in the end of time. But a movement leaving a more profound mark on Indian Islam as a whole began under the reign of Akbar's son, Jahangir. Sheikh Ahmad Sirhindi, the great Naqshbandi leader, declared himself *mujaddid,* the "renewer," understood by Muslims to come at the beginning of each Islamic century; but since Sirhindi lived through the thousandth year of the hegira, he was to be the renewer of the next Islamic millenium. For Sirhindi, the unitive Sufi experience—which in India had been taken to its most monistic, indeed Vedantic, extremes—appeared as an incomplete realization. So Sirhindi developed a new, dualistic integration of mysticism and Islamic law—one that has earned the respect of Muslim scholars far beyond the subcontinent.[14]

In revivifying traditional heritages, both the Hindu and Islamic movements oriented piety away from the transcendent visions emerging among the *sant*s and liberal Sufis of earlier centuries. The play of Krishna presents the familiar Hindu world as a place for divine enjoyment; the rule of Ram recognizes it as a field of sacred duty. Effectively directing their devotees' gaze out and down to traditional forms, these divinities offer an experience contrasting with that offered by the *sant*, who stands beyond all heritages and points upward toward the

Formless Lord. Among Muslims, Naqshbandis continued to contemplate the master's image, and sought the transcendent through ever higher stages of ascent. But they took the upward orientation of the earlier traditions to a radically different end: the Lord, according to Sirhindi, may be approached but never finally grasped; and since everything proceeds from Him, His will can be served through correct actions in the creation—which are made known in the institutions of Islam.

Emerging under the clash of contrasting heritages and quietly transformed in a period of religiocultural contraction, the *sant*s, along with other guru-oriented traditions, find their greatest resurgence under a new impact—that of the West. The Radhasoamis, who counted important adherents among nineteenth-century civil servants versed in Persian as well as English, are one of the oldest and most widespread of the guru-oriented movements found today. Yet even though *sant* tradition seems to flourish under broad-scale cultural impact, it has still persisted vitally through periods of general religiocultural reaction. For individuals and small-scale communities experience moments of impact and reaction of their own, encountering new cultures and seeking to preserve established heritages. In such situations, the continuing *sant* tradition often finds a creative role.

Increasingly Hinduized during the general religious reactions of the seventeenth century, the older *sant* lineages have still tended to thrive at the margins of Hindu society or within its interstices. The numerous Kabirpanthis entrenched in Chhatisgarh offer an elaborate but non-Vedic heritage in a region with a large tribal population, and the Dadupanthis of Rajasthan have presented local princes with a respectable lettered tradition grounded in the vernacular.[15] Both Dadupanthis and Sikhs, moreover, have let the un-Brahmanic image of their gurus become a focus for specialized military functions. At the same time, some individuals, dissatisfied with a ritualistic piety, may simply have un-Brahmanic personal sentiments: a few informants from rural Hindu families said matter-of-factly that they were attracted to some *panth* because they liked the aniconic worship practiced there.

Most of the later sants had less important popular roles than the earlier, illustrious ones, but appear to have carried on a continuous, if malleable, tradition of acquired spiritual practice, an aniconic tradition that can have an appeal of its own even if taken in a more Hinduized context. A figure like Charandas, moreover, can come out of a *sant* background to present a liberal, nonsectarian form of traditional Hinduism when the occasion demands. But all later *sant* poets, in adopting the literary conventions of *nirguṇ* poetry, sing at length of the guru and use a mixed Hindi-Vaishnava/Urdu-Sufi devotional vocabulary that reflects the exaltation of the holy man in the midst of an obviously continuing, if significantly less jarring, cultural interface.

Unpolished, didactic, and hybrid, sometimes esoteric and occasionally striking, the distinctive *sant* style of verse is venerated and still produced throughout North India today. Though the genre took shape in particular circumstances of cultural impact, it has nevertheless continued to provide a scriptural basis for a widespread and long-lived religious tradition. In its origins, *sant* verse reflects a characteristic attitude—at once yogic and devotional, always popular, at times iconoclastic. But different *sants* have given this attitude their own emphases, and lineages of disciples gave the diverging perspectives of great gurus varied institutional forms.

In formulating their doctrines and shaping their traditions, disciples have continuously dwelt on the mystery of the guru extolled in *sant* verse. The guru may be found in a finite scripture or an infinite divine truth, in one or many *sants* of the past, or in an entire lineage of devotees. And most crucially for disciples, the guru may be recognized in a living master at hand. These different facets of the guru, often invoked at the same time, reinforce each other: human dimensions revealing the practical meanings of esoteric knowledge; eternal truths that come down through a lineage giving depth to familiar human appearance.

The redemptive power of *sants* of the past is thus made available through the living guru. His words convey their instructions, explain the meaning of scripture, and make known the will of the highest divine. And as a direct manifestation of the divine guru within everyone, each of the master's outer actions is weighted with significance. For many who have realized the highest truth—including, perhaps, the poets themselves—the guru of *sant* songs may refer first of all to the Lord above, the one known to all masters and disciples. But devotees on the path are liable to know the Lord above through the living guru—who contains contradictions but exists beyond them, who lives in the world but remains unbound by conventions, appearing at once divine, human, and always somehow accessible.

Appendix

Spiritual Lineages: The Bauri *Paramparā* and the Radhasoami Masters

The purpose of the following genealogical charts is to clarify relationships among some of the *sant*s we have discussed. Members of the different lineages outlined who are not relevant to our discussion have been omitted.

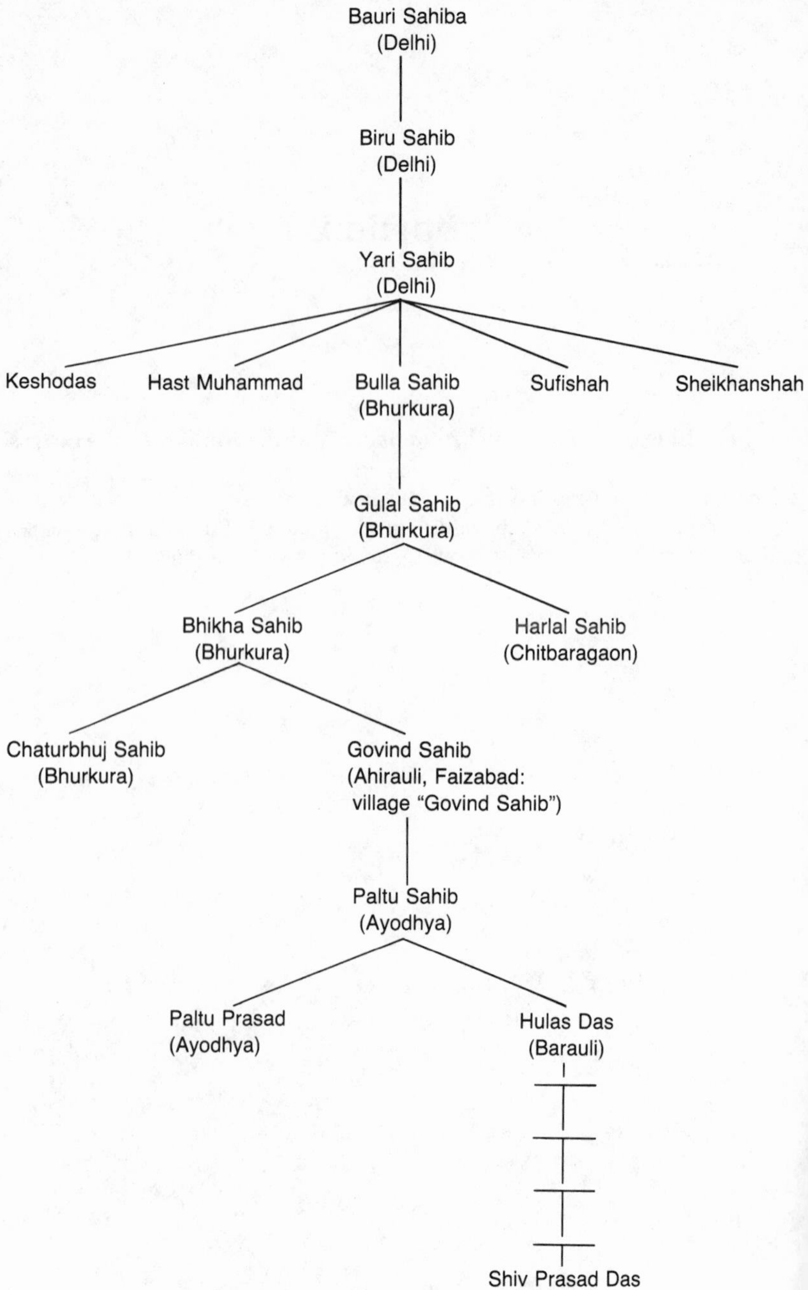

Fig. 2. *Sants* of the Bauri *Paramparā* according to Gulalpanthi tradition.

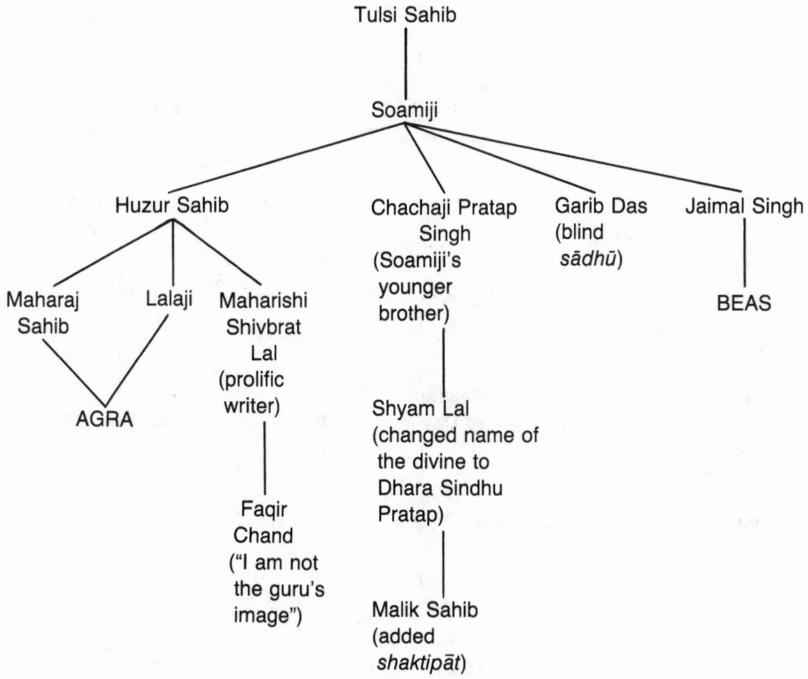

Fig. 3. The Radhasoami lineages: the beginnings and the minor sublineages.

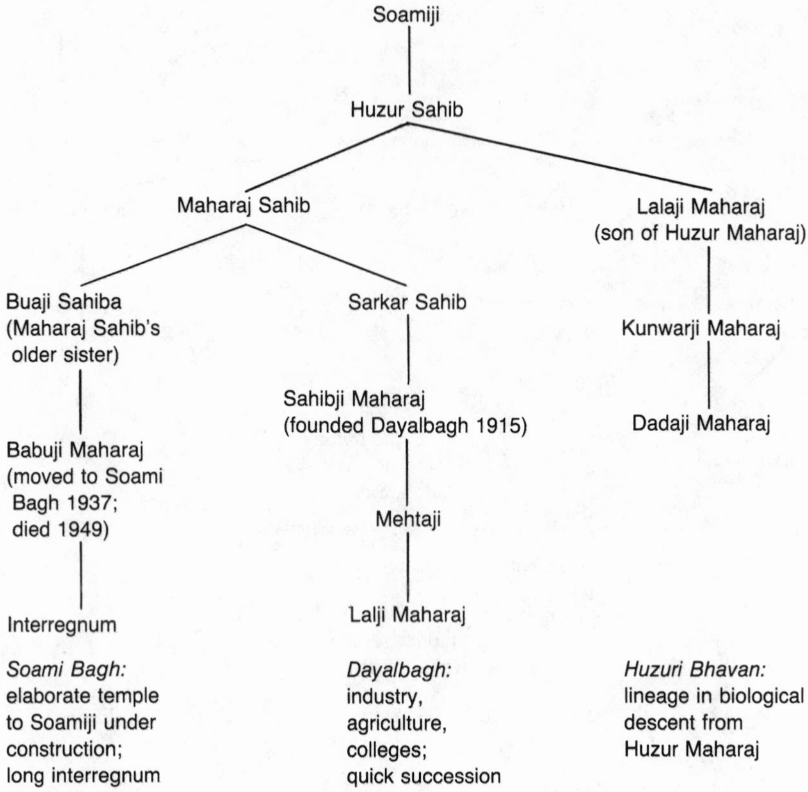

Fig. 4. The Radhasoami lineages in Agra.

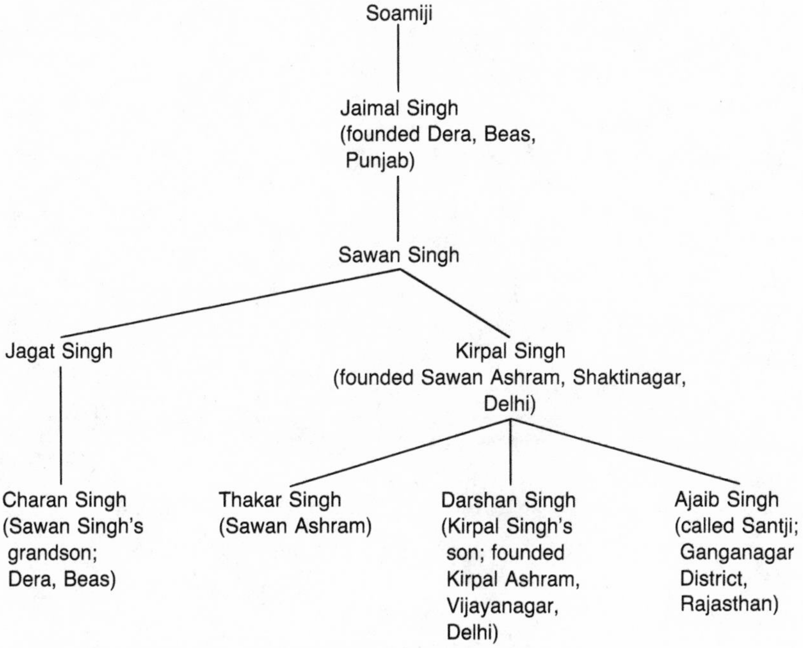

Fig. 5. The Beas sublineages of the Radhasoami line.

Notes

Introduction

1. The academic study of the *sants* was pioneered by Pitambar Datta Barthwal in *The Nirgun School of Hindi Poetry* (1936). Writing in English, Barthwal sorted out some different strands of *sant* tradition, typifying them in terms of classical Hindu philosophy. Parashuram Chaturvedi, however, has done the most comprehensive work on the *sants*, including an encyclopedic survey of *sant* lineages (1972) and a concise interpretation of themes from *sant* verse (1975). Identifying a common piety among Hindi *sants*—who are seen in continuity with earlier *sant* traditions to the south—Chaturvedi does not emphasize any close parallels between the *sants* and other forms of Indian religion. Other scholars have offered more daring, specific interpretations: Nagendra Nath Upadhyaya, contrasting the literature of *sants* and *nāth* yogis, stresses the similarity of *sant* piety to that found in the *Nāradīya bhakti sutras*; Ramamurti Tripathi, on the other hand, sees elements in *sant* verse deriving from the tantric yoga of Kashmir; Shashibhusan Dasgupta (pp. 346–66) has drawn parallels between the *sants* and the Buddhist *siddha* tradition that he studied. In the figure of Kabir, the Sufi and revolutionary side of the *sants* was presented to the West at the beginning of this century by Tagore and Westcott. The image remains: see recent works by Hedayatullah and Gafurova. The revolutionary aspects of the larger *sant* tradition have lately been examined by Kiran Nanda, who pays particular attention to their literary implications.

2. Kabir and Nanak in the fifteenth century and Dadu in the sixteenth, all sources of important sectarian traditions, have caught the attention of contemporary Western scholars. Charlotte Vaudeville's profusely annotated scholarly translation of Kabir's *sākhīs* (1974) is certainly of an order higher than any earlier Western work on Kabir. Her introduction to the volume is the best compact presentation of Kabir's epoch in English. More recent studies have focused on Kabir's piety (Dwyer) and his rhetoric (Hess 1983). A detailed review of the scholarship on the poet, in Indian as well as Western languages, can be found in the preface to Gafurova's Russian translation of Kabir's verses

from the Adigranth. The careful textual scholarship of W. H. McLeod has encompassed the life and teachings of Guru Nanak (1968) and Sikh hagiographical traditions (1980). From a more religiohistorical perspective, he has examined the evolution of the Sikh community (1976). The institutions of Sikhism in their historical development have been treated by Owen Cole (1982, 1984). The first Western scholar to look seriously at Dadu was W. G. Orr, a Scottish missionary whose presentation of Dadu's life, his works, and Dadupanthi tradition remains useful. More recently, Winand Callewaert (1974, 1977, 1978) has embarked on detailed research into Dadupanthi texts, and several others have followed his lead (Antoni, de Brabandere, Thiel-Horstmann [1983b]). For interesting studies of the modern Radhasoami movement see Babb (1981, 1983, and 1986 part 1) and Juergensmeyer (1986). Lorenzen (1981, 1986) has treated recent developments in the Kabir *panth*.

3. Different views on the problem of *sant* tradition were expressed at a conference on *sant*s held in Berkeley in 1978, and are presented in the belated (1986) conference volume edited by Schomer and McLeod. Schomer's introduction gives a balanced perspective on approaches taken in articles by Vaudeville, Juergensmeyer, and Gold. A revised version of Hawley's conference paper (1984, ch. 5) shows the place of *sant* themes in Sur Das, famous as an exponent of Krishna devotion.

4. On the significance of the sectarian compilations, see Schomer (1979) and Gold (1986). Callewaert (1978) has studied an important *sant* compiler.

5. Gold (forthcoming a).

Chapter 1

1. For the different ways in which Indian regions have been defined, see Cohn (1977), Schwartzberg, and Sopher (1980).

2. Tivari, *pada* section, pp. 26, 28, 115.

3. Of course, Lal Ded, the fourteenth-century poetess of Kashmir, lived probably before Kabir and certainly far away from Namdev. But the Bauls of Bengal are known to have flourished in the eighteenth century and, like the *sant*s, constitute a popular tradition deriving from yogic, Vaishnava, and Sufi sources. Vaishnava Gujarat knew Narsi Mehta; his dates remain problematic (see Joshi, pp. 11–15), but he may well have flourished with Kabir during the fifteenth century.

4. More than once, Kabir contrasts the virtuous *sant* with the debased *shākta*. See Vaudeville's translations (1974, pp. 185, 186, 242, 258).

5. The most important of these is the Jñāneshvarī (trans. V. G. Pradhan, 1967).

6. Thapar, p. 264.

7. As early as 1829 the resemblances between postclassical India and medieval Europe were dramatized by James Tod, "a careful and acute observer"

(Banerji, p. 109), but also a romantic. Since then, many social historians of India have questioned the appropriateness of the comparison. Fox (1971), pp. 133–38, discusses the literature on Indian feudalism. Coulborn, pp. 218–22, and Thorner, pp. 133–50, examine the Indian patterns against the general phenomenon of feudalism. Cohn (1977) presents the feudal model as one of several changing British perspectives on Indian social structures.

8. Wolpert, p. 112.

9. See Fox (1971), p. 19.

10. Graburn, p. 2. Emphasis in original.

11. Rudolph, p. 19.

12. Westcott, pp. 188–94, reports on the Kabirpanthis of Chhatisgarh.

13. *Sar Bachan* (*Prose*), pp. 218–21.

14. The closest parallel is the Dadupanthi Nagas; see Orr, pp. 199–209, and Gold (forthcoming b).

15. Narrated as hagiographical literature early in chapter 7.

16. Wach, p. 128.

17. Translation of songs featuring these analogies are given below, pp. 124, 132.

18. "*apne samān banā letā hai*" (*Shabda Kosh Sant Mat Vānī,* p. 268; see also *Hindi Shabdsāgar,* vol. 7, s.v. *bhrangī*).

19. Tivari, p. 3.

20. *Sār Bachan Rādhāsoāmī,* p. 76.

21. p. 26, v. 3.

22. *Sūrsāgar:* 2970 (vol. 2, p. 1002). Though Sur Das was particularly renowned for his descriptions of the child Krishna, there are also many amorous verses in the *Sūrsāgar,* the voluminous collection of lyrics attributed to Sur Das (see especially vol 2, pp. 985–1035). Important monographs treating the figure of Krishna in the *Sūrsāgar* have been written by Bryant, and Hawley (1983). Hawley (1979) has also written on text criticism in the *Sūrsāgar.* Hawley and Bryant together are preparing a critical edition.

23. *Kabīr Sāhib kī Shabdāvalī,* vol. 1, p. 4.

24. *Sūrsāgar:* 2848 (vol. 2, p. 975).

25. *Santbānī Sangrah,* vol. 2, p. 2.

26. See Barnett, Marriott, Inden, and Inden and Nicholas. The anthropological formulations these writers use derive from a crucial contrast between Indian and Western notions; see Inden and Nicholas, who acknowledge their debt to Schneider's work on American kinship (p. 14).

27. The seminal works have been Srinivas, Redfield and Singer, Singer and Cohn, and Singer (1972).

28. On *puṣṭimārgīya* sectarian tradition see Barz, Shah, and Jindel. On Vallabha's philosophy, called *shuddhādvaita,* see Marfatia and Bhatt.

29. Other causes for pollution include speaking a language other than *Vraj Bhāṣā* or Sanskrit and presenting a folded-hands salutation to anyone other than Krishna. For more details, see Jindel, pp. 58–61.

Chapter 2

1. Tod, vol. 1, pp. 419–24, gives a hyperbolic account of the richness of Nathdwara and its pilgrims during the early nineteenth century.

2. The life history of Shrinathji was recorded in *Vraj Bhāṣā* by Hariraiji, an important *gosāīṃ,* probably in 1685.

3. Mahabharata, bk. 3, ch. 80, vss. 40–60; in van Buitenen, vol. 2, pp. 374–75.

4. Chatterjee discusses the place of the *Puṣkara Mahātmya* in the Padma Purāṇa, pp. 190–94.

5. This description is based on conversations with disciples of Sant Ajaib Singh, known as Santji, one of three important successors to Sant Kirpal Singh of Delhi. His ashram is in Ganganagar district, Rajasthan.

6. *Sār Bachan Rādhāsoāmī,* p. 76.

7. *Sūrsāgar,* vol. 2, p. 990.

8. Jindel, pp. 86–87, gives statistics on the pilgrims to Nathdwara. *Baniyās* and Brahmans together constitute almost eighty-five percent; people coming from Gujarat and Bombay over fifty percent.

9. Jindel, pp. 114–15.

10. Jindel, pp. 75, 150.

11. *Souvenir in Commemoration of the First Centenary of the Radhasoami Satsang,* p. 171.

12. The versions of the story heard in the field and recounted in the popular literature (Agrawal, p. 27) have the Gujarin, logically enough, coming out of the cow's anus. According to the account given in the official Rajasthan District Gazeteer (1966), p. 736, she came out of the cow's womb.

13. *Sūrsāgar:* 744 (vol. 1, p. 303); cf. the commentary of Varma, p. 56, and Bryant's translation in *Poems to the Child God,* p. 161.

14. Bryant, p. xii.

15. *Sūrsāgar:* 728 (vol. 1, p. 299); cf. Varma, p. 55 and Bryant, pp. 159–60.

16. *Sūrsāgar:*733 (vol. 1, p. 300).

17. Weber (1964), p. 92.

18. See Mulji's accusations, pp. 144–49.

19. Paltu Sahib, *Palṭu Shabdāvalī,* p. 313; *Palṭu Bānī,* vol 3., p. 59. See also Feldhaus, who translates a thirteenth-century Marathi text describing the quixotic behavior of a holy man. as *The Deeds of God in Ṛddhipur.*

20. Shyam Lal (1952), vol. 2, pp. 132–33; Dhara Sindhu Pratap is the name Shyam Lal used for the Supreme Lord.

21. Puri, p. 234. Emphasis in original.

22. For further dimensions of the parallel between physical and spiritual seed, see O'Flaherty (1980a), pp. 17–61. For seeds as the potentiality of acts, see McDermott, p. 187.

23. Inden, pp. 24–25.

24. Shastri, p. 2.
25. See the descriptions of Macauliffe, vol. 2, pp. 1–48.

Chapter 3

1. The vast scholarship on Kabir is of highly varied quality. Hazariprasad Dvivedi (1973) has written the most influential Hindi monograph on Kabir. The poet's verses are available in several recent scholarly editions: Tivari's is authoritative, though limited; Shukdeo Singh's edition of the Bijak has too many printing errors, unfortunately, to be trustworthy as a critical edition in its present form (Hess [1983], appendix C, gives a list of corrections); Mataprasad Gupta offers a good selection with a valuable gloss. Vaudeville (1974) presents extensive and important treatments of the cultural-historical context, the textual tradition, and Kabirian scholarship; Hess (1983) examines Kabir's poetry as religious rhetoric. Both offer eminently readable translations of his verses: Vaudeville from Tivari's text, Hess from Singh's.

2. Kabir's dates are problematic. The early fifteenth-century floruit is Vaudeville's judgment (1974, pp. 36–39); she refers to the lengthy discussion of Chaturvedi (1972, pp. 845–70). There is, however, no reason to doubt the tradition that the Adigranth was compiled by Guru Arjan between 1603 and 1604; see McLeod (1976), p. 60.

3. Macauliffe recounts the story in vol. 6, pp. 120–22. According to another tradition, Sena came from Maharashtra, an origin also sometimes attributed to Sadhna; see Chaturvedi (1972), pp. 97–99, 232–35.

4. Particularly those of Beni. For translations, see Macauliffe, vol. 6, pp. 92–93.

5. Mishra and Maurya, pp. 9–31, review the scholarship on Namdev and present good arguments for accepting Namdev's traditional dates (1270–1350) as well as the identity of the Hindi Namdev with the Marathi one. A useful English summary of their review is given in Machwe, pp. 24–32. The thematic differences between the eastern and western recensions of Kabir are treated by Hess (1986). On the contrast between the two Western recensions see Schomer (1979), pp. 75–86.

6. Translated by Prabhakar Machwe, p. 88.
7. Translated by Prabhakar Machwe, p. 89.
8. Macnicol, p. 15; cited in Machwe, p. 38.
9. Keshavadas, p. 37.
10. Translated by Prabhakar Machwe, p. 93.
11. Hess (1983), p. 76, *shabda* 104.
12. Tivari, *pada* 144, pp. 84–85; cf. "the dyer-guru," p. 26, above.
13. Vaudeville (1974), pp. 81–89; Dvivedi (1973), p. 26; Briggs, pp. 44–61, 128–29, 135–36.

14. See Gold and Gold.

15. Modern low-caste movements invoking the names of past sants have been described by Juergensmeyer (1982) and Cohn (1969).

16. Raidas, Kabir, Pipa, Dhanna, and Sena are treated consecutively in Nabhaji's vss. 59–63.

17. There is also a popular etymology from *pal pal,* "every moment"; Paltu, they say, was constantly engaged in muttering the Lord's name.

18. The most widely circulated of Paltu's songs are published by the Belvedere Press, Allahabad: the *Bānī* in three volumes. The Paltu Akhara, Ayodhya, has published two collections based on the manuscripts they have preserved: the *Shabdāvalī* and *Palṭū Darshan.*

19. Radhakrishna Singh, p. 31, cites these references to Paltu's caste: *Paltū Bānī,* vol. 1, *kuṇḍaliyās* 58 and 255; vol. 2, *aril* 114; and vol. 3, *shabdas* 81, 118, and 131. The introductions to both *Palṭū Shabdāvalī* (p. 6) and *Palṭū Bānī,* vol. 1, give verses identifying Paltu's natal village as Nagpur Jalalpur.

20. The date is sometimes taken as that of Paltu's birth, but this is unlikely; Shukla discusses the problem, pp. 74–75.

21. Sakhopar, in Devariya district; see Radhakrishna Singh, pp. 38–39.

22. *Palṭu Shabdāvalī,* introduction, p. 8. A full recounting of the tale is here given by Jagannath Das, a former *mahant* of the Paltu Akhara and namesake of the Lord of Puri.

23. See *Palṭū Bānī,* vol. 3, *shabda* 5, pp. 2–3. Translated in Gold (forthcoming a, ch. 1).

24. *Palṭū Bānī,* vol. 1, *kuṇḍaliyā* 218, p. 90.

25. The reference to Vidura is from the Mahabharata, Udyoga Parvan, ch. 89; the relevant passage is accessible in Narasimhan, p. 103. The story of Shabari is told in the Valmiki Ramayana, Aranya Kanda, Canto 74. Later tradition embellishes Shabari's naiveté; to see if the berries are sweet she tastes each one first, thus polluting it. Ram accepts the selected berries, but the *munis* are outraged. The story of Swapacha does not seem to appear in the common Sanskrit versions of the Mahabharata's Ashvamedha Parvan, where one would expect it. But Charan Singh of Beas tells it twice: 1958, pp. 104–5, and 1977, pp. 23–25.

26. In addition to being discussed at length by Charan Singh (1958, 1977), the song has been included in *Sant Sangrah,* an anthology compiled by the second Radhasoami guru, known as Huzur Sahib, in 1886 (vol. 2, p. 150).

27. Ezekiel, p. 37.

28. *Palṭu Bānī,* vol. 1, p. 43.

29. Ramrupji (n.d.), p. 66.

30. *Bhaktisāgar,* p. 130.

31. Jogjit, p. 16; Sahajo Bai (1967), 50, 51.

32. Thanks to Joan Erdman for information on Jaipur Bhargavas. For the Bhargavas of the Mahabharata, see Goldman.

33. Wilson, p. 117; Grierson, p. 366; Sen, p. 145.

34. Some lists do differ in details, but at the older sectarian establishments scattered throughout Faizabad, Azamgarh, and Ballia districts memories are frequently kept straight by the accumulated tombs of former *mahant*s.

35. E.g., *Palṭū Bānī,* vol. 3, p. 5.

36. Thanks to Wendy O'Flaherty for pointing out to me the contrast between Shukdev and Vyasa.

37. The Upanishads include the Hamsanada, Sarva, Tattvayoga, Yogashikha, and Tejabindu. On the story of Nasiketa in the *Brahmāṇḍa Puraṇa,* see Grierson, p. 368.

38. See pp. 60–61.

39. *Bhaktisāgar,* p. 464.

40. Ramrupji (n.d.), pp. 163–68; Jogjit, pp. 215–17, 268–72. Charandas traveled as far as Ujjain and Lucknow.

41. See pp. 40–41.

42. Jogjit, pp. 166–90; Ramrupji, pp. 96–151. Both biographers present the journey to Vraj as the next major episode in Charandas' life after his exploits during Nadir Shah's invasion, which occurred when Charandas was thirty-six. Charandas' descriptive *Vrajcharitvarnan* begins the *Bhaktisgāgar,* pp. 2–14.

43. Rajesh Dixit, p. 65. For a Sanskrit litany of *siddha*s, see the *Kulārṇava Tantra,* ch. 6, vs., 65–66 (p. 76).

44. Ramrupji (n.d.), pp. 11–13, 115–51; Jogjit, pp. 19–24, 186–90.

45. Ramrupji (n.d.), p. 45. The date is found in Ramrupji, p. 57 and Jogjit, p. 79. The *saṃvat* year 1789 corresponds to A.D. 1732; *chaitra* falls in the hot season.

46. Grierson, p. 366; Wilson, p. 118; Crooke, vol. 2., p. 202.

47. Ramrupji (n.d.), p. 57, 62–66.

48. Ramrupji (n.d.), pp. 14–16, 23–32; Jogjit, pp. 25–28, 48–52.

49. Jogjit, p. 48.

50. T. N. Dixit 1961, pp. 1–24; 1966, pp. 1–7; Sahay, pp. 1–2.

51. Ramrupji (n.d.), pp. 81–92; Jogjit, pp. 147–58.

52. Ramrupji (n.d.), p. 90. According to Jogjit, p. 156, Nadir Shah said:

Know him as of the race of God
    And banish bigotry.
Whether he's a Hindu or a Turk
    He's still God's light.

53. *Bhaktisāgar,* pp. 176–77.

54. *Bhaktisāgar,* p. 220.

55. *Bhaktisāgar,* p. 338. For Paltu's song, see p. 103.

56. *Bhaktisāgar,* p. 3.

Chapter 4

1. T. N. Dixit (1961), pp. 340–41, gives some lists.

2. Jogjit, pp. 218–19. Sarasmadhuri's verse biography is published as an

introduction to the 1972 edition of Ramrupji's collected songs (*Mukti Mārg*), to which several of his verse narratives have been appended.

3. Ganga Das, p. xiii.

4. The account of Ghanshyam Das, the newly installed *mahant* of Sahajo's seat in Delhi, in his introduction to *Sahaj Prakāsh.*

5. Sahajo Bai (1967), p. 2. A description of the *bhrangī* guru begins the discussion of religiocultural contexts in ch. 1.

6. From the account of Ghanshyam Das, quoting a version of Jogijit that differs from the 1968 edition I have used.

7. Page 230.

8. I am grateful to Professor Shyam Sundar Shukla of Banaras Hindu University for sharing with me the fruits of his research. All of the unattributed specific facts in the present discussion have been communicated to me privately by Professor Shukla, who has done extensive work on the available Charandasi records.

9. Tulsi Sahib, vol. 1, p. 59.

10. Daya Bai (1976), pp. 14–26, "the Vinaya Malika."

11. From Chaturvedi (1967), pp. 200–201.

12. *Palṭū Shabdāvalī,* p. 200.

13. Present-day *mahant*s often say that this Ramananda was a *sādhū* who lived in a village in Gazipur, where the most important center of the tradition is located; this coincidence seems too convenient: Shukla discusses the problem, pp. 54–59.

14. Prabhudas Acharya, pp. 2–8. In 1980, Prabhudas was reigning as *mahant* at the Paltu Akhara, Ayodhya.

15. Radhakrishna Singh, pp. 139–42, describes four vital *maṭh*s in the sublineage of Paltu alone; I have visited six others in different sublineages and have heard *sādhū*s speak of several more. For more on the present-day state of the lineage, see Gold (forthcoming a, ch. 2).

16. These have no connection with the seventeenth-century Satnami rebellion; *sat nām,* "the true name," is a common expression for the highest divine principle among *sant*s, and has been used by different *sant* groups.

17. On the traditional accounts of Dadu's life, see Callewaert (1978), pp. 21–56, where important sources are given in translation.

18. The most influential Kabirpanthi metaphysical work is the *Anurāg Sāgar,* available in several editions.

19. About the Kabirpanthi *sādhū*s at Kabir Chaura, Sinha and Saraswati report "that all of them wanted us to write that Kabir was born in a Brahman family and that the popular version of his being born in a Moslem weaver family is the product of malicious propaganda by the rival sects" (p. 179). My own interviews with the Kabir Chaura *sādhū*s confirm this report.

20. Kedarnath Dvivedi, pp. 203–5.

21. Kedarnath Dvivedi, p. 204.

22. See pp. 163–64.

23. Tapswiji, pp. 671–768 (out of a 1050-page volume!); Barari, introduction, p. *ṭh.*

24. Wilson, p. 117.

25. Orr, p. 228; Wilson refers to the apparently defunct *panth*s of Sena and Sadhna, pp. 78–79, 119.

26. Kharsia, founded in 1933; details are given in Kedarnath Dvivedi, p. 346.

27. Above, pp. 44–47.

28. Maharaj Sahib, p. 456.

29. Shyam Lal (1927), p. xxii.

30. Chaturvedi (1972), pp. 159–61; Vaudeville (1974), p. 116.

31. Schomer 1979, p, 81; McLeod 1968, p. 197.

32. McLeod (1968), p. 197.

33. Vaudeville (1974), p. 159.

34. Tivari, 1:23, p. 139; 2:22, p. 145; cf. Vaudeville (1974), pp. 166, 157.

35. See the *Pādukāpanchakam* in Woodroffe (1964), pp. 481–500. For the Radhasoami's vision, see p. 47.

36. Sri Aurobindo (1972), pp. 79–80.

37. Puri, pp. 7, 17.

38. Mathur, pp. 75, 24.

39. Pratap Singh, pp. 6–7.

40. *Tulsi Sahib* (Beas edition), p. 8; Maheshwari (1979b), p. 20.

41. The possibility that Soamiji waited until Girdhari Das had died to open the *satsang* was suggested to me by the editor of the volume on Tulsi Sahib published at Beas. This possibility is given support by the narrative sequence of Chachaji Pratap Singh's biography of Soamiji, pp. 37–40, where the account of Soamiji's opening the *satsang* immediately follows a discussion of his relationship to Girdhari Das.

42. *Sār Bachan Rādhāsoāmī* 38:12, p. 351.

43. Pratap Singh, p. 17.

44. *Sar Bachan* (*Prose*), pp. 57–58, 218–21; *Sār Bachan Rādhāsoāmī,* pp. 178–85.

45. Dharmendra Brahmchari, p. 1.

46. The similarities between the cosmology of the Anurag Sagar and that of Tulsi Sahib, Soamiji's guru, have been pointed out by Juergensmeyer (1986); on the place of the *Anurāg Sāgar* in a modern Radhasoami sublineage, see ch. 6, note 27.

47. For a portrait of Chachaji Maharaj offered by a partisan of Huzur Maharaj, see Maheshwari (1979a), pp. 14–26.

Chapter 5

1. Pitambar Mishra, pp. 298–301.

2. Examples can be found in Maheshwari (1971), pp. 244, 246, 350, 353, and 358.

3. *Sār Bachan Rādhāsoāmī* 35:10, p. 297.

4. *Sār Bachan Rādhāsoāmī* 35:6, p. 295.

5. *Sār Bachan Rādhāsoāmī* 35:7, p. 295.
6. Vaudeville (1974), 9:37, p. 207
7. Vaudeville (1974), 9:8, p. 200; 9:21, p. 203.
8. Vaudeville, (1974), pp. 143–44.
9. H. P. Dvivedi (1973), pp. 13ff.
10. H. P. Dvivedi (1963), p. 37.
11. Vaudeville (1974), p. 143.
12. Barthwal, pp. 270–72. The early Dadupanthi text on which Barthwal largely based his glossary is presented by Callewaert (1974). Shashikala Pandey has recently prepared a useful philological and literary analysis of key terms in *sant* literature, including some from the technical vocabulary.
13. Barthwal, p. 156.
14. Also sometimes referred to as *sandhyā bhāṣā,* "twilight language"; Bharati, pp. 165–68, gives a history of the terminological controversy.
15. Eliade (1969), p. 253.
16. See Bharati, Snellgrove, and Kvaerne, who takes Eliade's insight a step further in his analysis of the *Caryāgīti.*
17. Bharati, pp. 168–73.
18. Dasgupta, pp. 413–24
19. Eliade 1969, p. 250.
20. Barthwal, p. 301, quoted in Vaudeville, p. 144. On the *sant*s' *ulaṭvāṃsī,* see Rameshchandra Mishra.
21. Eliade (1969), pp. 252–54.
22. Wayman, p. 165
23. Sri Aurobindo (1971), pp. 1–7.
24. See Bolle, p. 147.
25. Renou, p. 3.
26. Gonda, pp. 12–13, 27, 168.
27. Gonda, pp. 118, 135–36.
28. Tulsi Sahib, vol. 1, pp. 56–57.
29. Tulsi Sahib, vol. 1, p. 59.
30. Charan Singh (1976), p. 309.
31. Shyam Lal (1952), vol. 2, pp. 47–48.
32. Charan Singh (1976), p. 247.
33. Charan Singh (1976), p. 275.
34. *Mahātmāoṃ kī Bānī,* p. 22.
35. The word for "monastery" in the song is *maṭh,* which in the *sant bānī* often forms a compound with *ghaṭ,* used for "body": *ghaṭ-maṭh.*
36. *Mahātmāoṃ kī Bānī,* p. 22.
37. Maheshwari (1979a), pp. 160–61.
38. For example, the *Amighuṃṭ* of Keshavdas and the *Shabdsār* of Bulla.
39. The manuscript contains *shabda*s numbered up to 906, written on both sides of 361 folio pages.
40. *Mahātmāoṃ kī Bānī,* pp. 187–88.

41. *Mahātmāoṃ kī Bānī,* pp. 193–94.
42. *Mahātmāom kī Bānī,* pp. 205–6.
43. *Mahātmāoṃ kī Bānī,* p. 224.
44. *Mahātmāoṃ kī Bānī,* p. 33.
45. See Kvaerne, pp. 61–64, "An Essay on the Concept of Sahaja."
46. *Mahātmāoṃkī Bānī,* p. 33.
47. *Mahātmāoṃ kī Bānī,* p. 377.
48. *Mahātmāoṃ kī Bānī,* p. 166.
49. Some aspects of this later esoteric *sant* tradition have been sketched from Kabirpanthi sources by Juergensmeyer (1986), who wonders about its extent.
50. See p. 127.

Chapter 6

1. Maharaj Sahib, p. 479. On other anthropological dimensions of the religious life at Soami Bagh, see the very full account of Babb (forthcoming, chs. 1–3).
2. Maheshwari (1954), pp. 57–58, 123.
3. Maheshwari (1954), p. 67.
4. Maheshwari (1954), p. 68.
5. Maheshwari (1954), p. 122.
6. *Souvenir,* p. 119.
7. *Souvenir,* pp. 176–77.
8. *Souvenir,* preface, p. vi.
9. *Souvenir,* pp. 205–7.
10. *Souvenir,* p. 357.
11. *Souvenir,* p. 257.
12. *Souvenir,* p. 263.
13. Maheshwari (1954), pp. 123–24.
14. Mathur, p. 83; Dadaji Maharaj has written this book under his legal name.
15. Mathur, p. 24.
16. *Sar Bachan* (*Prose*), part 2, para. 250, pp. 215–16.
17. *Sar Bachan* (1974), part 2, para. 250, p. 156.
18. Kirpal Singh (1973a), p. 111.
19. On "crowds in heaven" see O'Flaherty (1976), pp. 248–71.
20. Kirpal Singh (1973b), pp. 20–35.
21. Sahai and Khanna, pp. 65–66.
22. Charan Singh (1976), pp. 221–22.
23. Kirpal Singh (1972), vol. 2, pp. 157–58.
24. *Sar Bachan* (*Prose*), part 1, para. 39, pp. 42–43.
25. Puri, p. 270.

26. Puri, pp. 240–41, 270.
27. Morrow, pp. 26–27. Morrow also refers to Kirpal Singh's mentioning Kabir as the first master of the world.
28. I write in the ethnographic present, but both Faqir Chand and Malik Sahib have passed on since my last meetings with them.
29. Faqir Chand, pp. 3, 17.
30. Faqir Chand, pp. 11, 20.
31. Pitambar Mishra, pp. 116–24.
32. See pp. 90–91.

Chapter 7

1. This aphorism of Shri Aurobindo has been taken as the title of a series of writings by M. P. Pandit.
2. Macauliffe, vol. 5, pp. 91–93.
3. Translated in Guenther, pp. 1–109.
4. Guenther, intro., p. v.
5. Guenther, pp. 53, 63.
6. Robinson, p. 105.
7. Babuji Maharaj, p. 404.
8. Coomaraswamy 1977, pp. 85, 93. On the yogic dimensions of sacred images in India, see also Zimmer.
9. Sri Aurobindo (1970), p. 389.
10. Coomaraswamy (1977), p. 83.
11. Thanks to Pat Pranke for arranging the interview and giving me other information on *tanka* painting.
12. The quote on Hindu visualizations is from Shiva C. V. Bhattacharya, vol. 2, p. 273; on degrees of plasticity in Buddhist meditation, see Beyer, pp. 69–76.
13. The reader who wants to study examples for the points made in this paragraph can compare the famous Buddhist meditation on Tara translated in Conze, pp. 133–39 (as well as in Bentoyosh Bhattacharya, pp. 169–75, and Coomaraswamy [1946], pp. 146–51) to the meditation on Adya Kalika in the Mahanirvana Tantra (Woodroffe [1963], pp. 115–19). For the Radhasoamis' subtle offering of the parts of their being, see ll. 3 and 4 of Soamiji's song #2 at the start of ch. 5; cf. vss. 42–46 of the Adya Kalika meditation.
14. Beyer, pp. 394–95.
15. Woodroffe (1963), p. 117, vs. 141. The oppositions in the personality of one Hindu deity are presented in a sophisticated and exhaustive study by Wendy O'Flaherty (1973).
16. Tucci 1969, pp. 4–6; see also Snellgrove, pp. 23–24.
17. *Essence of Refined Gold,* p. 40.
18. Ngawang Dhargyey, pp. 160–61.

19. The Sanskrit line is found in *Kulārṇava Tantra* ch. 12, v. 49, p. 154. Tucci (1980), p. 44, refers to it in a discussion of Tibetan tradition. The verse of Kabir is given on p. 156.

20. Babu Shyam Lal of Gwalior and Maharishi Shivbrat Lal of Gopiganj.

21. See p. 82; the different planes of Radhasoami experience, moreover, are felt to correspond to different points in the head.

22. Shiva C. V. Bhattacharya, vol. 2, pp. 211–12.

23. Vishnu Tirth, p. 133.

24. These strategies were particularly well developed in T'ien Tai; see Takakusu, pp. 136–40.

25. Tucci (1980), p. 34, discusses the innovative Tsonkhapa as a highly remarkable *exception:* "Very rarely [does] a creative mind [attempt] to break through the framework of a tradition regarded as sacrosanct."

26. Quoted by Shiva C. V. Bhattacharya, vol. 2, p. 203.

27. Shiva C. V. Bhattacharya, vol. 2, p. 209.

28. On the elaboration of the parental metaphor, see Schimmel (1975), p. 103. Turner, pp. 65–68, treats important Western discussions of *baraka.*

29. Maneri, p. 95.

30. Nizami (1974), pp. 218–19. The story, from the *Siyar al Auliyā'*, an important hagiographical collection, is told often: see Rizvi (1978), pp. 157–58.

31. Bolshakoff (pp. 181–82) describes the humbling discipline practiced by the Russian *starets* Leonid of Optino. The institutionalization of such discipline in Western Christianity can be seen in *The Rule of the Master,* p. 158. Vivid descriptions of the ecstatic, apparently mad behavior of Vaishnava *bhakta*s can be found in Feldhaus and Mahendranath Gupta.

32. On the *qalandariyas* in India, see Digby (1984) and Rizvi (1978), pp. 300–11.

33. Schimmel 1975, p. 105; Eaton, p. 245.

34. On Naqshbandi tradition see Friedmann (1971), Fusfeld, Schimmel (1979), and Rizvi (1980).

35. Nizami (1974), pp. 179–86, gives oft-cited examples.

36. The reports are from the *Fawā'id-al-Fu'ād;* see Nizami (1955), pp. 105–6, and Rizvi (1976), pp. 69–75.

37. Friedmann, pp. 69–75.

38. Eaton, p. 148. On the role of lights and colors in Sufi meditation, see Valiuddin, pp. 84, 114.

39. An intricate meditation on Arabic letters from an eighteenth-century Indian Naqshbandi source is translated by Schimmel (1975, p. 421).

40. Nawab Gudri Shah, pp. 12–13.

41. Schimmel (1975), pp. 205–6.

42. Sirhindi's statement is from letter 11 of *Maktubāt-i Imām Rabbānī;* Rizvi (1965, pp. 210–11) gives a translation. Naqshbandi *tawajjoh* is discussed by Fusfeld, pp. 185–190.

43. *Sar Bachan* (*Prose*), pp. 42–43.

44. Schimmel (1975), p. 362.

45. Eaton, pp. 244–53. At the beginning of the nineteenth century, Shah Isma'il Shahid, grandson of the great Naqshbandi Shah Wali Allah, continued the discussion of the problem of *sijda* (Shahid, pp. 48–50).

46. Rizvi (1978), p. 231.

47. Digby, pp. 33, 42, 62.

48. Roy, pp. 159–63; the citation is from Sheikh Mansur's *Sirr Nama.*

49. Nawab Gudri Shah, p. 14.

50. Eaton, p. 307, presents an example of such a certificate; he describes it in context on pp. 291–92.

51. Woodroffe (1963), p. 149.

52. From the *Kulārṇava Tantra;* quoted by Shiva C. V. Bhattacharya, vol. 2, p. 208. Cenkner, chs. 6–7, gives a full treatment of the guru-disciple relationship in the classical Hindu context.

53. On Abhinavagupta's gurus see Kanti Chandra Pandey, pp. 11–13. Ramakrishna's different paths are vividly described by Mahendranath Gupta. Malik Sahib's two lineages are sketched in the last section of ch. 6.

54. Beyer, pp. 398–99.

55. Tucci (1980, p. 43) stresses the liberality of Vajrayana masters in this respect.

56. Rizvi (1978), p. 150.

57. Nizami (1955, pp. 98–99) translates the *khilāfat nāma* given by Baba Farid to Nizamuddin.

58. A case history is given by Eaton, pp. 205–9.

59. Maneri, pp. 80–81; Maneri also treats the topic from another point of view, pp. 37–38.

60. A *hadīth* frequently cited by Sufis. See Maneri, p. 25. Hujwiri, p. 55, and Schimmel (1975), p. 101.

60. Rizvi (1978), p. 243.

62. Rizvi (1978, p. 177) cites four traditional sources for this story. Valiuddin, p. 61, cites similar instructions from Naqshbandi tradition.

Chapter 8

1. The *siddhas* seem to have been the first to sing yogic songs in a middle Indic vernacular, and their usage has left its mark on later traditions. In particular, the widespread use among *sants* of the terms *sunna* (Skt. *shunya,* "void") and *sahaj,* "unconditioned," may well have roots in the popularization through song of the *siddhas*' particular Buddhist esoteric vocabulary. For translations and discussion of the *siddhas*' songs, see Kvarene.

2. Hess (1986) gives a statistical analysis of the divine names in the different collections of Kabir.

3. Vaudeville (1974), p. 144.

4. Vaudeville (1974), pp. 147–48. The word *kāl* means "time" and for *sants* suggests the impermanence of life in the world.

5. Nawab Gudri Shah, p. 10.

6. Nawab Gudri Shah, pp. 7–8.

7. Ajudhya Prasad, Huzur Maharaj's son, gives us the earliest written account of the story, pp. 31–32. It is also found in Maheshwari (1971), pp. 87–89, and in the Dayalbagh *Souvenir,* p. 42.

8. On Sufi stories in relation to *sant* tradition and the similarities of Sufi and *sant* experience, see Lawrence (1986).

9. See Eaton, pp. 165–67, and Nizami (1974), pp. 205–14.

10. Nizami discusses evidence of *khanqa*s outside cities (1974, p. 261) and gives reports of yogis in *khanqa*s. He also translates the story about preaching from *Fawā'id al Fu'ād* (1974, pp. 179–80).

11. Orr, pp. 52–66.

12. Rizvi (1971) discusses the processes of conversion in India in historical detail (on the treatment of prisoners of war, see p. 21). Hodgson, vol. 2, pp. 555–59, gives a broad view within the greater Islamic context. Lawrence (1984) identifies the roles early Indian Sufis were seen to play in conversion to Islam. Eaton, pp. 155–64, describes the functions of Indian Sufis within the slow process of Islamization. Zelliot documents a modern low-caste conversion to Buddhism. On conversion to Islam in general, see Levtzion's edited volume.

13. See Babineau for an interpretation of Tulsi Das' Ramayana as an integration of ecstatic devotion with traditional social values. For the impact of Islam on Tulsi Das, see Turbiani.

14. Rizvi (1965) offers an account of Saiyid Muhammad and the Mahdavi movement, pp. 68–124, and a long discussion of Sirhindi, pp. 202–329. To balance Rizvi's negative approach to the latter, see also Friedmann (1971).

15. See Lorenzen (1981, 1986) for the socioreligious roles of the Kabirpanthis, and Gold (forthcoming b) for those of the Dadupanthis. Through the title they have given themselves, the Sufi side of *sant* tradition is still invoked by the publications committee of one small Hinduized *panth:* T. N. Dixit's book on Malukdas (1965), which contains a useful sectarian biography, was published by the *Sant-Sufi Sāhitya Saṃsthān*—a name that brings Sufism together with Sanskrit euphony.

Bibliography

Agrawal, Paramanand Mohan. N.d. *Shrī Puṣkar Rāj Mahātmya*. Pushkar: Bhakti Jnana Mandir.

Ajudhya Prasad. 1928. *Jīvan Charitra Param Puruṣ Pūran Dhanī Huzūr Mahārāj Sāhab*. Agra: Kuṃvar Gurprasad.

Antoni, Petra. "Garībdās' *Anabhai Prabodh:* The Introductory Stanzas." In *Bhakti in Current Research* (*see* Thiel-Horstmann 1983a).

Anurāg Sāgar. n.d. Calcutta: Loknath Pustakalaya.

———. 1968. Allahabad: Belvedere Press.

———. 1974. Bombay: Venkateshwar Press.

———. 1982. See *Ocean of Love*.

[Sri] Aurobindo. 1970. *Letters on Yoga*. Part I. Pondicherry: Sri Aurobindo Ashram.

———. 1971. *The Secret of the Veda*. Pondicherry: Sri Aurobindo Ashram.

———. 1972. *On Himself*. Pondicherry: Sri Aurobindo Ashram.

Babb, Lawrence Alan. 1981. "Glancing: Visual Interaction in Hinduism." *Journal of Anthropological Research* 37:387–401.

———. 1983. "The Physiology of Redemption." *History of Religions* 22:293–312.

———. Forthcoming. *Redemptive Encounters: Three Modern Styles in the Hindu Tradition*. Berkeley and Los Angeles: University of California Press.

Babineau, Edmour J. 1979. *Love of God and Social Duty in the Rāmcharitmānas*. Delhi: Motilal Banarsidass.

Babuji Maharaj. 1977. *Discourses*. Translated by S. D. Maheshwari. Soami Bagh, Agra: S. D. Maheshwari.

Banerji, Anil Chandra. 1962. *Lectures on Rajput History*. Calcutta: Firma K. L. Mukhopadhyaya.

Barari, Sukrit Das. 1977. *Satkabīr Mahāpurāṇ*. Bangalore: Satkabir Sahitya Prakashan Samiti.

Barnett, Steve. 1976. "Coconuts and Gold: Relational Identity in a South Indian Caste." *Contributions to Indian Sociology* 10:133–56.

Barthwal, Pitambar Datta. 1936. *The Nirgun School of Hindi Poetry*. Banaras: Indian Press Ltd.

Barz, Richard. 1976. *The Bhakti Sect of Vallabhacharya*. Faridabad, Haryana: Thomson Press [India], 1976.

Beyer, Stephan. 1973. *The Cult of Tara: Magic and Ritual in Tibet*. Berkeley: University of California Press.

Bhaktisāgar. 1966. Edited by Triloki Narayan Dixit. Lucknow: Navalkishore Press. Collected works of Sant Charandas.

Bharati, Agehananda. 1975. *The Tantric Tradition*. New York: Samuel Weiser.

Bhatt, G. H. 1980. *Shri Vallabhacharya and His Doctrines*. Delhi: Butala & Co.

Bhattacharya, Bentoyosh. 1924. *Indian Buddhist Iconography*. Calcutta: Oxford University Press.

Bhattacharya, Shiva Chandra Vidyarnava. 1978. *Principles of Tantra*. 2 vols. Edited by Sir John Woodroffe. Madras: Ganesh and Co. First published in 1913.

Bolle, Cornelis Willem [Kees]. 1961. "Tantrism and Sri Aurobindo's Philosophy." Ph.D. diss., University of Chicago.

Bolshakoff, Sergius. 1976. *Russian Mystics*. Kalamazoo, Michigan: Cistercian Publications.

Briggs, George Weston. 1938. *Gorakhnath and the Kanphata Yogis*. Calcutta: Y.M.C.A. Publishing House. Reprinted Delhi, 1973.

Bryant, Kenneth E. 1978. *Poems to the Child-God*. Berkeley: University of California Press.

Bulla Saheb. 1973. *Shabdsār*. Allahabad: Belvedere Press.

Callewaert, Winand M. 1974. "The Anabhay Prabodh of Garibdas." *Orientalia Lovaniensa Periodica* 5:187–96.

———. 1977. "Key for Understanding Mystical Literature." *Orientalia Lovaniensa Periodica* 8:309–30.

———. 1978. *The Sarvangi of the Dadupanthi Rajab*. Louvain, Belgium: Department of Oriental Studies, Catholic University.

Cenkner, William. 1983. *A Tradition of Teachers: Śankara and the Jagadgurus Today*. Columbia, Mo.: South Asia Books.

Charan Singh. 1958. *Light on Sant Mat*. Beas, Punjab: Radhasoami Satsang.

———. 1976. *Divine Light*. 4th ed. Beas, Punjab: Radhasoami Satsang.

———. 1977. *Two Poems of Saint Pāltu*. Beas, Punjab: Radhasoami Satsang.

Chatterjee, Asoke. 1967. *Padma Puraṇa: A Study*. Calcutta Sanskrit College Research Series, no. 58. Calcutta: Sanskrit College.

Chaturvedi, Parashuram. 1967. *Sant Kāvya*. 3rd ed. Allahabad: Kitab Mahal. Anthology of Sant Poetry.

———. 1972. *Uttarī Bhārat kī Sant Paramparā*. 3rd ed. Allahabad: Leader Press.

———. 1975. *Sant Sāhitya kī Preṛnā Srot*. New Delhi: Rajpal.

Cohn, Bernard. 1967. "Regions Subjective and Objective." In *Regions and Regionalism in South Asian Studies* (*see* Crane).

———. 1969. "The Changing Status of a Depressed Caste." In *Village India.* Edited by McKim Marriott. Chicago: University of Chicago Press.

———. 1977. "African Models and Indian Histories." In *Realm and Region in Traditional India* (*see* Fox 1977).

Cole, W. Owen. 1982. *The Guru in Sikhism.* London: Darton, Longman, and Todd.

———. 1984. *Sikhism and its Indian Context 1479–1708.* London: Darton, Longman, and Todd.

Conze, Edward. 1969. *Buddhist Meditation.* New York: Harper & Row.

Coomaraswamy, Ananda. 1946. *Figures of Speech or Figures of Thought.* London: Luzac and Co.

———. 1977. "The Part of Art in Indian Life." In vol. 1 of *Coomaraswamy.* Edited by Roger Lipsey. Princeton: Princeton University Press.

Coulborn, Rushton. 1965. *Feudalism in History.* Hamden, Conn.: Archon Books.

Crane, Robert I., ed. 1967. *Regions and Regionalism in South Asian Studies.* Program in Comparative Studies on South Asia, Monograph no. 5. Durham, N.C.: Duke University.

Crooke, William. 1896. *Tribes and Castes of the Northwestern Provinces and Oudh.* Calcutta: Superintendent of Government Printing.

Dasgupta, Shashibhusan. 1969. *Obscure Religious Cults.* Calcutta: Firma K. L. Mukhopadhyaya.

Daya Bai. 1976. *Dayā Bāī kī Bānī.* Allahabad: Belvedere Press.

De Brabandere, Godelieve. 1983. "The Haridāsa of the Dādūpanthī *Pancavāni.*" In *Bhakti in Current Research* (*see* Thiel-Horstmann 1983a).

Dharmendra Brahmchari, Shastri. 1954. *Santkavi Dariyā: Ek Anushīlan.* Patna: Bihar Rastrabhasa Parisad.

Digby, Simon. 1975. "Abd Al-Quddus Gangohi (1456–1537 A.D.): The Personality and Attitudes of a Medieval Indian Sufi." In *Medieval India: A Miscellany.* Bombay: Asia Publishing House.

———. 1984. "Qalandars and Related Groups: Elements of Social Deviance in the Religious Life of the Delhi Sultanate of the Thirteenth and Fourteenth Centuries." In *Islam in Asia,* vol. 1 (*see* Friedmann 1984).

Dixit, Rajesh. 1969. *Navanāth Charitra Sāgar.* Delhi: Dehati Pustak Bhandar.

Dixit, Triloki Narayan. 1961. *Sant Charandās.* Allahabad: Hindustani Academy.

———. 1965. *Sant Kavi Malukdās.* Allahabad: Sant Sufi Sahitya Samsthan.

———. 1966. Introduction to *Bhaktisāgar, q.v.*

Dvivedi, Hazari Prasad. 1963. *Hindī Sāhitya kī Bhūmikā.* Bombay: Hindi-Granth-Ratnakar [Private] Limited.

———. 1973. *Kabīr.* 2nd ed. Delhi: Rajkamal Prakashan.

Dvivedi, Kedarnath. 1965. *Kabīr aur Kabīr Panth.* Prayag (Allahabad): Hindi Sahitya Sammelan, 1965.

Dwyer, William, J., S.J. 1981. *Bhakti in Kabir.* Patna: Associated Book Agency.

Eaton, Richard Maxwell. 1978. *The Sufis of Bijapur.* Princeton: Princeton University Press.

Eliade, Mircea. 1969. *Yoga: Immortality and Freedom.* 2nd ed. Bollingen Series, no. 56. Princeton: Princeton University Press.

Essence of Refined Gold. 1978. Translated by Glenn H. Mullin. Dharamshala: Tushita Books. Composed by the third Dalai Lama.

Ezekiel, Isaac A. 1977. *Saint Paltu.* Beas, Punjab: Radhasoami Satsang.

Faqir Chand Ji Maharaj. n.d. *The Art of Happy Living.* Translated by B. R. Kamal. Hoshiarpur, Punjab: Faqir Library Charitable Trust.

Feldhaus, Anne. 1984. *The Deeds of God in Ṛddhipur.* New York: Oxford University Press.

Fox, Richard G. 1971. *Kin, Clan, Raja, and Rule.* Berkeley: University of California Press.

———. 1977. *Realm and Region in Traditional India.* New Delhi: Vikas.

Friedmann, Yohanan. 1971. *Shaikh Ahmad Sirhindi: An Outline of His Thought and a Study of His Image in the Eyes of Posterity.* Montreal: McGill-Queen's University Press.

Friedmann, Yohanan, ed. 1984. *Islam in Asia.* Vol. 1: South Asia. Boulder, Colo.: Westview Press.

Fusfeld, Warren. "The Shaping of Sufi Leadership in Delhi: The Naqshbandiyya Mujaddidiyya." Ph.D. diss., University of Pennsylvania.

Gafurova, Nelli Babadzhanovna. 1976. *Kabir i ego Nasledie.* Moscow: Nauka.

Ganga Das. 1977. "The Eighteenth-Century Mira: Sahajo Bai" (in Hindi). Radio Address. Rpt. in Sahaj Prakash 1979, pp. xii–xvi.

Ghanshyam Das. 1979. Introduction to *Sahaj Prakāsh* (*see* Sahajo Bai).

Gold, Daniel. 1986. "Clan and Lineage among the Sants." In *The Sants: Studies in a Devotional Tradition of India* (*see* Schomer and McLeod). In press.

———. Forthcoming a. *Comprehending the Guru: Towards a Grammar of Religious Perception.* Decatur, Ga.: Scholars Press.

———. Forthcoming b. "The Dadupanth and Princely Power in Rajasthan." In *Rajasthan: The Making of a Regional Identity.* Edited by Karine Schomer et al.

Gold, Daniel, and Ann Grodzins Gold. 1984. "The Fate of the Householder Nath." *History of Religions* 24:113–32.

Goldman, Robert P. 1977. *Gods, Priests, and Warriors: The Bhrigus of the Mahabharata.* New York: Columbia University Press.

Gonda, Jan. 1963. *The Vision of the Vedic Poets.* The Hague: Mouton.

Graburn, Nelson. 1971. *Readings in Kinship and Social Structure.* New York: Harper & Row.

Grierson, George. 1911. "Charandasis." In vol. 3 of *Encyclopedia of Religion and Ethics.* Edited by James Hastings. New York: Charles Scribner's Sons, 1908–26.

Guenther, Herbert V. 1963. *The Life and Teaching of Naropa.* Oxford: Oxford University Press.

Gupta, Mahendranath. 1964. *The Gospel of Shri Ramakrishna.* Translated by Swami Nikhilananda. Mylapore, Madras: Sri Ramakrishna Math.

Gupta, Mataprasad. 1969. *Kabīr Granthāvalī.* Allahabad: Lokbharati Prakashan.

[Goswami] Harirayji. 1905. *Shri Govardhan Nāthjī ke Prākatya kī Vartā.* Edited by Mohanlal Vishnulal Pandya. Bombay: Shri Venkateshwar Press.

Hawley, John Stratton. 1979. "The Early Sur Sagar and the Growth of Sur Tradition." *Journal of the American Oriental Society* 99:64–72.

———. 1983. *Krishna, the Butter Thief.* Princeton: Princeton University Press.

Hawley, John Stratton. 1984. *Sur Das: Poet, Singer, Saint.* Seattle: University of Washington Press.

Hedayatullah, Muhammad. 1977. *Kabir: The Apostle of Hindu-Muslim Unity.* Delhi: Motilal Banarsidass.

Hess, Linda. 1983. *The Bijak of Kabir.* Berkeley: North Point Press. Translated with Shukdeo Singh.

———. 1986. "Three Kabir Collections: A Comparative Study." In *The Sants: Studies in a Devotional Tradition of India* (*see* Schomer and McLeod). In press.

Hindī Shadbsāgar. 1965–75. Varanasi: Kashi Nagari Pracharani Sabha.

Hodgson, Marshall G. S. 1974. *The Venture of Islam.* Chicago: University of Chicago Press.

al-Hujwiri, 'Ali B. 'Uthman Al-Jullabi. 1936. Translated by Reynold A. Nicholson. London: Luzac and Co.

Huzur Sahib (Rai Saligram). 1886. (see *Sant Sangrah*).

Inden, Ronald B. 1976. *Marriage and Rank in Bengali Culture.* Berkeley: University of California Press.

Inden, Ronald B., and Ralph W. Nicholas. 1977. *Kinship in Bengali Culture.* Chicago: University of Chicago Press.

Jagannath Das. 1950. Introduction to *Palṭū Shabdāvalī* (*see* Paltu Sahib 1950).

Jindel, Rajendra. 1976. *Culture of a Sacred Town.* Bombay: Popular Prakashan.

Jogjit. 1968. *Shrī Līlā Sāgar.* Jaipur: Shri Shukcharandasiya Sahitya Prakashak Trust. Composed in 1762.

Joshi, Bhramarlal. 1968. *Sūrdās aur Narsingh Mehtā: Tulnātmak Adhyāyan.* Ahmedabad: Gurjar Bharati.

Juergensmeyer, Mark. 1982. *Religion as Social Vision.* Berkeley: University of California Press.

———. 1986. "The Radhasoami Revival of the Sant Tradition." in *The Sants: Studies in a Devotional Tradition of India* (*see* Schomer and McLeod). In press.

Kabīr Sāhib kī Shabdāvalī, vols. 1–4. 1966–73. Allahabad: Belvedere Press.

Keshav Das (medieval poet). 1979. *Amighuṃt.* Allahabad: Belvedere Press.

[Sadguru Sant] Keshavadas (modern devotee). 1977. *Lord Pandurang and His Minstrels.* Bombay: Bharatiya Vidya Bhavan.

Kirpal Singh. 1972. *Heart to Heart Talks*. 2 vols. Delhi: Ruhani Satsang.

———. 1973a. *A Great Saint: Baba Jaimal Singh*. Delhi: Ruhani Satsang.

———. 1973b. *A Brief Life Sketch of Hazur Baba Sawan Singh Ji*. Delhi: Ruhani Satsang.

Kulārnava Tantra. 1975. Edited by Taranatha Vidyaratna and Arthur Avalon (Sir John Woodroffe). Delhi: Motilal Banarsidass.

Kvaerne, Per. 1977. *An Anthology of Buddhist Tantric Songs*. Oslo: Universitetsforlaget.

Lawrence, Bruce B. 1984. "Early Indo-Muslim Saints and Conversion." In *Islam in Asia* (*see* Friedmann 1984).

———. 1986. "The Sant Movement and North Indian Sufis." In *The Sants: Studies in a Devotional Tradition of India* (*see* Schomer and McLeod). In press.

Levtzion, Nehemia, ed. 1979. *Conversion to Islam*. New York and London: Holmes & Meier.

Lorenzen, David. 1981. "The Kabir Panth: Heretics to Hindus." In *Religious Change and Cultural Domination*. Ed. David N. Lorenzen. Mexico City: El Colegio de Mexico.

———. 1986. "The Kabir Panth and Social Protest." In *The Sants: Studies in a Devotional Tradition of India* (*see* Schomer and McLeod). In press.

Macauliffe, Max Arthur. 1909. *The Sikh Religion: Its Gurus, Sacred Writings, and Authors*. 6 vols. Oxford: The Clarendon Press; rpt. New Delhi: S. Chand, 1963.

Machwe, Prabhakar. 1968. *Namdev: Life and Philosophy*. Patiala: Punjabi University.

Maharaj Sahib. 1978. *Discourses of Maharaj Saheb*. Translated by S. D. Maheshwari. Soami Bagh, Agra: S. D. Maheshwari.

Mahātmāoṃ kī Bānī. 1933. Bhurkura, Gazipur: Baba Rambaran Das Saheb.

Maheshwari, S[ant] D[as]. 1954. *Radhasoami Faith: History and Tenets*. Soami Bagh, Agra: S. D. Maheshwari.

———. 1971. *Biography of Huzur Maharaj*. Soami Bagh, Agra: S. D. Maheshwari.

———. 1979a. *Bhaktmal of the Radhasoami Faith*. Soami Bagh, Agra: S. D. Maheshwari.

———. 1979b. *Param Sant Tulsi Saheb*. Soami Bagh, Agra: S. D. Maheshwari.

Maneri, Sharafuddin. 1980. *The Hundred Letters*. Translated by Paul Jackson, S.J. New York: Paulist Press.

Marfatia, Mridula. 1967. *The Philosophy of Vallabhacharya*. Delhi: Munshiram Manoharlal.

Marriot, McKim. 1976. "Hindu Transactions." In *Transaction and Meaning*. Edited by Bruce Kapferer, Philadelphia: Institute for the Study of Human Issues.

Mathur, Agam Prasad [Dadaji Maharaj]. 1974. *Radhasoami Faith*. Delhi: Vikas.

McDermott, James P. 1980. "Karma and Rebirth in Early Buddhism." In *Karma and Rebirth in Classical Hindu Traditions* (*see* O'Flaherty 1980b).

McLeod, W. H. 1968. *Guru Nanak and the Sikh Tradition.* Oxford: Oxford University Press.

———. 1976. *The Evolution of the Sikh Community: Five Essays.* Oxford: Oxford University Press.

———. 1980. *Early Sikh Tradition: A Study of the Janam Sakhis.* Oxford: Oxford University Press.

Mishra, Bhagirath, and Rajnarain Maurya. 1964. *Sant Nāmdev kī Padāvalī.* Puna, Maharashtra: Puna University.

Mishra, Pitambar. 1973. *Divya Charitāmrit.* New Delhi: S. K. Chopra, 9 Shankar Market.

Mishra, Rameshchandra. 1969. *Ulatvāmsī Sāhitya.* New Delhi: Arya Book Depot.

Morrow, Steve. 1978. "A Long Journey." *Sant Bānī: The Voice of the Saints.* (Journal Published by Santji's disciples in Franklin, N.H.), April–May.

Mulji, Karsondas. 1865. *History of the Sect of the Maharajas.* London: Trubner and Co.

Nabhaji. 1965. *Bhaktmāl.* Varanasi: Thakurdas and Sons. With commentary by Priyadas.

Nanda, Kirana. 1983. *Santa kāvya meṃ vidroha kā svarg.* New Delhi: Nachiketa Prakashana.

Narasimhan, Chakravarti V. 1965. *The Mahabharata.* New York: Columbia University Press.

Nawab Gudri Shah. 1978. *The Path of the Tasawwuf* (*Mysticism*). The Hague: East-West Publications (Fonds B.V).

[Geshe] Ngawang Dhargyey. 1978. Commentary on *The Fifty Stanzas of Guru Devotion* by Ashvaghosa, in *The Mahamudra Eliminating the Darkness of Ignorance.* Translated by Alexander Berzin. Dharamshala, Himachal Pradesh: Library of Tibetan Works and Archives.

Nizami, Khaliq Ahmad. 1955. *The Life and Times of Shaikh Farid-ud-din Ganj-i-Shakar.* Delhi: Idarah-i Adabiyat-i Dilli.

———. 1974. *Some Aspects of Religion and Politics in India During the Thirteenth Century.* 2nd ed. Delhi: Idarah-i Adabiyat-i Dilli.

The Ocean of Love: The Anurag Sagar of Kabir. 1982. Translated by Raj Kumar Bagga, edited by Russell Perkins, under the direction of Sant Ajaib Singhji, with illustrations by Michael Raysson. Sanbornton, N.H.: Sant Bani Ashram.

Oddie, G. A., ed. 1977. *Religion in South Asia: Religious Conversion and Revival Movements in South Asia in Medieval and Modern Times.* Delhi: Manohar.

O'Flaherty, Wendy Doninger. 1973. *Asceticism and Eroticism in the Mythology of Shiva.* London: Oxford University Press.

———. 1976. *The Origins of Evil in Hindu Mythology*. Berkeley and Los Angeles: University of California Press.

———. 1980a. *Women, Androgynes, and Other Mythical Beasts*. Chicago: University of Chicago Press.

———. 1980b. *Karma and Rebirth in Classical Hindu Traditions*. Berkeley: University of California Press.

Orr, W. G. 1947. *A Sixteenth-Century Indian Mystic*. London: Lutterworth Press.

Paltu Sahib. 1950. *Shrī Palṭū Sāheb Kṛit Shabdāvalī* [*Palṭu Shabdāvalī*]. Ayodhya: Mahant Jagannath Das Ji Maharaj [of the Paltu Akhara].

———. 1965–67. *Palṭū Sāhib kī Bānī* [*Palṭu Bānī*]. 3 vols. Allahabad: Belvedere Press.

———. 1977. *Palṭū Darshan*. Ayodhya: Shriman Mahant Ramsumer Dasji Maharaj [of the Paltu Akhara].

Pandey, Kanti Chandra. 1963. *Abhinavagupta: An Historical and Philosophical Study*. 2nd ed. Varanasi: Chowkhamba Sanskrit Series Office.

Pandey, Shashikala. 1981. *Santa-Sāhitya ki Paribhāṣik Shabdāvalī*. Allahabad: Anamika Prakashan.

Pandit, M. P. 1967–70. *All Life Is Yoga*. Pondicherry: Dipti Publications.

Prabhudas Acharya. 1976. *Govind Sāhab kā Sankṣipt Itihās*. Govind Sahib, Faizabad, Uttar Pradesh: Mahant Shri Ramkomal Das Sahab.

Pradhan, V. G., trans. 1967. *Jñaneshvarī*. Edited by H. M. Lambert. London: George Allen and Unwin.

[Lala] Pratap Singh Seth. 1978. *Biography of Soamiji Maharaj*. Translated by S. D. Maheshwari. Soami Bagh, Agra: S. D. Maheshwari.

Puri, Lekh Raj. 1972. *Radha Swami Teachings*. 2nd ed. Beas, Punjab: Radhasoami Satsang.

Rajasthan District Gazeteer, March 1976. Ajmer.

Ramrupji. n.d. *Guru Bhakti Prakāsh*. Jugalghat, Vrindavan: Virakt Vaishnav Rupmadhuri Sharan.

———. 1972. *Mukti Mārg*. Jaipur: Shri Shukcharandasiya Sahitya Prakashak Trust.

Redfield, Robert, and Milton Singer. 1962. "The Cultural Role of Cities." In *Human Nature and the Study of Society*. Edited by Robert Redfield. Chicago: University of Chicago Press.

Renou, Louis. 1955. "Les Pouvoirs de la Parole dans le Rigveda." In vol. 1 of *Etudes Védiques et Paninéennes*. Paris: Publication de l'Institute de Civilisation Indienne.

Rizvi, Saiyid Atthar Abbas. 1965. *Muslim Revivalist Movements in North India in the Sixteenth and Seventeenth Centuries*. Agra: Agra University, 1965.

———. 1976. *Religious and Intellectual History of the Muslims in Akbar's Reign*. Delhi: Munshiram Manoharlal.

———. 1977. "Islamic Proselytization." In *Religion in South Asia* (*see* Oddie).

———. 1978. *A History of Sufism in India.* Vol. 1. Delhi: Munshiram Manoharlal.

Robinson, James B., trans. 1979. *Buddha's Lions: The Lives of the Eighty-Four Siddhas.* Berkeley: Dharma Publishing. Translation from the Tibetan of Abhayadatta's *Chaturashita-siddha-pravritti.*

Rudolph, Susanne. 1963. "The Princely States of Rajputana." *Indian Journal of Political Science* 24:14–32.

Rule of the Master. Translated by Luke Eberle. Kalamazoo, Mich: Cistercian Publications, Inc., 1977

Sahai, B. M., and Radha Krishna Khanna. 1968. *The Saint and His Master.* Delhi: Ruhani Satsang.

Sahajo, Bai. 1967. *Sahajo Bāī kī Bānī.* Allahabad; Belvedere Press.

———. N.d. *Sahaj Prakāsh.* Published with an introduction by Ghanshyam Das. Delhi: Shri Shyamcharandras Prakashan Karyalaya, 1979. This edition is based directly on the Belvedere Press text.

Sahay, Paramsant Dr. Chaturbhuj. 1959. *Guru-bhaktā Sahajobāī.* Mathura: Haimendra Kumar, Sadhan Karyalaya.

Santbānī Sangrah. 1955–70. 2 vols. Allahabad: Belvedere Press. Anthology of *sant* verses.

Sant Sangrah. 1976–78. 2 vols. Soami Bagh, Agra: Radhasoami Satsang. Compiled by Rai Saligram, the second Radhasoami guru.

Sār Bachan. 1974. Translated by Sardar Seva Singh. Beas: Radhasoami Satsang. Prose works by Radhasoami Sahib, Beas Version.

Sār Bachan (Prose). 1958. Translated by S. D. Maheshwari. Soami Bagh, Agra: S. D. Maheshwari. Prose works of Radhasoami Sahib, Agra version.

Sār Bachan Rādhāsoāmī. 1976. Beas, Punjab: Radhasoami Satsang. Hindi verses of Radhasoami Sahib.

Schimmel, Annemarie. 1975. *Mystical Dimensions of Islam.* Chapel Hill: University of North Carolina Press.

——— 1979. "The Golden Chain of 'Sincere Muhammedans'." In *The Rose and the Rock: Mystical and Rational Elements in the Intellectual History of South Asian Islam.* Edited by Bruce Lawrence. Duke University Programs in Comparative Studies on Southern Asia, no. 15. Durham, N.C.: Duke University.

Schneider, David M. 1968. *American Kinship: A Cultural Account.* Englewood Cliffs, N.J.: Prentice-Hall.

Schomer, Karine. 1979. "Kabir in the Guru Granth Sahib: An Exploratory Essay." In *Sikh Studies.* Edited by Mark Juergensmeyer and N. Gerald Barrier. Berkeley Religious Studies Series, no. 1. Berkeley: Graduate Theological Union.

———. 1986. "Introduction: The Sant Tradition in Perspective." In *The Sants: Studies in a Devotional Tradition of India* (*see* Schomer and McLeod). In press.

Schomer, Karine, and W. H. McLeod, eds. 1986. *The Sants: Studies in a*

Devotional Tradition of India. Berkeley Religious Studies Series. Berkeley: Graduate Theological Union. In press.

Schwartzberg, Joseph E. 1967. "Prolegomena to the Study of South Asian Regions and Regionalism." In *Regions and Regionalism in South Asian Studies* (*see* Crane).

Sen, Kshiti Mohan. 1936. *Medieval Mysticism of India.* London: Luzac and Co.

Shah, Jethalal G. 1969. *Shri Vallabhacharya: His Philosophy and Religion.* Nadiad, Gujarat: The Pushtimargiya Pustakalaya.

Shahid, Shah Ismail. 1969. *Support of the Faith.* Translated by Mir Shahmat Ali. Edited by M. Ashraf Darr. Lahore: Shah Muhammad Ashraf.

Shabda Kosh Sant Mat Vānī. 1970. Soami Bagh, Agra: Radhasoami Satsang.

Shastri, Satyanarayan. 1964. *Puṣṭimārgīya Āchārya aur Unkī Paramparāyeṃ.* Nathdwara: Shri Krishna Bhandar.

Shukla, Bhagvati Prasad. 1972. *Baurī Panth Ke Hindī Kavi.* New Delhi: Arya Book Depot.

Shyam Lal [Data Dayal]. 1927. *Retransformation of Self.* Lashkar, Gwalior: G. S. Nivas.

———. *Shabdāmrit Dhārā.* 1952. 2 vols. *Lashkar, Gwalior: Shabd Pratap Satsang.*

Singer, Milton. 1972. *When a Great Tradition Modernizes.* New York: Praeger.

Singer, Milton, and Bernard S. Cohn, eds. 1968. *Structure and Change in Indian Society.* Chicago: Aldine.

Singh, Radhakrishna. 1966. *Sant Palṭu aur Palṭu Panth.* Delhi: Surya Prakashan.

Singh, Shukdeo. 1972. *Kabīr Bījak.* Allahabad: Nilabh Prakashan.

Sinha, Surajit, and Baidyanath Saraswati. 1978. *Ascetics of Kashi: An Anthropological Exploration.* Varanasi: N. K. Bose Memorial Foundation.

Snellgrove, D. L. 1959. *The Hevajra Tantra.* Part 1. London: Oxford University Press.

Sopher, David E. 1980. "The Geographical Patterning of Culture." In *An Exploration of India.* Edited by David Sopher. Ithaca: Cornell University Press.

Souvenir in Commemoration of the First Centenary of the Radhasoami Satsang. 1977. 2nd ed. Dayalbagh, Agra: Radhasoami Satsang.

Srinivas, Mysore N. 1952. *Religion and Society among the Coorgs of South India.* London: Oxford University Press.

Sūrsāgar. 1965. 2 vols. Edited by Jagannath Das "Ratnakar." Varanasi: Kashi Nagari Pracharini Sabha.

Tagore, Rabindranath, trans., assisted by Evelyn Underhill. 1915. *Songs of Kabir.* New York: Macmillan.

Takakusu, Junjiro. 1975. *The Essentials of Buddhist Philosophy.* Delhi: Motilal Banarsidass.

Tapaswiji. 1976. *Kabīr Satya Prakāsh*. Limbri, Saurashtra: Shri Tapaswi Saheb.

Thapar, Romila. 1966. *A History of India*. Baltimore, Md.: Penguin.

Thiel-Horstmann, Monika, ed. 1983a. *Bhakti in Current Research, 1979–1982*. Berlin: Dietrich Reimer.

———. 1983b. "The *Bhajan* Repertoire of the Present-Day Dadupanth." In *Bhakti in Current Research* (see Thiel-Horstmann 1983a).

Thorner, Daniel. 1965. "Feudalism in India." In *Feudalism in History* (*see* Coulborn).

Tivari, Parasnath, ed. 1961. *Kabīr Granthāvalī*. Prayag: Hindi Parishad.

Tod, James. 1914. *Annals and Antiquities of Rajastahan*. London: Routlege and Kegan Paul. Rpt. New Delhi: M. N. Publishers, 1978.

Tripathi, Ramamurti. 1975. *Tantra aur Sant*. Allahabad: Sahitya Bhavan, Ltd.

Tucci, Giuseppe. 1969. "Nomina Numina." In *Myths and Symbols*. Edited by Joseph M. Kitagawa and Charles H. Long. Chicago: University of Chicago Press.

———. 1980. *The Religions of Tibet*. Translated by Geoffrey Samuel. Bombay: Allied Publishers Private Limited.

Tulsi Sahib. 1976–77. *Ghaṭ Rāmāyana*. 2 vols. Allahabad: Belvedere Press.

Tulsi Sahib. 1977. Beas: Radhasoami Satsang. Biography and selected translations of the eighteenth-century *sant* presented by devotees from Beas.

Turbiani, Enzo. 1983. "The Impact of Islam on Tulsidas' Thought and His Poetical Work." In *Bhakti in Current Research* (see Thiel-Horstmann 1983a).

Turner, Bryan S. 1974. *Weber and Islam*. London: Routledge and Kegan Paul.

Upadhyaya, Nagendranath. 1965. *Nāth aur Sant Sāhitya*. Varanasi: Vishvavidyalaya Prakashan.

Valiuddin, Mir. 1980. *Contemplative Disciplines in Sufism*. London and The Hague: East-West Publications.

Van Buitenen, J. A. B, ed. and trans. 1973–78. *The Mahābhārata*. 3 vols. Chicago: University of Chicago Press. Vol 1, 1973; vol 2, 1975; vol 3, 1978.

Varma, Dhirendra. 1977. *Sūrsāgar Sār Saṭīk*. Allahabad: Sahitya Bhavan, Ltd.

Vaudeville, Charlotte. 1974. *Kabir*. Oxford: Oxford University Press.

———. 1986. "*Sant-Mat:* Santism as the Universal Path to Sanctity." In *The Sants: Studies in a Devotional Tradition of India* (see Schomer and McLeod). In press.

[Swami] Vishnu Tirth. 1962. *Devātmā Shakti*. 2nd ed. Bombay: Shri Sadhan Granthmala Samiti, Behramji Mansion.

Wach, Joachim. 1944. Sociology of Religion. Chicago: University of Chicago Press.

Wayman, Alex. 1973. *The Buddhist Tantras*. New York: Samuel Weiser.

Weber, Max. 1958. "The Social Psychology of the World Religions." In *From Max Weber: Essays in Sociology*. Translated and edited by H[ans] H. Gerth and C. Wright Mills. New York: Oxford University Press.

———. 1964. *The Sociology of Religion.* Translated by Ephraim Fischoff. Boston: Beacon Press.

Westcott, G. H. 1907. *Kabir and the Kabir Panth.* Kanpur, Christchurch Mission Press.

Wilson, H. H. 1977. *Hindu Religions.* Delhi: Bharatiya Book Corporation. First published 1862.

Wolpert, Stanley. 1977. *A New History of India.* New York: Oxford University Press.

Woodroffe, John [Arthur Avalon], trans. 1963. *The Great Liberation.* 4th ed. Madras: Ganesh and Co. Translation of the *Mahānirvāṇa Tantra.*

———. 1964. *The Serpent Power.* 7th ed. Madras: Ganesh and Co. Translation of *Ṣaṭ-cakra-nirūpaṇa* and *Pādukā-panchaka,* with extensive commentary.

Zelliot, Eleanor. 1977. "The Psychological Dimension of the Buddhist Movement in India." In *Religion in South Asia* (*see* Oddie 1977).

Zimmer, Heinrich. 1984. *Artistic Form and Yoga in the Sacred Images of India.* Translated by Gerald Chapple and James B. Lawson in collaboration with J. Michael McKnight. Princeton: Princeton University Press. Translation of *Kunstform und Yoga im indischen Kultbild.* Berlin, 1926.

Index